AF545131

The Gardener's Guide to Australian Plants

By the same author:

Australian Plants for Small Gardens and Containers
Fun with Australian Plants
Colour Your Garden with Australian Plants

Gwen Elliot

The Gardener's Guide to Australian Plants

First published in 1985 by
Hyland House Publishing Pty Limited
10 Hyland Street,
South Yarra
Melbourne
Victoria 3141
Reprinted 1989

National Library of Australia
Cataloguing-in-publication data:

Elliot, Gwen.
The gardener's guide to Australian plants.

Bibliography.
Includes index.
ISBN 0 908090 79 X.
1. Wild flower gardening — Australia. I. Title.

635.9'676'0994

Illustrated by Sue Elliot
Colour plates and jacket designed by Peter Yates
Typeset by Acton Graphic Arts Pty Ltd, 8a Church Street, Hawthorn, Victoria 3122
Printed and bound in Singapore by Singapore National Printers Ltd.

Contents

SECTION 2

Acknowledgements

The seeds of inspiration for this book were originally sown by Anne Godden and Al Knight of Hyland House, who felt the need for such a publication on the propagation and cultivation of Australian plants, and to whom I am grateful for having been asked to work on the project.

I appreciate very sincerely the assistance given to me by my husband Rodger, in reading through the manuscript and for his many helpful suggestions. His support and encouragement have been invaluable. I thank him also for supplying the majority of the colour photographs used.

Sincere thanks are expressed to Brian Crafter for his photographs of *Calocephalus brownii*, *Clematis microphylla*, *Conostylis aculeata* and *Correa pulchella*, and to John Clasper of *Your Garden* magazine for the photographs of *Eremophila glabra* and *Isotoma fluviatilis*.

The line drawings have come from the pen of Sue Elliot who undertook the task with dedication and patience. A number of the black and white photographs are from the files of *Your Garden* magazine, and the helpful assistance of the Editor, Allan Balhorn, is very much appreciated.

No book of this nature could ever be written without the assistance of the many people who are keen growers of Australian plants, and who are willing to share their knowledge and experiences of their successes and failures in the cultivation of particular plant species. For assistance in this regard and also for allowing the photography of plants growing in their gardens I would like to thank Keith and Sue Alcock, John and Beth Armstrong, Neville and Elizabeth Bonney, Brian and Judy Crafter, David and Margaret Darbyshire, Ian and Helen Hamilton, Neil and Jane Marriott, Fred and June Rogers, Glyn and Peg Sago, Rex and Dawn Shields, Ken Stuckey, Alice Talbot, the staff at Billanook College, Mooroolbark Vic, Burrendong Arboretum, Wellington NSW and Monash University, Clayton Vic, and also Ray Collett and staff at the Arboretum, University of California, Santa Cruz USA, which is renowned for its magnificent collection of Australian plants.

I would finally again thank Anne Godden and Al Knight for their practical assistance in editing and design. If the end result is a publication which will be of help to all who wish to successfully grow Australian plants in their gardens, our prime objective will be fulfilled.

Gwen Elliot

Introduction

Gardening and the growing of plants is one of the most enjoyable and relaxing pastimes available today. It is an activity which has been enjoyed by millions in past years, and undoubtedly will continue to provide pleasure in the future.

The pleasure we gain from gardening does however depend on the achievement of at least some good results. There will always be frustrations caused by the failure of seeds to germinate or cuttings to strike, the frequent germination and good growth of weeds, damage to plants caused by garden pests, or even the death of some treasured plants. Generally, however, our frustrations are only minimal compared with the pleasures we are able to enjoy through seeing plants grow to maturity, and flower or fruit in the appropriate seasons.

To some gardeners success seems to come easily, whilst others struggle with a higher than average percentage of problems.

Many of the dificulties we experience can be averted with an understanding of basic gardening 'know-how'. It is this sort of information that this book seeks to provide.

Chapter One takes an overall look at gardening through 'Ten Basic Steps to Successful Garden Cultivation'. Chapters 2 to 12 then cover a wide range of topics related to the successful growing of plants. Chapter 13 is devoted to 'Encouraging Birds to Your Garden' which is a fascinating and highly important aspect of Australian plant cultivation. The remaining chapters cover a variety of topics related to the growing of Australian plants, including plants for specific situations and concluding with three chapters on the important topic of propagation.

Throughout the book approximately 500 plant species are mentioned. Detailed descriptions will be found in Section 2. To enable as much information as possible to be provided in the space available, a code (see the beginning of Section 2) has been used to signify cultivation requirements. Some of the most important of these requirements have also in some cases been mentioned in the text.

Section 1

1—Ten Basic Steps to Successful Garden Cultivation

1. GET TO KNOW YOUR OWN GARDEN CONDITIONS

Study and make a note of aspects such as —

(a) your general soil structure, whether sandy, mountain loam or clay, etc.;
(b) the amount of sunshine received in different parts of the garden — in all seasons;
(c) the amount of moisture in areas of the garden throughout the year;
(d) areas which already have dense root growth from existing trees in your own or neighbouring properties;
(e) features of the property, such as power lines and drainage pipes, which must be considered when selecting suitable plants.

2. UNDERSTAND YOUR GENERAL, AND SPECIFIC, CLIMATIC CONDITIONS

General climatic conditions, such as whether the area is tropical or temperate and the annual average rainfall, have a marked bearing on the range of plants which can be grown with success.

Specific conditions within the garden also require consideration. These will include the aspects of north, south, east and west, the usual wind direction and force, and susceptibility to frost. Conditions such as these may not be the same throughout the whole garden.

Planning is also most important in coastal gardens receiving strong, salt-laden winds. Are any parts of the garden sheltered?

3. CHOOSE HARDY, WELL-TRIED PLANT SPECIES FOR YOUR BASIC GARDEN STRUCTURE

Plants such as screening shrubs, windbreaks and shade trees should be selected with extreme care. They will form the basis of the garden structure and their death could cause much inconvenience. Similarly, they could cease to serve the purpose intended if the wrong plants are chosen and they grow larger than required.

Assistance in making appropriate selections can be gained from this and other books (see Bibliography) and from discussions with nurserymen and other experienced gardeners.

4. PLANT ANY RARE, NEW, OR HARD-TO-GROW SPECIES IN POSITIONS WHERE THEY ARE NOT NEEDED FOR A VITAL FUNCTIONAL SERVICE

We are all tempted from time to time by a particular plant which we may have seen illustrated in a book or magazine, or for some other reason we may wish to 'give it a go'. Often we know right from the start that the plant is not ideally suited to our conditions, but we are prepared to accept that risk.

Whilst still trying to place the plant in a position which gives it the required conditions, we should also look for a situation which will cause minimum inconvenience to the general appearance and function of the garden should the plant fail to survive.

5. ENSURE ADEQUATE GARDEN PREPARATION

In some cases garden preparation may be minimal or even unnecessary, but items such as the provision of adequate drainage, soil conditioning if required and the removal of weeds from the area should receive attention before planting.

If the garden preparation prior to planting is good, many of the problems which can later beset gardeners will be avoided. Further details on this topic will be found in Chapter 3.

6. FOR BEST RESULTS, PLANT HEALTHY, WELL-DEVELOPED STOCK

Weak, 'leggy' or rootbound plants are less likely to develop into good garden specimens than healthy, vigorous young plants. On the other hand, vigorous and lush plants which have been grown in a glasshouse or in other very sheltered conditions, or taken directly from an 'indoor' location, may suffer a severe setback when planted out in an open garden situation.

When buying plants, choose a nursery which uses treated soil or potting mixes, to avoid bringing root fungus or other diseases into your garden. Look for specimens which have healthy, vigorous growth and are hardened to outdoor conditions. See further information in Chapter 4.

7. USE CORRECT PLANTING TECHNIQUES

This step is closely related to Step 5, but involves the actual digging of the hole and the planting. It is a relatively simple procedure, but nevertheless if done incorrectly it can lead to the failure of the plant to survive. Further details regarding this step will be found in Chapter 4.

8. MOISTURE CONTROL AND SUPPLEMENTARY WATERING

A very large number of garden plant deaths result from either under- or over-watering. Chapter 5 is devoted to this very important aspect.

9. GENERAL GARDEN MAINTENANCE

If the previous steps have been followed, the need for general garden maintenance will be greatly reduced. However, to obtain best results and maximum satisfaction from your garden, a programme of on-going care should be provided, involving such aspects as weeding, mulching, fertilising, pruning, and staking if necessary.

10. CONTROL OF PESTS AND DISEASES

The majority of garden pests and diseases can be controlled naturally in a well-balanced garden, particularly if there are plenty of native birds in the area.

From time to time however there will be particular infestations which require some attention to avoid permanent damage to a plant or plants, and we should be on the look-out for such attacks. Further details will be found in Chapter 12.

2—Basic Garden Planning and Construction

GARDEN PLANNING

The planning of a garden can be an exciting exercise. It is also extremely important if we hope to establish a garden which will be both attractive and functional.

We should initially consider our own lifestyle and needs. Do we wish to spend a good deal of time in the garden, or are we looking for a low-maintenance area? Do we enjoy outdoor living and require space for a barbecue or pool, surrounded by paving or lawn? Are medium to large, shade-providing trees considered desirable, or is there a need for more open space? All these aspects, along with others such as the need for a clothes line or incinerator should be thought out thoroughly before any garden construction begins.

It often helps to put down our thoughts on paper. Start with a plan of the property, to scale if possible, and draw in the house. Add any other fixtures such as buildings, paved or concrete pathways and existing plants which you wish to retain. Draw in any overhead electricity or telephone wires, and any underground drains and gas or water supply pipes. Mark in the North, South, East and West aspects of the property.

From this point you can use tracing paper to draft out rough garden plans. The tracing paper should be placed over the basic garden plan and the sheets can be altered or re-sketched several times if necessary before a final garden layout is decided upon.

Begin by drawing in proposed functional and outdoor living areas as mentioned above. Don't overlook the need for access to water, gas and electricity meters. The next items to be plotted will be the driveways and pathways. Allow ample width for these areas to avoid always having to prune back shrubs from them. See also Chapter 17, 'Establishing a Narrow Garden Screen'.

Take into account the natural contours of the land. Drains may be needed to allow good drainage for plants, or to cope with excess water on sloping blocks. Think about the direction in which water will flow. The neighbours won't thank you if their land becomes waterlogged as a result of your drains flowing in the wrong direction! Draw in proposed drains on your plan.

Finally you can sketch in proposed planting areas and plants. Begin by considering the aspects of north, south, east and west and the availability of sun and/or shade in the garden. You should then draw in any trees or large shrubs required for shade, screen or windbreak purposes. (Make sure these plants are not placed close to overhead wires or underground pipes.) Consideration should also be given to the effect any large trees may have on neighbouring properties.

The selection of suitable species will depend to a great extent on the soil and climatic conditions of your area. It is particularly important that any large shrubs or trees which are to perform a major function in the garden should be hardy, and well suited to the conditions available.

Smaller shrubs, groundcovers and herbaceous plants can be added after the basic framework of the garden has been decided upon. These species should also be chosen having regard to the individual requirements of each species. This is particularly important in regard to watering, and is discussed further at the beginning of Chapter 5.

You may want colour in your garden all the year round. Don't forget the plants that have a lovely scent and the plants that encourage birds to your garden. What else *must* you have for *your* garden? Have fun!

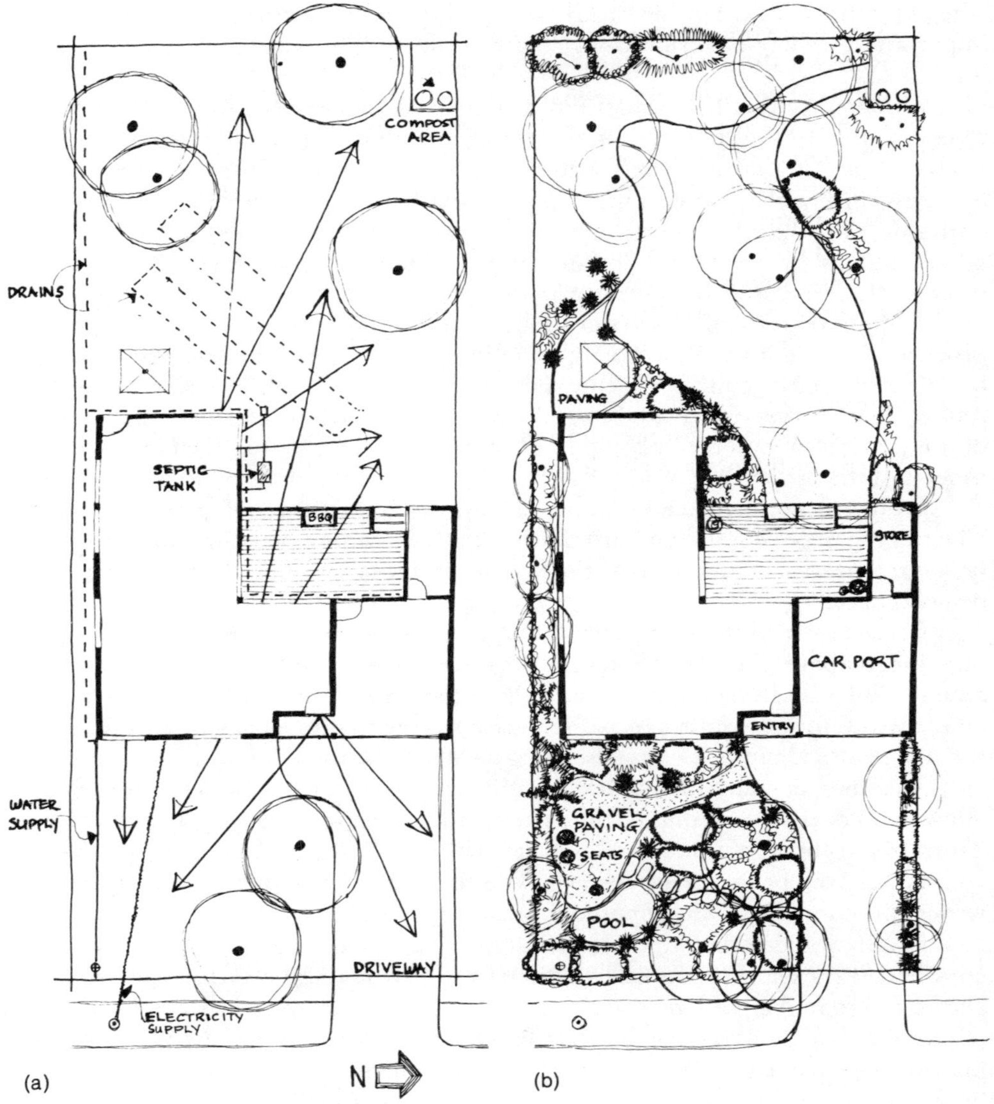

(a) (b)

GARDEN CONSTRUCTION

The following steps are recommended as a general guideline for the construction of a new garden, or reconstruction of an existing garden area.

1. Decide on the first area to be constructed. Usually it is better to concentrate on one area at a time. This will help you control weeds more easily and effectively.
2. Mark any plants that are to be retained, so they will not be damaged when work is carried out. These can include existing native trees and shrubs, or any plants already growing in the garden. It can also include dormant bulbs and species such as many of our small native lilies and orchids. If these are present they should, if possible, be marked when they are in leaf or flower, perhaps some months before construction takes place, and saved. Many of these plants can be difficult to re-establish, which makes it even more important to retain them if possible.
3. Remove all rubbish. Eradicate and remove weed growth or unwanted plants. The task of future maintenance will be greatly reduced if all or most of the weeds can be removed at the time of construction. It is also very much easier to eradicate weeds before planting than when they are growing amongst established plants. Further information on 'Weeds and Weed Control' will be found in Chapter 11.

   If possible the area should be left fallow for a few weeks after clearing and weed eradication to allow for any weed regeneration and further eradication.
4. Mark out garden features according to your layout plan and construct any pathways, drains, etc., adding topsoil you have removed to the garden areas.
5. Undertake any soil preparation of the garden areas, see Chapter 3, in readiness for the planting of selected plants, as outlined in Chapter 4.

The illustration opposite shows stages in the drawing of a garden plan, on land measuring 50 m x 20 m.

(a) Shows lines of vision from the house, plus existing trees, drainage lines and services.
(b) Shows semi-completed plan, having regard to the features in (a).

3—Soil Preparation

Some garden soils require very little preparation, whilst in other places this is of major importance if successful results are to be achieved.

Basically, a minimum of preparation is needed in any area if you are proposing to grow plants which are native to that particular region. It is when you seek to cultivate species which are used to growing in different soil structures that the need for thorough preparation of the garden area arises.

SANDY SOILS

Many of the commonly cultivated Australian native plants come from the sandy, well-drained regions of this country. Two such areas noted for their wide range of colourful wildflowers are the south-west corner of Western Australia and the Sydney sandstone region.

A wide range of native plants can therefore be cultivated with very good success in areas of sandy soils.

One of the problems which does occur is that sandy soils do not usually retain water well and once fine sand dries out completely the surface can become water-repellent and any rain or other water will run off the top without penetrating.

Adding organic material such as peat moss, leaf litter, grass clippings or compost can improve the moisture-retaining ability of sandy soil. A surface mulch will help prevent drying out of the upper layer of the sand and allow better penetration of water (see Chapter 6).

A second problem in sandy areas is that, as the water passes through the porous sand, it carries with it the natural nutrients or garden fertilisers needed for good plant growth. This is called leaching. Adding compost, cow manure or horse manure to the soil will both provide nutrients for the plants and also improve its texture and moisture-retaining ability.

Lechenaultia formosa.

Chart 1 — Plants suitable for cultivation in sandy soils

(a) Groundcovers and plants to around 1 m high: A selection of 20 species

Plant Name	Height x width	Brief comment — for further description see Section 2
Acacia aculeatissima	Prostrate to 0.5 m x 1-2 m	Has slightly prickly foliage and yellow flowers.
Anigozanthos bicolor	0.3-0.6 m x 0.5-1 m	Kangaroo paw with deep red with green flowers.
Anigozanthos humilis	0.2 m x 0.5-1 m	Cat's paw. Flowers creamy yellow, orange, pink or red.
Anigozanthos viridis	0.3 m x 0.5 m	Green kangaroo paw flowers.
Boronia filifolia	0.3-0.5 m x 1-2 m	Has slender, purplish leaves and pink flowers.
Conostylis aculeata	0.2-0.4 m x 0.5 m	Clumping plant with tubular yellow flowers.
Conostylis bealiana	0.2 m x 0.3 m	Tufting plant with tubular yellow flowers.
Darwinia lejostyla	1 m x 1 m	Small shrub with pinkish-red, bell-shaped flowers.
Eriostemon spicatus	0.5-1.5 m x 0.5-1.5 m	Has small leaves and spikes of pink to mauve flowers.
Grevillea acanthifolia	0.5-2.5 m x 2-4 m	Has prickly leaves and mauve-pink flowers.
Grevillea brownii	Usually 0.5 m x 1-3 m	Has clusters of very bright red flowers.
Grevillea x *gaudichaudii*	0.3 m x 2-5 m	Has reddish new foliage. Flower-heads dark red to burgundy.
Grevillea thelemanniana	Prostrate or 1-2 m x 2-3 m	Leaves green or greyish. Flowers bright red.
Helichrysum baxteri	0.5 m x 1 m	Has white with yellow everlasting daisies.
Hemiandra pungens	Prostrate x 1-2 m	Has narrow, prickly leaves and mauve-pink flowers.
Lechenaultia biloba	0.5-1 m x 0.5-1 m	Has very showy blue flowers.
Lechenaultia formosa	0.1-0.6 m x 0.5-1 m	Flowers can be yellow, orange, pinks or reds.
Micromyrtus ciliata	0.1-1 m x 1-2 m	Profuse small white flowers deepen with age to red.
Pultenaea pedunculata	0.5 m x 1-2 m	Has profuse pea-flowers. Several colour forms available.
Verticordia plumosa	1 m x 1 m	Has grey-green foliage and mauve-pink flower-heads.

Chart 1 — Plants suitable for cultivation in sandy soils

(b) Medium shrubs around 1-4 m high: A selection of 20 species

Plant Name	Height x width	Brief comment — for further description see Section 2
Acacia buxifolia	2-4 m x 2-4 m	A hardy wattle with profuse yellow flower-heads.
Acacia gracilifolia	2.5-5 m x 2-5 m	Has long, narrow foliage and clusters of golden flower-heads.
Acacia suaveolens	1-3 m x 2-5 m	Has fragrant, pale yellow flower-heads.
Banksia baueri	2-5 m x 2-4 m	Has large mauve-grey or orange-brown flower-heads.
Banksia baxteri	3-4 m x 3-5 m	Has dome-shaped, yellow-green flower-heads.
Beaufortia sparsa	2-4 m x 1-3 m	Has bright reddish-orange flower-heads.
Callistemon macropunctatus	2-4 m x 2-4 m	Bottlebrush flower-spikes are red tipped with gold.
Calothamnus quadrifidus	2-4 m x 2-5 m	A variable species. Has red flower-spikes.
Calytrix aurea	1-2 m x 1-1.5 m	An upright shrub with fragrant, yellow, starry flowers.
Chamelaucium sp. 'Walpole'	1.5-3 m x 1.5-3 m	Flowers are initially white then age to pink or purple.
Darwinia citriodora	1.5 m x 1-2 m	Has fragrant foliage and yellow-green and red flower-heads.
Grevillea banksii	2-5 m x 2-3 m	Leaves are greyish. Flower-heads are bright red.
Grevillea 'Robyn Gordon'	1-2 m x 2-3 m	Long-flowering, with bright red flowers.
Grevillea sericea	2.5 m x 2.5 m	Has pink to mauve or white flowers most of year.
Grevillea speciosa	1.5-3 m x 1.5-3 m	Has bright red, wheel-like flower-heads.
Lambertia formosa	2-3 m x 2-3 m	Has dark green, pointed leaves. Tubular flowers are orange to red.
Lambertia inermis	2-4 m x 1.5-2.5 m	Has clusters of yellow to red flowers over long period.
Melaleuca fulgens	1.5-3 m x 1.5-3 m	Has scarlet, deep pink or salmon-pink brushes.
Persoonia pinifolia	3-5 m x 2-4 m	Has pine-like leaves and yellow flower-spikes.
Pimelea ferruginea	0.5-1.5 m x 0.5-1.5 m	Has shiny, oblong leaves and terminal pink flower-heads.

Eucalyptus caesia fruits.

Chart 1 — Plants suitable for cultivation in sandy soils

(c) Tall shrubs or trees over 4 m high: A selection of 20 species

Plant Name	Height x width	Brief comment — for further description see Section 2
Acacia elata	10-20 m x 5-10 m	A large wattle with pale yellow flowers in summer.
Angophora costata	10-30 m x 6-15 m	Has smooth-barked trunk. Flowers white to cream.
Banksia ericifolia	3-6 m x 2-5 m	An adaptable banksia with flower-heads commonly orange.
Banksia occidentalis	3-8 m x 2-5 m	Flower-heads are cream to yellow with red.
Banksia prionotes	4-6 m x 4 m	A spectacular banksia but *must* have well-drained soils.
Banksia speciosa	3-6 m x 3-8 m	Has large, yellowish flower-heads.
Casuarina equisetifolia	5-20 m x 5-10 m	A graceful, drooping she-oak.
Dryandra formosa	3-8 m x 2-5 m	Has attractive foliage and orange-yellow flower-heads.
Eucalyptus caesia	5-10 m x 3-5 m	Has decorative foliage and pink flowers tipped with gold.
Eucalyptus eremophila	3-5 m x 3-6 m	Has reddish bud-caps and yellowish flowers.
Eucalyptus ficifolia	6-10 m x 5-8 m	The spectacular and variable Red Flowering Gum.
Eucalyptus sepulcralis	4-8 m x 3-8 m	Has smooth, white trunk, pendulous foliage and pale yellow flowers.
Eucalyptus torquata	5-9 m x 4-6 m	Decorative buds are reddish. Flowers usually pink.
Hakea laurina	3-6 m x 3-5 m	Pincushion flowers are cream and red.
Hakea multilineata	3-5 m x 1.5-3 m	Has showy, pale to deep pink flower-spikes.
Lagunaria patersonii	8-13 m x 3-6 m	A single-trunked tree with pink, open-petalled flowers.
Nothofagus cunninghamii	5-15 m x 3-6 m	Has shiny, oval, toothed leaves with reddish new growth.
Polyscias sambucifolius	4-6 m x 1-3 m	Has small greenish flowers and translucent bluish berries.
Stenocarpus sinuatus	6-15 m x 3-5 m	A spectacular tree with red, wheel-like flower-heads.
Syzygium coolminianum	5-10 m x 3-5 m	Has shiny, dark green leaves and pink to purplish fruits.

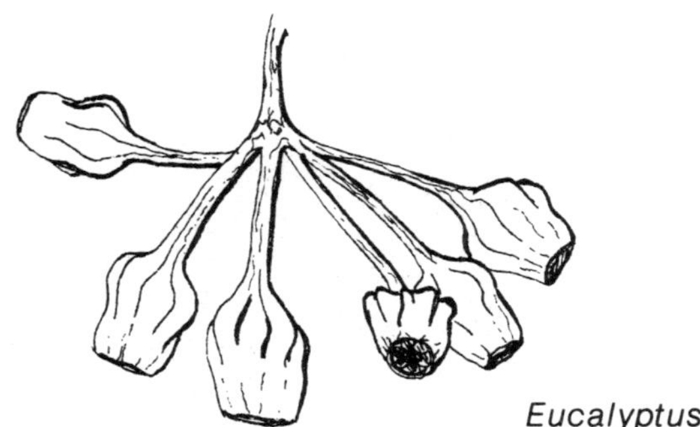

Eucalyptus torquata fruits.

HEAVY CLAY-LOAM AND CLAY SOILS

Once again there are many plants which grow naturally in heavy soils and therefore can be cultivated very successfully in these conditions with a minimum of soil preparation.

In clay soils the particles are very fine. If the area dries out the clay will set hard and surface cracking frequently occurs. Plant roots can be damaged.

In wet seasons moisture is retained by clay for long periods and the soil becomes sloppy and waterlogged. Unless plants are able to cope with waterlogging they are not likely to survive.

Clay soils can be improved by digging in organic material such as leaf litter, compost or peat moss to help separate the fine clay particles. Coarse river sand is also useful, but large quantities are required before there is any benefit. Any material added in this way must be mixed thoroughly with the natural soil to avoid the formation of layers or pockets in which the moisture will collect and cause waterlogging.

Gypsum (hydrated calcium sulphate) is one of the most useful substances for the treatment of clay soils. This is the material from which plaster of Paris is made. When incorporated into the soil it causes the fine clay particles to join together into groups allowing better penetration of moisture and improving the aeration of the soil. Gypsum should always be added when the soil is slightly moist. The recommended rate is 1 to 1.5 kg per square metre. Gypsum is readily obtainable from suppliers of gardening materials.

For best results, treatment of clay soils with a combination of organic matter and gypsum is recommended.

Wherever possible, clay-loam or clay soils should be dug by hand or a deep ripper should be used as this results in an uneven base to the cultivated soil and assists good drainage. Rotary hoeing is not recommended as it can break down the soil structure and also leaves a hard pan base through the action of the rotating blades. Plant roots can have difficulty in penetrating through this layer.

Surface mulching is useful in areas of heavy clay soils. It will reduce moisture loss during hot, dry weather and thus help to prevent the formation of cracks in the soil.

In moist clay areas, where water is retained in the soil for extended periods, it may be necessary to improve the drainage before successful plant growth can be expected. Further information on this aspect will be found below under 'Poorly Drained Areas', and also in Chapter 15, 'Growing Plants in Wet Areas'.

Correa reflexa.

Chart 2 — Plants suitable for cultivation in heavy clay-loam and clay soils

(a) Groundcovers and plants to around 1 m high: A selection of 20 species

Plant Name	Height x width	Brief comment — for further description see Section 2
Anigozanthos flavidus	0.5-1 m x 1 m	Kangaroo paw with green, yellow, orange, pink or red flowers.
Astroloma humifusum	0.1-0.5 m x 0.5-1.5 m	Has pointed leaves and bright red, tubular flowers.
Brachyscome multifida	0.5 m x 1-1.5 m	Has white, pink, blue-mauve or purple daisies.
Brachysema praemorsum	Prostrate to 1 m x 1-3 m	Pea-flowers are cream then deepen to red.
Brachysema sericeum	Prostrate to 1 m x 1-4 m	Pea-flowers are yellow-green, cream or blackish.
Correa reflexa	Variable	The bell-shaped flowers are in many colour combinations.
Dampiera rosmarinifolia	0.4 m x 1-3 m	Low shrub with spikes of blue or mauve flowers.
Eremophila serpens	Prostrate x 1.5-3 m	Has purple and lime-green flowers most of year.
Grevillea confertifolia	Prostrate to 0.5 m x 3 m	Has mauve to pink flower-heads.
Grevillea tridentifera, prostrate form	0.5 m x 2-4 m	Has light green foliage and dense clusters of cream flowers.
Helichrysum apiculatum	0.3-0.6 m x 1-2 m	Has silvery foliage and clusters of bright yellow flower-heads.
Homoranthus papillatus	0.5-1 m x 1-2 m	Has small, greyish-green leaves and small yellow flowers.
Leptospermum humifusum	0.2-1 m x 1-2 m	Leaves are small and dark green. Has white tea-tree flowers.
Melaleuca thymifolia	0.5-1.5 m x 1-1.5 m	A small shrub with mauve to purple flowers.
Patersonia occidentalis	0.5-0.8 m x 0.5 m	A clumping plant with purple flowers.
Pratia pedunculata	Prostrate x 0.5-2 m	Mat plant with small blue or white, starry flowers.
Pultenaea pedunculata	0.5 m x 1-2 m	Has profuse pea-flowers. Several colour forms available.
Scaevola 'Mauve Clusters'	Prostrate x 1-2 m	A dense groundcover with profuse mauve flowers.
Spyridium parvifolium 'Austraflora Nimbus'	Prostrate x 0.5-1 m	Has small, white to cream flowers.
Stypandra ceaspitosa	0.3-0.5 m x 0.5 m	A tufting plant with blue or cream flowers.

Chart 2 — Plants suitable for cultivation in heavy clay-loam and clay soils

(b) Medium shrubs around 1-4 m high: A selection of 20 species

Plant Name	Height x width	Brief comment — for further description see Section 2
Acacia decora	2-5 m x 3-5 m	Has grey-green foliage and golden flower-heads.
Acacia pulchella	0.5-1.5 m x 1-2 m	Has prickly foliage and profuse golden flowers.
Astartea fascicularis	1-2.5 m x 2-3 m	Pink buds open to white, open-petalled flowers.
Baeckea linifolia	1-3 m x 1-2.5 m	Has small leaves and profuse small white flowers.
Banksia spinulosa, dwarf forms	1-2 m x 1-3 m	Flower-heads are yellow or honey-coloured.
Beaufortia orbifolia	2-3 m x 2-3 m	Flower-heads are lime-green with red tips.
Callistemon 'Burgundy'	2-4 m x 2-4 m	Has deep red to burgundy bottlebrushes.
Callistemon 'Mauve Mist'	2-4 m x 2-4 m	Bottlebrush flower-spikes are mauve.
Callistemon phoeniceus	2-4 m x 3-5 m	Has brilliant red or pink bottlebrushes.
Callistemon 'Reeves Pink'	2-4 m x 2-4 m	Bottlebrush flower-spikes are pink tipped with gold.
Callistemon viridiflorus	1-3 m x 1-2 m	An upright plant with yellow-green brushes.
Calothamnus quadrifidus	2-4 m x 2-5 m	Foliage is grey-green and flower-spikes are red.
Grevillea aquifolium	0.2-3 m x 1-4 m	Has holly-like leaves. Flower-heads red and green.
Grevillea 'Clearview David'	2-3 m x 2-4 m	Has prickly green leaves and red with white flowers.
Grevillea 'Poorinda Constance'	1.5-3 m x 1.5-3 m	Has red flowers during most of the year.
Grevillea 'Poorinda Firebird'	1.5-3 m x 1.5-3 m	Has clusters of bright red flowers.
Hakea nodosa	2-3 m x 2-3 m	Yellow flowers are fragrant.
Leptospermum nitidum 'Copper Sheen'	2.5 m x 2-3 m	Foliage is reddish. Flowers are lime-yellow.
Melaleuca incana	2-3 m x 2-3 m	Foliage is grey-green. Has pale yellow brushes.
Melaleuca violacea	1-2 m x 1-2 m	Leaves are greyish-green. Flowers purple to violet.

Chart 2 — Plants suitable for cultivation in heavy clay-loam and clay soils

(c) Tall shrubs or trees over 4 m high: A selection of 20 species

Plant Name	Height x width	Brief comment — for further description see Section 2
Acacia acuminata	6-10 m x 3-5 m	Has bright yellow, rod-like flower-heads.
Acacia fimbriata	5-8 m x 4-6 m	Globular flower-heads are deep cream to yellow.
Acacia retinodes	3-5 m x 3-6 m	Has lemon-yellow flowers for most of the year.
Acacia saligna	3-10 m x 3-6 m	Has profuse, golden-yellow flower-heads.
Allocasuarina littoralis	4-8 m x 2-4 m	A slender she-oak with fine foliage.
Allocasuarina torulosa	8-25 m x 5-10 m	Foliage colour can be reddish to almost black.
Brachychiton acerifolius	10-40 m x 10-15 m	Has bright red flowers and the common name Flame Tree.
Brachychiton populneus	6-20 m x 3-6 m	Has cream or pink, bell-shaped flowers.
Eucalyptus astringens	5-25 m x 4-10 m	Flowers are cream-yellow.
Eucalyptus erythronema	4-9 m x 4-7 m	Has red or sometimes yellow flowers.
Eucalyptus maculata	Usually 15-30 m x 8-15 m	Smooth-barked trunk is spotted. Flowers white.
Eucalyptus megacornuta	6-15 m x 5-10 m	Has a smooth trunk and yellow-green flower clusters.
Eucalyptus tesselaris	10-25 m x 5-12 m	Trunk is smooth and cream. Flowers are white to cream.
Hymenosporum flavum	5-10 m x 1.5-5 m	Yellow and cream flowers are highly fragrant.
Jacksonia scoparia	3-5 m x 1.5-3 m	Has greyish foliage and profuse orange to yellow pea-flowers.
Lophostemon confertus	10-35 m x 6-12 m	Has dark green, shiny leaves and feathery, white flowers.
Melaleuca leucadendron	15-25 m x 8-15 m	Bark is papery. Flower-spikes are cream.
Melaleuca styphelioides	4-15 m x 3-8 m	Has papery bark and creamy white flower-spikes.
Melaleuca viridiflora	8-18 m x 4-10 m	Flower-spikes are pale green or red.
Tristaniopsis laurina	3-15 m x 2-15 m	Has smooth, grey bark and yellow flowers.

POORLY DRAINED AREAS

Some plants are well suited to wet or even waterlogged and swampy conditions, but the majority of species are not. Extended periods of inundation can cause suffocation of the roots and the plants may die as a result.

In poorly drained areas we have the choice of either restricting plant cultivation to those species which will tolerate the moist conditions or improving drainage to remove excess moisture.

The planting of moisture-loving plants does of course also assist in the drainage of the area. The plants absorb the water through their root systems and excess moisture is released as water vapour into the atmosphere by the leaves. This process is called transpiration. A large tree can give off as much as 400 to 500 litres on a hot day.

Many evergreen Australian trees and shrubs have been grown for this purpose, both here and overseas. Deciduous species (such as weeping willows) do not have the same value in this regard when grown in temperate regions, as their moisture requirements are at a minimum during winter when they are without leaves, yet rainfall and waterlogging is then at a peak.

In slightly sloping or even flat areas the digging of surface drains may be all that is necessary to improve the drainage to an acceptable level.

A surface drain. The topsoil removed is added to nearby garden areas.

Garden beds can be built up to make drier areas for planting. Topsoil removed in digging surface drains can be used for this, as can other soil which may have been removed during the construction of pathways, garden pools or building excavations.

In areas of heavy soil, raised garden beds can be further improved by the addition of organic matter or coarse river sand.

In many places, however, the only adequate way to achieve effective drainage is by the formation of underground drains.

A drain can be constructed using a base layer of rubble, such as broken bricks or coarse screenings. Alternatively an agricultural pipe will increase the efficiency of the drain. Terracotta pipes have been used for this purpose for many years. Perforated polythene pipes are also now obtainable. They are extremely easy to install and will provide good drainage if laid correctly. See the diagram.

Always check to ensure that drains work effectively and that the water will flow in the desired direction. It will help if you use a line level during construction.

Chart 3 — Plants which will reduce moisture levels in poorly drained soils

A selection of 20 species

Plant Name	Height x width	Brief comment — for further description see Section 2
Acacia stenophylla	5-20 m x 3-8 m	Has pendulous foliage and cream to yellow flower-heads.
Agonis juniperina	5-10 m x 3-5 m	Has clusters of small, white flowers.
Allocasuarina luehmannii	8-25 m x 5-10 m	Bark is dark and furrowed. Foliage is long and narrow.
Allocasuarina pusilla	0.5-3 m x 1-2 m	An adaptable, dwarf she-oak.
Banksia robur	0.5-3 m x 0.5-2 m	Flower-heads are rich blue-green to yellow-green.
Callistemon citrinus	2-8 m x 2-6 m	Has showy, bright red bottlebrush flowers.
Callistemon speciosus	2-4 m x 1-3 m	Flower-spikes are deep red, tipped with gold.
Casuarina cunninghamiana	10-30 m x 10-12 m	A tall tree with fine, pendulous foliage.
Casuarina glauca	8-30 m x 4-12 m	A hardy she-oak. Can sucker to form a copse.
Eucalyptus camaldulensis	20-40 m x 10-25 m	A large tree with a decorative trunk.
Eucalyptus crenulata	6-15 m x 5-10 m	Leaves are grey-green. Has clusters of white flowers.
Eucalyptus globulus	15-55 m x 10-25 m	A quick-growing tree with profuse white to cream flowers.
Eucalyptus occidentalis	12-20 m x 5-10 m	An adaptable tree with pale yellow flowers.
Eucalyptus robusta	20-25 m x 10-15 m	A quick-growing tree with creamy yellow flowers.
Eucalyptus stellulata	5-15 m x 5-15 m	A sub-alpine tree with cream flowers.
Melaleuca decussata	2-4 m x 2-4 m	Small leaves are grey-green and flower-brushes are mauve.
Melaleuca ericifolia	4-8 m x 2-4 m	Has papery bark, fine leaves and small, cream flower-brushes.
Melaleuca leucadendron	15-25 m x 8-15 m	Has papery bark, broad leaves and cream flower-brushes.
Melaleuca quinquenervia	15-25 m x 3-10 m	Has papery bark, broad leaves and cream flower-brushes.
Viminaria juncea	4-6 m x 2-4 m	Branchlets are pendulous. Has sprays of yellow pea-flowers.

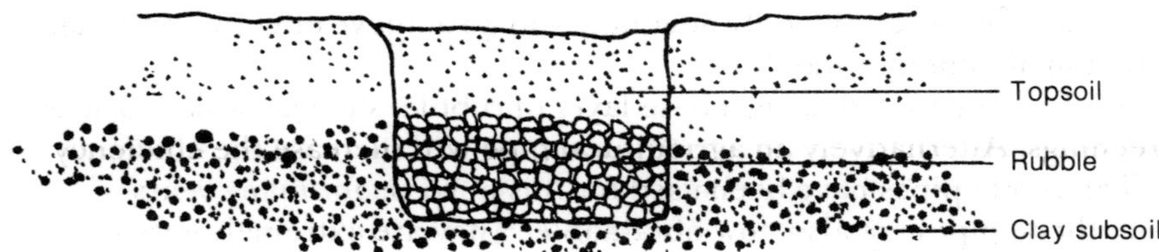

A rubble drain extending down into the clay subsoil. The base layer is of coarse screenings or rubble, and this is then covered with topsoil.

SALINE SOILS

Coastal areas are affected frequently by an excess of salts in the soil. This is caused by salt spray deposited by the strong winds over a long period.

Inland areas can also suffer from salinity. This is common in flat land where the water table lies close to the surface. In some areas salt lakes are formed.

Excessive salinity has a detrimental effect on plant growth. One method of improving the soil is by planting species which will tolerate these conditions. If enough are planted the water table will be lowered through transpiration and then any water received will flow through the soil, dissolving and carrying with it some of the salt.

The following chart lists plants which are suitable for soils with a moderate degree of salinity. For areas severely affected by this problem, advice can be sought from your state Department of Agriculture or Soil Conservation Authority.

ACID OR ALKALINE SOILS

These terms are commonly used in gardening reference books.

Soil acidity or alkalinity is measured on a pH scale, with measure readings of 0-14.

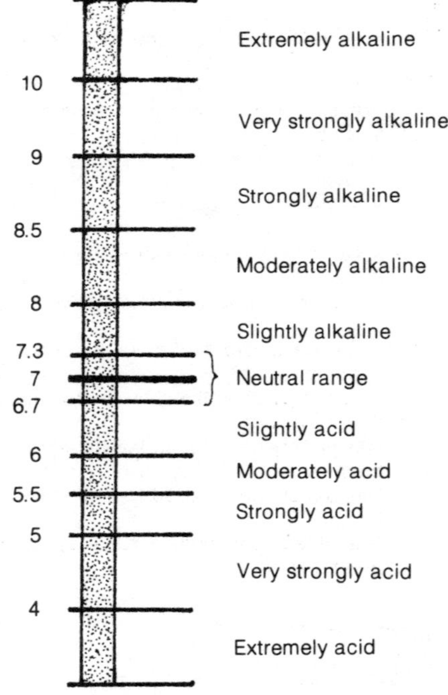

pH Chart.

Neutral soil has a pH reading of about 7. Alkaline or limey soils with an excess of calcium salts have a high pH reading, frequently between 7 and 10. Acid soils are at the bottom of the pH scale. Readings between 5 and 7 are common but they can also be lower.

Simple soil testing kits are obtainable and, by following the instructions given, it is possible for the home gardener to carry out tests to determine soil pH.

1 *Above:* A garden pathway planted with pink *Pimelea ferruginea*, a deep red form of *Lechenaultia formosa* and *Grevillea* 'Robyn Gordon' with lighter red flower-heads. A grey-foliaged form of *Dampiera linearis* provides colour contrast.

2 *Top right:* In this garden of low-growing plants the purple flowers of *Patersonia occidentalis* combine with golden *Helichrysum amplexans* and the white everlasting daisy, *Helichrysum baxteri*.

3 *Below:* Tree sections can provide informal seats. Here the blue of *Dampiera rosmarinifolia* combines attractively with yellow *Conostylis aculeata*.

4 *Bottom right: Grevillea lavandulacea* provides a contrast of grey-green foliage and bright red flowers. The white-flowered groundcover is *Kunzea pomifera* while *Eucalyptus preissiana* with its yellow flowers is seen in the background.

Opposite:
5 *Top left:* A colourful low garden featuring the red-flowered *Kennedia glabrata* and the blue *Dampiera linearis.*

6 *Top right:* The Native Violet, *Viola hederacea*, is an ideal groundcover for rock gardens and crevices. It is seen here with a cream-yellow form of the everlasting daisy, *Helichrysum bracteatum*, the white *Helichrysum baxteri* and the Blue Lechenaultia, *Lechenaultia biloba*, plus several other small plants providing a colourful display.

7 *Bottom left: Acacia iteaphylla* is a showy and long-flowering Wattle. The narrow phyllodes are a bluish green, and often have pink to purplish new growth.

8 *Bottom right:* Stems and trunks can be an important and decorative feature of a garden. Seen here are the smooth trunks of *Eucalyptus spathulata.*

9 *Top right:* A colourful groundcover display featuring yellow *Hibbertia*, blue *Dampiera linearis* form and a pale pink form of *Baeckea ramosissima.*

10 *Bottom right: Eucalyptus leucoxylon* is a variable and attractive species with flowers in shades from white through pink to red. The dwarf forms are extremely popular in cultivation.

11 *Hymenosporum flavum* has the common name of Native Frangipani, because of the delightful fragrance of its cream to deep yellow flowers.

12 *Brachyscome multifida* 'Break of Day' is a selected form of *B. multifida.* This low-growing plant is rarely without a colourful display of blue-mauve daisy flowers.

13 A low-growing form of *Helichrysum apiculatum* with papery, golden flower-heads which are excellent for use in dried flower arrangements.

Chart 4 — Plants suitable for use in saline soils

A selection of 20 species

Plant Name	Height x width	Brief comment — for further description see Section 2
Acacia ligulata	2-5 m x 4-7 m	Has globular, bright yellow to orange flower-heads.
Acacia salicina	4-10 m x 3-5 m	Branches are pendulous. Has pale yellow flower-heads.
Atriplex cinerea	1-2 m x 2-3 m	Has decorative silver-grey foliage.
Atriplex rhagodioides	0.5-2 m x 1-2 m	A hardy species with silver-grey foliage.
Callistemon salignus	5-15 m x 3-5 m	New growth bright pink. Flowers white to deep pink.
Carpobrotus modestus	Prostrate x 1-3 m	Pigface. Leaves are succulent. Flowers are light purple.
Casuarina cristata	8-25 m x 5-10 m	Fine foliage is greyish.
Casuarina glauca	8-30 m x 4-12 m	A hardy she-oak. Can sucker to form a copse.
Eucalyptus botryoides	12-40 m x 8-20 m	Quick-growing large tree. Flowers cream.
Eucalyptus erythrocorys	5-8 m x 3-6 m	Bud caps are red, flowers yellow.
Eucalyptus kondininensis	8-15 m x 5-10 m	Has profuse, white to cream flowers.
Eucalyptus occidentalis	12-20 m x 5-10 m	Has pale yellow flowers.
Eucalyptus platypus var. *heterophylla*	4-10 m x 5-10 m	Flowers are cream to yellow-green.
Eucalyptus sargentii	6-12 m x 5-8 m	Has a profuse display of cream flowers.
Eucalyptus spathulata	6-12 m x 4-8 m	Has a smooth trunk and narrow leaves. Flowers cream.
Eucalyptus stricklandii	6-12 m x 5-10 m	Has bright yellow flowers.
Melaleuca halmaturorum	4-6 m x 2-4 m	Has papery bark and white flower-brushes.
Melaleuca lanceolata	3-8 m x 2-6 m	Trunk has hard, dark bark. Flower-brushes white to cream.
Melaleuca styphelioides	4-15 m x 3-8 m	Paperbark tree with white to cream flowers.
Myoporum insulare	3-5 m x 4-8 m	A bushy shrub with white, starry flowers.

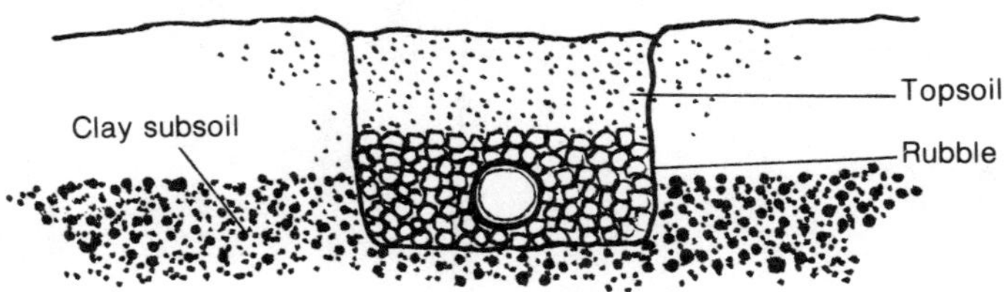

An agricultural pipe drain, with a layer of coarse screenings or rubble surrounding the pipe.

ACID SOILS

The majority of Australian plants grow best in slightly acid soils, or from pH 7 (neutral) down to pH 5.5. High degrees of acidity occur in moist, peaty areas.

Soils with a reading of less than 5.5 can be improved by the addition of lime or dolomite. If lime is being used it is best to add small amounts over a period of time. The addition of large quantities can cause problems with plant growth, which may be difficult to rectify.

For extremely acid soils it is best to choose plants that are known to survive under such conditions.

ALKALINE SOILS

Alkaline soils are fairly common in the arid zones of Australia.

It is not easy to lower the pH of highly alkaline soils. Specific texts on the topic are obtainable and their use is recommended for gardeners who may have this problem. Again, quite a number of Australian plants do occur naturally in limestone regions and these are of great value for the basic garden structure plants in alkaline areas. Throughout the charts in this book the code reference CA has been used to indicate those species which will grow in calcareous or alkaline soils.

The following chart lists a selection of species which are tolerant of alkalinity; all are worthy of cultivation for their decorative form, foliage, flowers or fruits.

Callistemon 'Harkness'. (Photograph by courtesy *Your Garden* magazine.)

Chart 5 — Plants suitable for use in alkaline soils

A selection of 20 species

Plant Name	**Height x width**	**Brief comment — for further description see Section 2**
Acacia calamifolia	2-5 m x 2-4 m	Has long, narrow foliage and golden flower-heads.
Acacia iteaphylla	3-5 m x 3-6 m	Has blue-green foliage and pale yellow flower-heads.
Allocasuarina verticillata	4-11 m x 3-6 m	Bark is dark and furrowed. Long, narrow-foliage is pendulous.
Araucaria bidwillii	30-50 m x 10-20 m	A handsome tree with glossy foliage.
Baeckea behrii	0.5-2 m x 0.5-0.8 m	A slender shrub with small white flowers.
Brachychiton populneus	6-20 m x 3-6 m	Has cream or pink bell-shaped flowers.
Callistemon 'Harkness'	3-6 m x 2-6 m	Bright red flower-spikes are very showy.
Callistemon teretifolius	1-3 m x 2-4 m	New growth is silky. Has crimson flower-brushes.
Cassia nemophila	1-3 m x 1-2 m	Has green or silvery leaves and yellow flowers.
Correa alba	0.5-2 m x 1-2 m	A variable dense shrub with white, starry flowers.
Eremophila glabra	Prostrate to 1.5 m x 1-3 m	A variable species with yellow, red or green flowers.
Eremophila maculata	0.5-3 m x 1-3 m	Variable. Flowers cream, pink, yellow, orange, red or purplish.
Eucalyptus forrestiana	4-6 m x 3-5 m	Has bright orange to red buds and fruits. Flowers yellow.
Eucalyptus kruseana	3-4 x 3-4 m	Has blue-grey oval leaves. Flowers yellow.
Eucalyptus leucoxylon, dwarf forms	5-8 m x 5-8 m	Has attractive trunk. Flowers cream to deep pink.
Grevillea lavandulacea	0.5-2.5 m x 0.5-3 m	Variable species. Has greyish foliage and pink to red flowers.
Hakea suaveolens	3-6 m x 3-5 m	Has prickly foliage and white to cream flowers.
Melaleuca elliptica	3-5 m x 2-5 m	Has oval, grey-green leaves and red flower-brushes.
Myoporum floribundum	2.5-4 m x 2-3 m	A graceful shrub with white flowers.
Templetonia retusa	1.5-2.5 m x 1-2 m	Has bright pink or red pea-flowers.

Correa alba.

4—Planting

CHOOSING WELL-DEVELOPED AND HEALTHY STOCK

This is one of the ten major requirements of successful gardening, as outlined in Chapter 1.

It is not necessary for a plant to be perfect. If some of the leaves have been chewed by caterpillars, this is not likely to affect its future development, apart from perhaps making it more bushy. Similarly plants can recover and thrive after light damage by frost.

However, it is desirable that any plants purchased be sturdy and well developed, whilst not being over-grown and pot-bound. They should also be healthy and free from disease.

HOW TO RECOGNISE PLANTS WHICH ARE NOT WELL-DEVELOPED

If new tips are wilted whilst the soil in the pot is quite moist, it can indicate that the plant has been allowed to dry out, or it may have been moved from a very sheltered location to a more open position. Perhaps the roots had extended through the base of the pot and were recently damaged or removed.

If plants have been heavily fertilised they will frequently produce considerable new growth and consequently their demand for moisture will be high. This need must be met or the plant will soon wither or die. An unbalanced use of fertilisers can lead to excessive top growth, without corresponding root development.

Plant growth which is 'forced' by fertilisers is usually very soft, even on species which normally have quite woody stems. The space between the leaf nodes is frequently greater than usual, because of the forced growth. Young trees may have had to be staked in the pots, because they had insufficient strength to remain upright without support. For best results avoid buying plants which have been overfertilised. Better results will usually be obtained from sturdy specimens, even if they are smaller at the time of planting.

Diseased plants can often be recognised by yellowing, blackening or distortion of the leaves.

Root diseases are not as easy to see; however, if your plant nursery maintains hygienic nursery conditions and uses a sterilised potting mix, the risk of introducing root disease to your garden will be minimised.

It is usually possible to judge, through observation, the cleanliness of any plant nursery. Nurseries which belong to the various state branches of the Australian Nurserymen's Association will have undergone at the time of admission an inspection, which includes cleanliness amongst other considerations. To find out if a nursery uses treated potting mixes the easiest method is simply to ask. The proprietors will be happy to tell you if this precaution against the spread of disease is being undertaken.

The introduction of weeds to a garden through soil brought in with plants purchased is really more than just a minor irritation. Many gardeners very much regret having learnt this lesson too late. If the roots of perennial weeds have become intertwined throughout the root system of a garden plant, their eradication can be a major problem.

Learn to recognise the major problem weeds, some of which are described in Chapter 11.

If you wish to purchase a plant and can see that the pot does contain one or more of the problem weeds (even if its top leaf growth has been recently removed), it is wise to remove all the soil and weed roots from the plant as soon as you get it home. This can be done by gently washing the root system in a bucket of water. The plant should then be repotted into fresh soil and allowed to become re-established by being placed in a sheltered position before being planted into the garden. The old soil and weed growth should be disposed of outside the garden and not added to the compost, etc., where further problems will be created. As an alternative, it might be sensible to seek out another nursery which can be relied on to supply weed-free plants.

CONTAINER SIZE AND THE SELECTION OF PLANTS

Best results are usually achieved if the depth of the container does not exceed the depth of topsoil in the place where the plants will be planted.

If you have very shallow topsoil it may be necessary to build up your garden beds in order to take plants from larger containers. If you just extend the planting hole down into heavy subsoil and then fill it with a lighter potting mix, a sump may form and the water will lie at the base of the plant for extended periods, damaging the roots.

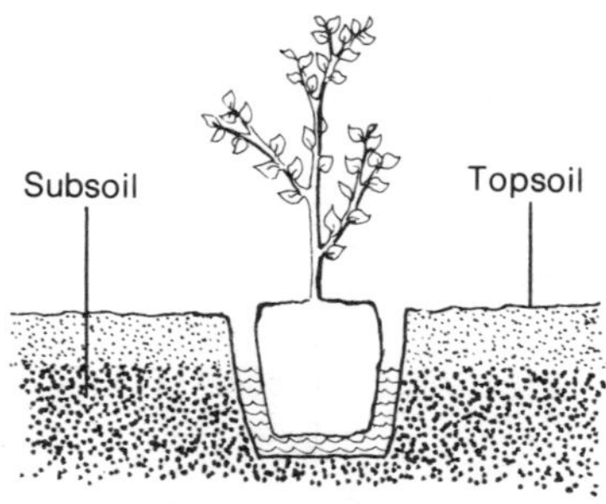

If the planting hole is dug down into the subsoil a sump can be formed, and plants can suffer from excess moisture around the roots.

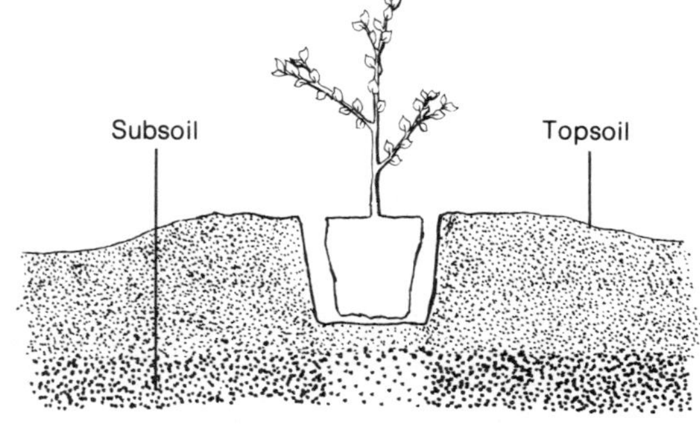

A raised garden bed in an area with shallow topsoil.

WHEN TO PLANT

In most parts of Australia native plants can be planted throughout the year. This is, of course, not the case in alpine regions, where snow covers the ground in winter.

There are nevertheless optimum times for achieving the best results. In temperate zones this is usually in autumn or spring, when the soil is both warm and moist. Autumn often provides the most favourable time, because young plants can become established during the following winter and spring, and will then be sufficiently hardy to survive the heat or dry conditions of the following summer. However, frost-tender species are likely to need some protection during their first winter, particularly if they are just becoming established (see Chapter 10). Young plants planted during spring will require regular watering during their first summer and, if this is not provided by natural rainfall, hand watering will be necessary for their survival.

Although optimum planting time certainly varies from region to region according to climatic variations, with the majority of evergreen Australian plants there is no particular time when they must, or must not, be planted.

If you have just purchased or been given plants for the garden it is not always necessary to plant them out immediately. For practical reasons this may not be possible anyway. In the meantime they should be cared for in the manner recommended for Australian plants in containers, Chapter 25. When the time comes for them to be planted into the garden, check that the roots have not become twisted or coiled and follow the instructions under 'Planting Techniques' in this chapter.

If a plant is in full bloom at the time of planting, or if it has recently produced a considerable amount of soft, new foliage growth, it is often desirable to prune it lightly to reduce the demands being made on the root system during the initial stages of establishment. This is particularly desirable if the removal of twisted or coiled roots has been necessary. However, for plants which are generally healthy and well developed, with a light to medium number of flowers, there is no need for these to be removed, and it is not necessary to wait until the plants have ceased flowering for them to be planted.

PLANTING TECHNIQUES

Before beginning the process of planting make sure that the plants to be planted are thoroughly watered. It will be easier to handle them if this is done several hours before planting.

Step 1
Dig the planting hole approximately twice as wide as it is deep.
Step 2
If the soil is dry, pour water into the hole and allow it to drain. This is best done a few days prior to planting.

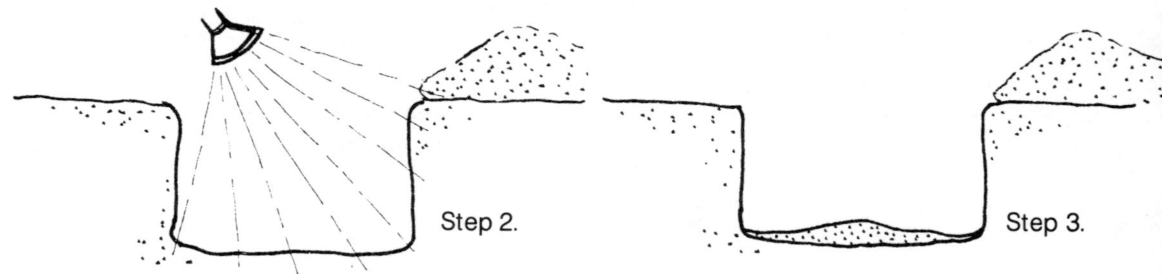

Step 3
Mix a small amount of a slow-release fertiliser evenly through the soil at the base of the hole. Mound the loose soil slightly to allow the plant roots to point down.
Step 4
Remove the plant carefully from the container.

Plants can be tipped from containers with sloping sides, e.g. rigid plastic pots.

Plants in flexible plastic bags will often slide out or the bags can be torn down one side.

Straight-sided tins should be cut with tinsnips to reduce root damage to the plants, although it is best to avoid plants grown in such containers.

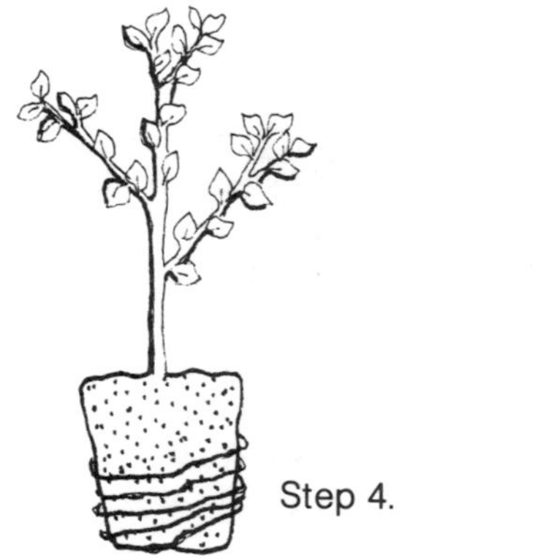
Step 4.

Step 5.

Step 5
Remove any weeds or weed roots, then inspect the roots of the plant.

Straighten any curled roots and prune with secateurs if they are excessively long.

Prune away any broken or damaged roots.

If the roots have formed a mat around the exterior of the soil ball, lightly loosen the root tips and the outside of the soil ball so that the roots can easily grow outwards into the garden soil.
Step 6
Place the plant in the hole, maintaining the same surface level as that of the original plant container. Spread the roots evenly.

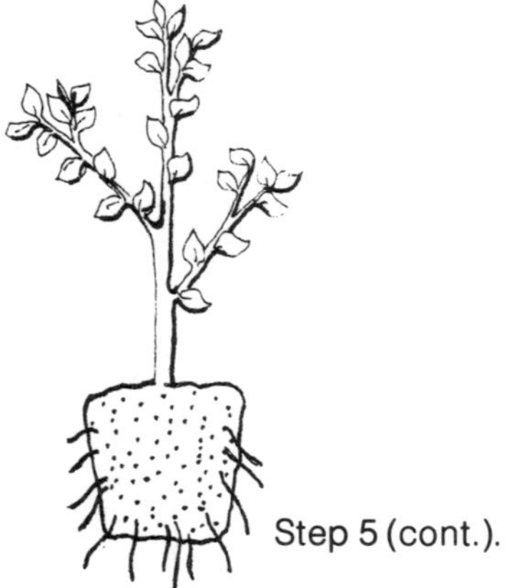
Step 5 (cont.).

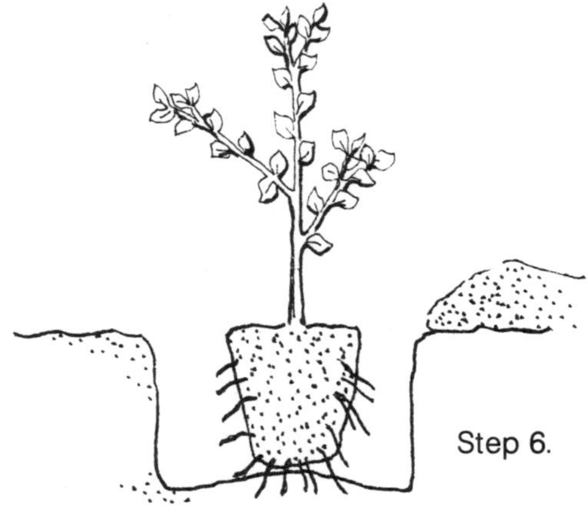
Step 6.

Step 7
Fill the hole with soil and firm it around the plant.
Step 8
Water thoroughly, using about one bucket (approx. 10 litres) of water. This can be poured in 2 to 4 stages to avoid too much water running away. If you add to the water a fungicide, a root stimulant, and a seaweed-base fertiliser it will help to establish young plants.

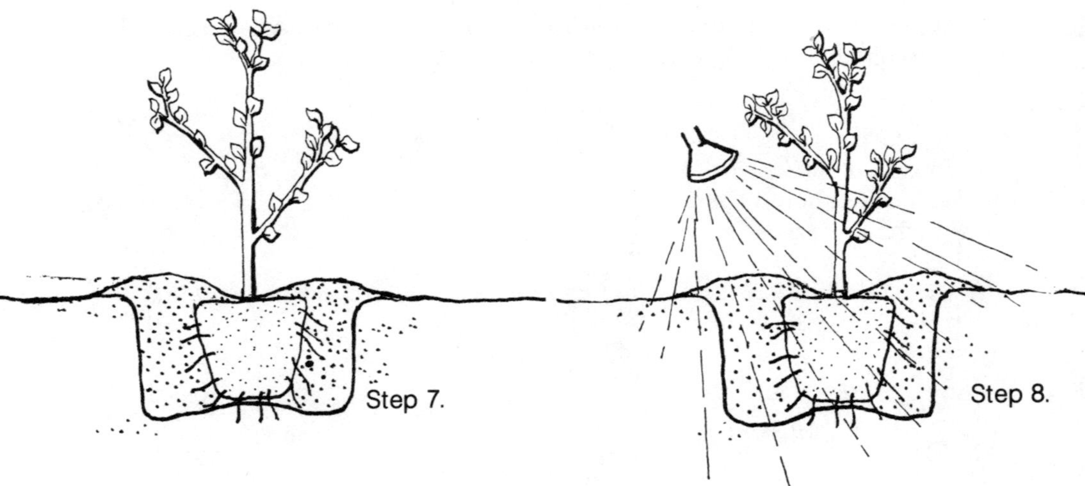

Staking of young plants is usually unnecessary (see Chapter 8). Information about staking methods is also provided in Chapter 8.

Many gardeners mulch after planting. Mulches can be extremely important for the conservation of moisture in the topsoil and have a highly beneficial effect on the development of young plants. Information on the various types of mulches available will be found in Chapter 6.

5—Watering

This is one of the most comon areas of concern amongst gardeners.

How much water do plants need?

How often should I water?

Insufficient or excessive watering is also one of the main reasons plants die in cultivation.

Watering is therefore a subject of considerable importance if we hope to be able to grow plants successfully.

BASIC GARDEN LAYOUT

Without any doubt the best time to consider the topic of watering is at the time of garden planning and preparation. Some parts of the garden may be naturally dry or even very dry. Improvements to the soil can be carried out (see Chapter 3) and plants which are likely to grow well under dry conditions should be selected for these areas. Similarly, if a section of the garden holds moisture for excessive periods, plants which grow naturally in moist regions are likely to prove the most successful. Chapter 3 gives information on soil preparation, together with details of plants suitable for a number of different soil types.

If you plan to grow a particular plant species, always try to find out about its need for moisture before planting. This will help you avoid the problems associated with growing a plant in the wrong position.

For minimum maintenance gardening, endeavour to group together plants which require similar conditions. For example, plants such as the Brown Boronia (*Boronia megastigma*), which appreciate a cool, moist root area throughout the year, will thrive in an easterly location, combined with most Mint Bushes (*Prostanthera* species), Native Violets (*Viola* species) and ferns. You can then keep this area moist by regular watering, without the need to water the entire garden. Many species will survive with a minimum of water during summer months, even with no manual watering at all, and these also should be grouped together.

This type of planning reduces watering to a minimum, increases the chances of plant survival during vacations, and also saves the unnecessary consumption of that valuable resource — water.

Often, despite planning and garden preparation, problems do occur as a garden matures. Large shrubs or trees become well-established and their need for moisture causes the soil in their vicinity to become extremely dry. This situation can of course be caused by plants on adjacent properties as well as plants in your own garden. Deep and thorough watering techniques should be used if hand watering is necessary. See 'How to Water Correctly', later in this Chapter.

Chapter 20 provides information on 'Replanting Amongst Existing Trees and Shrubs'.

MULCHING FOR WATER CONSERVATION

Mulching plays a very significant role in reducing the need for watering. It helps by shielding the topsoil from the direct heat of the sun, thus minimising loss of water through evaporation. The need to water plants during periods without rain is then reduced. Chapter 6 contains further information on mulching and the various mulching materials available.

TIME OF PLANTING

The time of year when new plants are planted out also has considerable bearing on the need for watering.

In temperate regions and particularly in large gardens where hand watering is not practicable, it is recommended that planting be undertaken after the first good soaking rains of autumn. This allows the young plants to become established during the autumn-winter-spring period, so they are more likely to be able to cope with the following summer than if they were planted later in the year.

In areas where there are heavy frosts, an exception may need to be made, particularly in regard to frost-tender species. These plants can be planted later in the year, or special protection can be given to the young plants during the winter (see Chapter 10).

HOW TO CHECK WHETHER PLANTS NEED WATERING

Usually it is possible to find out if plants need watering by simply poking into the soil with your finger. If it is moist at a depth of 2 to 3 cm down, watering is not necessary.

Plants will sometimes show symptoms of lack of moisture by wilting of the foliage. This does not always indicate dryness, however, so check before reaching for the hose. A young plant which is growing rapidly will frequently have wilted tips on a hot day, simply because it is unable to take in moisture quickly enough, even though that moisture is available in the soil. If the soil is damp, additional watering is not needed and the plant will usually regain its normal condition overnight.

It is simply not possible to make a general recommendation on how often watering may be necessary in periods when there is no natural rainfall. With young plants or species requiring a high level of moisture it may be once every three days or once a week. For other well-established species it may be once a month, or hand watering may not be needed at all.

You just have to use you own judgment, remembering that many Australian plants are very hardy and tolerant of extended periods of dryness. Don't feel that you *must* water the garden regularly.

If knowing when to water becomes a major problem for you, you can buy relatively inexpensive moisture-meters of various types, which will assist in making these judgments.

For information on the watering of plants grown in containers, see Chapter 25.

HOW TO WATER CORRECTLY

Often we simply do not stop to consider what happens when we water our gardens. If we are in a hurry, there is a strong temptation to give the garden 'just a quick watering' with the promise of more thorough attention next time. If this occurs frequently, the plants will develop roots primarily in the uppermost layer of the soil, just to where the water usually penetrates.

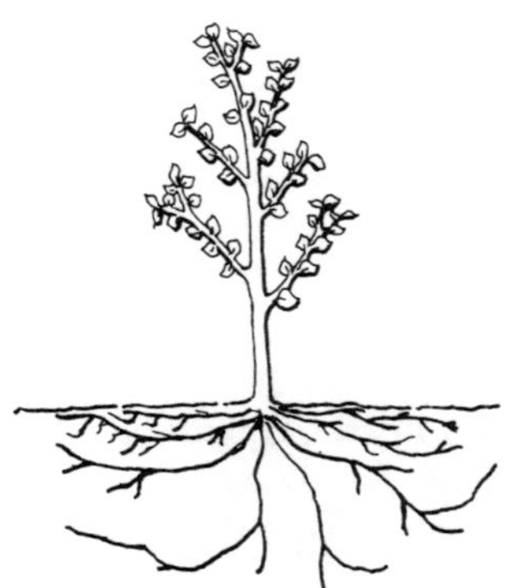

Dense root growth in surface layer of soil can be caused by frequent light watering.

Deep soaking promotes a good root system which extends down into the soil.

If we go on holiday or for other reasons there is no hand watering or rainfall, it is this upper layer of soil which will dry out first. Then those plants with roots near the surface will be unable to cope and die through lack of moisture.

We should therefore ensure that in all manual watering we give the area a thorough soaking. As the moisture penetrates right down into the soil, so too will the plants' roots and thus their chances of survival in times of stress will be considerably increased.

Unfortunately it is not possible to generalise and state in simple terms just how much water is required to achieve this deep soaking of the soil. Soils with a high organic content have better moisture-retaining ability than sandy soils, and are also better able to absorb moisture at surface level. Dry sandy soils can become impervious so that the water will sit on the surface or run off and will not be able to penetrate readily, and a similar barrier can be created in heavier clay soils by a hard, compacted surface. Applying a mulch or lightly hoeing the surface can help to reduce these problems. The number of plants being grown in an area, and their sizes, will also have a considerable bearing on the amount of water needed to achieve a thorough soaking of the garden.

It should be remembered that the need for deep soaking of garden areas does not only exist in summer. Soils can also dry out during the cooler months if rainfall has been only light. It is important to maintain the moisture level in the subsoil, to support the feeder roots in that area.

Never water the foliage of plants whilst they are exposed to hot sunshine.

Check before using a hose in summer to ensure that the water coming through the spray is cool. Water can reach very high temperatures in a hose which has been lying in the sun.

Water gently. Don't use a strong spurt of water at the base of small plants. It is likely to dislodge soil and expose the small feeder roots.

OVER-WATERING

We frequently make the mistake of killing our plants with 'kindness'. Far more Australian native plants die from over-watering than from neglect in this regard.

Our continent is renowned for the dry to very dry conditions which exist over most of the country and many of the native plants have adapted to cope with these conditions. Some of the most spectacular and showy species grow best in arid or semi-arid areas. We can use these plants in our gardens, in the interests both of labour-saving gardening and also water conservation.

The succulent foliage of *Carpobrotus* spp., Pigface, enables plants to survive in areas which can be hot and dry for extended periods.

DANGERS OF SUMMER WATERING

Plants from areas of little or no summer rainfall can often die if watered during hot weather. Unfortunately death may also occur as a result of heavy summer rainfall or humidity, as well as from manual watering.

These plants have adapted to tolerate hot, dry conditions, but not a combination of heat plus excessive moisture. Several *Banksia* species native to south-western WA are good examples.

There are many aspects to plant adaptation. For example, the roots of *Cassia* and *Eremophila* species are extremely efficient at absorbing any available moisture.

The silvery foliage of many desert plants will reflect rather than absorb heat, and other species have succulent leaves which retain moisture.

Trees and shrubs from tropical rainforest areas are almost the opposite. Because of the high moisture levels and humidity the leaves are usually very efficient at the process of transpiration.

Another problem with summer watering is that the combination of moisture and high temperatures provides ideal conditions for the spread of root fungal diseases, particularly in soils that are not well drained. Whilst some plant species have adapted to withstand such attacks, the majority of plants from low rainfall regions are either susceptible or highly susceptible, and death can result. A major problem disease in this regard is the Cinnamon Fungus (*Phytophthora cinnamomi*).

It is recommended that summer watering be done during cool weather if at all possible.

If it is necessary to water during warm periods, avoid spraying the foliage.

As mentioned earlier, make sure any watering is of a deep, soaking nature and avoid frequent, light waterings. (See 'How to Water Correctly', above.)

SUMMER WATERING OF YOUNG PLANTS

Young plants need to be kept moist throughout hot weather until they have become well established. As their moisture requirement during the period of early growth is greater than that of mature plants, they are able to tolerate the additional intake of water. Juvenile foliage also differs from the mature leaves in many species, allowing for excess moisture to be released into the atmosphere.

WATERING SYSTEMS FOR THE HOME GARDEN

When considering any form of watering system, we should be conscious of the need for water conservation as well as our desire to maintain plant growth.

A fixed sprinkler system can be installed in the garden, but there are several disadvantages to this method. It usually involves a considerable amount of run-off and wasted water and the spray may be blown away from the garden on a windy day so that the plants remain dry. Tall sprinklers are more of a problem in this regard than the lower types.

If you wish to use fixed sprinklers, it is certainly better if the plants which require moisture are grouped together so that the water is sprayed only where necessary.

Trickle irrigation provides an excellent and economical alternative for the home gardener. Water is fed to the plants through a series of very small plastic tubes at a slow drip rate. Consequently there is no excessive run-off and the timing mechanism can be adjusted so that the plants receive exactly the amount of moisture they need. Such a system may take a little time to install, but you will be well rewarded by its efficiency.

Trickle irrigation is useful for general garden plants, the vegetable garden and for plants growing in containers. If some plants require more moisture than others, two or more micro-tubes can be fitted instead of just the one, or alternatively dripping nozzles which can be regulated are easily installed.

Your nearest Department of Agriculture office can tell you where further information on trickle irrigation and other plant watering systems can be obtained. There are also listings of garden and agricultural sprinkler suppliers in the telephone books of all major Australian cities.

In times of water shortage, methods which involve the watering of individual plants are desirable. Upturned bottles placed beside plants requiring regular watering will allow the moisture to seep slowly into the soil. Specially designed plastic spikes (such as 'Aquaspikes') which fit into the neck of a bottle are available as an aid to the flow of water. Alternatively, you can bury a plant pot in the soil beside a chosen plant, then fill the pot with water at regular intervals. Trenches can also be dug near plants to hold water and ensure that waste through run-off is minimal.

RECYCLING HOUSEHOLD WATER FOR GARDEN USE

Recycled domestic water can be valuable for garden maintenance if you live in an area where only tank or bore water is available. It can also be of considerable use in times of drought, when the use of reticulated water for the garden may be restricted.

In suburban areas serviced by a sewerage system, there may be restrictions on the recycling of water. Regulations usually state that all kitchen water must be discharged through the sewerage system. It is, however, possible to make use of bath and laundry water for watering the garden.

Any recycled water should of course be allowed to cool before use on plants. The mild soaps generally used in bath water are unlikely to have any detrimental effect in the garden. Laundry detergents can cause some problems. The harmful ingredients are primarily boron and sodium compounds and boron toxicity can result in major damage to plant foliage. Continued use of waste water with a high sodium content would raise the pH of some soils to an undesirable degree. See 'Acid or Alkaline Soils' in Chapter 3.

To avoid these problems you can use only the rinse water from the washing machine for the garden, or alternatively buy a laundry detergent which does not contain these ingredients.

It is perhaps not until we go through a period of drought or water shortage that we realise the true value of water. It is a vital asset and its conservation should be encouraged at all times. We should also try to avoid any possible causes of water pollution.

6—Mulching

A mulch is a layer of material placed over the surface of the soil. There are different types of mulches and we will be looking at a number of them here.

A woodchip mulch helps to conserve moisture and prevent weed growth around small, clump-forming garden plants.

WHY MULCH?

The main benefits of good mulching are as follows.

(a) To conserve moisture during hot or dry weather.
(b) To maintain a fairly constant temperature in the root area.
(c) To prevent crusting of the soil and to enable better penetration of surface water.
(d) To allow plants to gain greater benefit from the upper layer of topsoil.
(e) To assist in weed control.

All areas of garden maintenance are of course related to each other through the total development of the plants. Mulching is directly related to watering, which has just been covered in Chapter 5.

As well as allowing droplets of water to penetrate through to the soil instead of draining away, mulching will reduce evaporation by shielding the soil from the direct rays of the sun.

Mulching also plays a very significant role in regard to weed control. This is discussed both later in this chapter and also in Chapter 11.

MULCHING MATERIALS

Mulching materials are listed in Chart 6. They vary from inorganic materials such as sand, gravel or even plastic sheeting, through to a wide range of organic materials, including bush litter, grass clippings, sawdust and compost. Low groundcover plants can also assist as 'living mulches', because they help shield the soil from the sun's rays.

Coarse sand or gravel is undoubtedly one of the best mulches available for garden use. The relatively high cost of these materials is the main drawback.

In areas of heavy frost it is not wise to use organic mulches as they retain moisture which becomes frozen at low temperatures, so mulching with sand or gravel is certainly best.

A major function of most mulches is to act as a weed deterrent. However, mulches do not in most cases eliminate weed growth and in areas badly infested with weeds some other form of control should be used in conjunction with a mulch to achieve good results. Nevertheless a thick layer of mulch will usually reduce weed growth and make weed control easier.

Sand mulches do not act as weed deterrents. In fact they provide ideal conditions for weed seeds to germinate and become established. If regular checks are made, however, young weed seedlings can be easily removed. Of course, the same conditions can be used to your advantage if desired and plants such as Flannel Flowers (*Actinotus* species) or annual Everlasting Daisies (*Helipterum* species) can be encouraged to self-sow in the sand to form attractive drifts in a garden.

When using organic materials, the mulch should not be placed close to the trunk of a tree or shrub. In particular, the common practice of placing grass clippings around tree trunks is not recommended as the disease known as 'collar rot' can result. This causes damage to the area of the plant just above ground level.

Sawdust is a material commonly used for garden mulching. Hardwood sawdust is generally better than softwood. Never use a mulch of sawdust from timber which has been treated with preservatives (e.g. treated pine). The chemicals can have an adverse effect on garden plants.

As sawdust mulches break down, nitrogen is used in the decomposition process and plants in that area can suffer from nitrogen deficiency. This shows in a

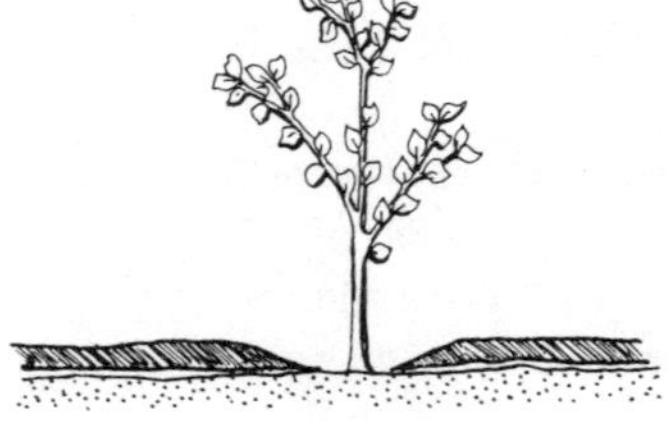

Do not place organic mulches right against the trunks of plants. In this illustration the mulch is a suitable distance away.

yellowing of foliage and can be counteracted by application of blood and bone or another similar fertiliser.

A sawdust mulch should be trampled firmly with the feet after spreading. The mulch should then be watered thoroughly to avoid the sawdust being blown away by every light breeze. A light covering of coarse sand or crushed rock will help prevent removal by the wind.

Sawdust mulches, although excellent in many respects, should never be used in places where there is a high fire risk. Fire can travel below the surface of the mulch, then break through some distance away from the initial outbreak.

Some mulching materials (e.g. sawdust and pine needles) can prevent water soaking down into the soil. If this occurs, a light layer of coarse sand spread over the mulch will help.

Among the comparatively recent introductions to the shelves of nurseries and garden stores is a black, spun bonded, continuous polyester fibre material, sold under the registered name of 'Marix'. It is said to have a mulch value equivalent to 20 cm of loose straw, and is durable and resistant to rot, as well as being light and easy to use. Both air and water are able to permeate through the fabric to allow good plant growth, whilst at the same time the material restricts the development of weeds.

A woven polypropylene fabric with similar qualities to the material described above is also available. It is sold under the name of 'Rheem Weed Stop', and can be obtained in widths of up to 5 m.

Mulch materials of this type can be used in garden beds, and circles of the fabric can also be cut and placed around the base of container-grown plants.

Chart 6 — Materials used as garden mulches

Mulch	Durability	Depth	Comments
Bush litter	Very good	5-10 cm	An excellent mulch but will need some replenishing as material breaks down. If gathered from the bush, collect only from areas known to be free from Cinnamon Fungus.
Carpet	Good to very good	—	Old carpet placed beneath a mulch such as pine bark or wood chips can help to smother weeds. Carpets which allow air and moisture penetration are better than rubber-backed types, which are not recommended.
Coffee bean husks	Fair	5 cm	A good mulch but can become messy as the husks break down. Is best incorporated with the soil.
Compost	Short	5-10 cm	Is mainly valuable for incorporation with the soil. If used as a mulch it needs replenishing as the material breaks down.
Grass clippings	Short	5-10 cm	A good mulch but should not be placed or piled around trunks. Heat is created in piles of green clippings. Moisture permeability is poor in a thick mulch of dry clippings. Valuable for incorporation with soil.
Gravel	Excellent	5-7.5 cm	Highly recommended. Does not adversely affect plants if placed next to stems and trunks but should be kept to a depth of 5 cm around trunks.
Hay	Fair	5-10 cm	See Straw.
Lawn clippings	Short	5-10 cm	See Grass clippings.

Mulch	Durability	Depth	Comments
Mulch from garden shredder	Good	5-10 cm	An excellent material but will need some replenishing as material breaks down. Prunings from diseased plants should not be used in this way.
Mushroom compost	Fair	5-7.5 cm	A good mulch but should not be placed near trunks of plants. Moisture permeability is poor when dry. Best incorporated with soil.
Newspaper	Fair	—	Several thicknesses of newspaper placed beneath a mulch such as pine bark or wood chips can help to control annual or perennial weeds in some situations. It should be borne in mind that the paper will gradually break down.
Peanut shells	Good	5-7.5 cm	A good mulch, if available.
Pine bark	Very good	5-7.5 cm	A good mulch with excellent moisture retention and temperature control. Should not be placed right against trunks of plants.
Pine needles	Good	5-10 cm	A fair mulch. Penetration of moisture is very slow unless the material has been put through a mulching machine.
Plastic sheeting	Very good	—	Not recommended as a mulching material. It can help create sour soil in poorly drained areas. Although useful on large, sloping areas with a covering of pine bark, etc., weeds can become difficult to eradicate if holes occur, or the plastic breaks down.
Polyester mulch fabric	Excellent	—	Spun or woven polyester fabric, prepared specifically as a garden mulching material. Highly recommended. Can be covered with a thin layer of pine bark, wood chips, etc.
Sand, coarse	Excellent	5-7.5 cm	Highly recommended, even though it can be expensive. Sand can provide ideal conditions for seed germination so weeds should not be allowed to set seed.
Sand, fine	Excellent	5-7.5 cm	A fair mulch. The main problem is that water will run off when the sand is dry. See Sand, coarse, above, re seed germination.
Sawdust, hardwood	Fair	5-25 cm	A good mulch but breaks down and will need replenishing. Soil can become deficient in nitrogen, which can be corrected by application of blood and bone. Mulch should not be placed against trunks of plants.
Screenings	Excellent	5-7.5 cm	See Gravel.
Straw or hay	Fair	5-10 cm	A good mulch, ideal for embankments. Moisture permeability can be poor when mulch is dry. The main problem (particularly with hay) is the germination of seed from grain crops and weeds.
Tan bark	Very good	5-7.5 cm	An excellent mulch, but rarely obtainable due to modern tanning methods which has led to a reduction in the use of bark.
Underfelt	Fair	—	See Carpet.
Wood chips, hardwood	Very good	5 cm	Highly recommended as a mulch, but not always easily available.
Wood shavings, hardwood	Good	5-25 cm	An excellent mulching material, but moisture permeability is poor when the mulch is dry. It is recommended that the surface be covered with a thin layer of coarse sand. This allows water to penetrate and also prevents the mulch from blowing away.
Wood shavings or chips, softwood	Fair	5-7.5 cm	A very good mulch. Commonly creates a nitrogen deficiency as it breaks down but this can be corrected by the application of blood and bone.

7—Fertilising

All home gardeners know that plants require an intake of nutrients in order to grow well. Such nutrition is available through air, water and the soil. Beyond this basic information, many of us are somewhat 'hazy' as to the more specific needs of our plants and how they can best be provided. We are told that without adequate food intake plants may become stunted or die and that deaths can also result from over-fertilising. How then can we achieve the happy medium?

Generally it is possible for us to use a fertiliser which will assist plant growth by simply purchasing a recommended product and following the directions on the packet. Thus we can find on nursery shelves packs of 'Tomato Fertiliser', 'Lawn Fertiliser', 'Rhododendron Fertiliser', and so on.

A problem does arise, however, when we want to assist the growth of plants for which no specific product is available. At the present time there are very few fertilisers packaged specifically for Australian plants and most of those available are marked simply as being suitable for native plants in general. As there are thought to be around 10 000 different species in cultivation from a wide range of natural habitats, the needs of these plants will obviously vary considerably. We will be looking at the needs of some particular plant genera later in this chapter.

For information on the fertilising of plants grown in containers, readers should refer also to Chapter 25.

A selection of plant fertilisers. (Photograph by courtesy *Your Garden* magazine.)

TYPES OF FERTILISERS

It is interesting and helpful to know something of the nutrients required by plants. With this information we can select a fertiliser suited to our requirements or correct specific deficiencies within our garden.

Element	Symbol	
Carbon —	C	Obtained from air/water.
Oxygen —	O	
Hydrogen —	H	
Nitrogen —	N	Known as the 3 macro nutrients or major elements. Available in the soil and contained in various proportions in garden fertilisers.
Phosphorus —	P	
Potassium —	K	
Sulphur —	S	Also major elements. Usually contained in the soil to an adequate degree.
Calcium —	Ca	
Iron —	Fe	
Magnesium —	Mg	
Manganese —	Mn	
Zinc —	Zn	Known as trace elements, or minor elements. Required only in very small quantities.
Copper —	Cu	
Boron —	Bo	
Chlorine —	Cl	
Molybdenum —	Mo	
Cobalt —	Co	

Fertilisers which are labelled as 'complete' or 'general garden' fertilisers usually contain nitrogen, phosphorus and potassium in stated proportions, e.g. N:P:K — 10:9:8, which would indicate 10 per cent nitrogen, 9 per cent phosphorus and 8 per cent potassium. Many variations occur, both in the elements contained and in their ratio. Blood and bone may supply nitrogen and phosphorus at a ratio of 6.5N:4P, whilst some hoof and horn fertilisers contain the same elements with a ratio of 12N:1P. For those Australian plants which react adversely to excessive phosphorus, the latter provide a more suitable fertiliser.

Nitrogen rich fertilisers encourage lush foliage growth. If applied in excessive quantity, over-development will occur and plants may become weakened as a result.

Fertilisers with a higher ratio of phosphorus and potassium will encourage flowering and fruiting. Such fertilisers are used widely in the cultivation of fruit and vegetable crops, with superphosphate being commonly used as the phosphorus fertiliser.

Fertilisers containing some or all of the major elements can be obtained in various forms from powders through granules and pellets to fertiliser sticks. Several of these products are coated with compounds which allow the nutrients to be released slowly over a period of weeks or months, instead of all at the time of application. These are known as 'slow-release fertilisers'. Here again it is important to read the manufacturers' instructions at the time of use to avoid over-fertilising by too frequent applications.

ANIMAL MANURES

The three major elements are also available through animal manures. Cow and horse manure are high in nitrogen, followed by potassium, with some phosphorus. Poultry manure is high in nitrogen and phosporus, with some potassium.

Fresh manure should be stored for some months before use to avoid burning the plant roots. Organic material including animal manures should never be placed agains the trunks of trees or shrubs, as collar rot and other diseases can result.

One problem with animal manures is that they frequently contain seeds and so introduce grasses and weeds into the garden. This is less of a problem when they are stored before use.

As well as supplying nutrients, animal manures are of value in improving the texture of the soil. See Chapter 3, 'Soil Preparation'. Organic material such as manure or compost will help retain moisture in sandy areas and improve drainage in heavy clay soils.

LIQUID FERTILISERS

Liquid fertilisers are used mainly when a rapid or short-term result is desired. Because the fertiliser is in a soluble form it can be absorbed readily by the plant roots or the young foliage.

A wide range of fertilisers can be applied in this way, including soluble chemical compounds and organic preparations involving animal manures or seaweed, etc.

Liquid fertilisers are useful for correcting specific mineral deficiencies in plants, such as the use of chelated iron to correct yellowing of foliage caused by iron deficiency.

As with other forms of fertiliser, it is important to know just what is contained in any liquid fertiliser and to avoid over-fertilising plants.

CORRECT APPLICATIONS OF FERTILISERS

The first and most important rule in regard to fertiliser application is that fertilisers, particularly inorganic ones, should never be added to dry soil.

Garden areas or containers should be well watered before the addition of fertilisers. This rule is particularly important in regard to granules or pellets of slow-release fertiliser. If these are exposed to moisture and then dry out the coating can crack, allowing the total nutrient to be released immediately, instead of giving the normal slow release over a period of weeks or months.

The soil should similarly be moist before any liquid fertilisers are applied.

Fertilisers can be added at the time of planting and information regarding this will be found in Chapter 4.

Usually, once native plants have become established in the garden there is little or no need for regular applications of fertiliser. It may be possible to achieve a quicker growth rate through the use of fertilisers, but if this results in a plant which is leggy, or weak, or may be blown out by the wind as it nears maturity, then quick growth will have been a disadvantage rather than desirable.

The aim should be to ensure that sufficient nutrients are available for the development of healthy and sturdy plants with natural vigour.

As a generalisation, applications of one-half to one-third of the recommended rates should be ample for most Australian plants. Young, recently purchased plants may still have adequate fertiliser reserves and won't need any more at planting time.

General fertilising of entire native garden areas is not usually recommended once the plants have become established. An exception may occur if for some reason a complete area has become deficient in a particular element. Nitrogen deficiency can, for example, develop if a garden bed has been mulched with fresh sawdust, see Chapter 6.

If individual plants need fertilising they can be treated by raking or digging lightly around the root area and adding the fertiliser. The area should then be covered again with soil, or a mulch, and watered well. (Warning! The application of blood and bone in this way can encourage dogs to dig and scratch in the area.)

Liquid fertilisers provide another means of adding nutrients to particular plants within a garden.

WHEN TO FERTILISE

There is little point in applying fertilisers when plants are in a period of dormancy or minimum growth. The optimum time for good results will vary from area to area and also frequently from season to season.

Choose a time when new growth is beginning to appear and make sure that the area is moist before the fertiliser is applied.

Fertilisers should *not* be used in autumn in regions of heavy frost during winter. Any new growth encouraged at this time of year will quickly be burnt by the cold and under severe conditions the plant could die.

If fertilisers are used during the winter, when plants are unable to utilise them adequately due to lower temperatures, the plants may react adversely.

SOME PARTICULAR AUSTRALIAN PLANTS AND THEIR NEEDS

In general, plants which occur naturally in regions of high organic content, such as in rainforests or wet sclerophyll forests, have adapted to grow in and utilise a high degree of the major nutrients. They therefore respond well to applications of complete fertiliser.

All annual species which grow quickly, flower and then die, and plants which become dormant for a period between each flowering season will respond well to the use of fertilisers. Many of the native everlasting daisies can be included in this category.

Most Kangaroo Paws (*Anigozanthos* species) respond well to generous watering and regular fertilising during the spring-summer flowering period, although drainage should be good to allow excess moisture to get away.

The Bottlebrushes (*Callistemon* species) have been found to respond favourably to applications of fertiliser. If this is applied following the spring flowering season and in conjunction with summer watering, a second flowering period in autumn will frequently result.

Species of *Leptospermum* and *Melaleuca* which are in the same family as *Callistemon* will respond favourably to fertilising, although their growth rate is normally adequate without this treatment. Fertilisers are also used with success on species which are grown for the cut flower trade and therefore pruned heavily each year.

Species of Australian plants which occur naturally in regions of low rainfall and poor soils do not respond as well to fertilising.

Many members of the Proteaceae family have adapted extremely well to conditions much less favourable than we supply in our gardens. A particular type of root development, called 'proteoid roots', makes the plants extremely efficient in their intake of whatever small amount of nutrient may be available. Thus if larger than normal amounts are applied through fertilisers these plants can suffer from the excessive intake. An excess of phosphorus is one of the main dangers and the result is commonly known as phosphorus toxicity. (See Chapter 12 under paragraph 13, 'Mineral Deficiencies or Excesses'.)

Some commonly cultivated members of the Proteaceae family are *Banksia, Dryandra, Grevillea, Hakea, Isopogon* and *Petrophile.* They will appreciate a light application of a slow-release fertiliser at the time of planting, but will rarely need further treatment. In some cases yellowing of foliage may occur and this can be corrected by the use of chelated iron.

Members of the family Rutaceae, including *Boronia, Correa* and *Eriostemon*, are noted for their dislike of overdoses of inorganic fertilisers. In general, fertilisers should be kept to a minimum with these species. However, Correas often occur in naturally alkaline soils and it has been found that the development of young plants can be encouraged by a light application of dolomite or ground limestone.

Dryandra formosa. (Photograph by courtesy *Your Garden* magazine.)

8—*Staking and the Use of Plant Guards*

STAKING

Most Australian native plants do not need stakes to support them as they grow. The movement of a plant in the wind is both natural and healthy. It encourages the strengthening of the trunk and root system to resist and survive the local climatic conditions.

In areas of strong winds the need for staking can be reduced by planting small trees and shrubs at an early stage of their development. Larger plants may need initial support from stakes.

Staking may be necessary if plants are transplanted from one area to another, or if plants become top-heavy due to an unbalanced programme of fertilisation and excessive foliage growth. Established plants may require staking if they are suddenly exposed to strong winds by the removal of previous protection, such as that provided by buildings or other plants.

The pruning of plants to promote bushy growth can reduce the need for staking and help to promote sturdier plants. One Australian native plant which can be treated in this way is the large-flowered *Eucalyptus caesia* 'Silver Princess'. Its long, pendulous branches can become very heavy when laden with flowers and the main trunk may even snap with the weight. Pruning, staking, or a combination of both is often needed for the successful cultivation of this beautiful small tree.

Large rocks and logs can also be used to provide support for plants. This method can be of value with established plants which have been transplanted and also in cases where plants have been blown over by strong winds and partially uprooted. The rocks or logs can be placed around the base of the plant and will help to support it until the root system re-develops. This use of rocks and logs can be combined with staking and also pruning to provide maximum assistance to the plant.

CORRECT STAKING METHODS

Firstly it is important to choose good staking materials. Stakes should be durable so that they will not rot quickly when in the ground. Always use a coarse material for tying the plant. Strips of cloth or discarded pantihose are suitable and cause little or no damage to the bark. If you use wire or fine string, it should be encased in a protective outer coating such as a length of plastic or rubber hose. See illustrations.

Place the stake in the ground, avoiding damage to plant roots. This is best done at the planting stage. Do not position the stake too close to the trunk, or they may rub against each other causing damage to the plant. If possible place the stake on the windward side of the plant so that the plant will be blown away from the stake rather than against it. In most areas the prevailing winds come primarily from one direction.

Never tie plants tightly. Always allow for some movement of the trunk to encourage natural development and strengthening of the plant. If this is done the plant will be better able to support itself when the stake is removed.

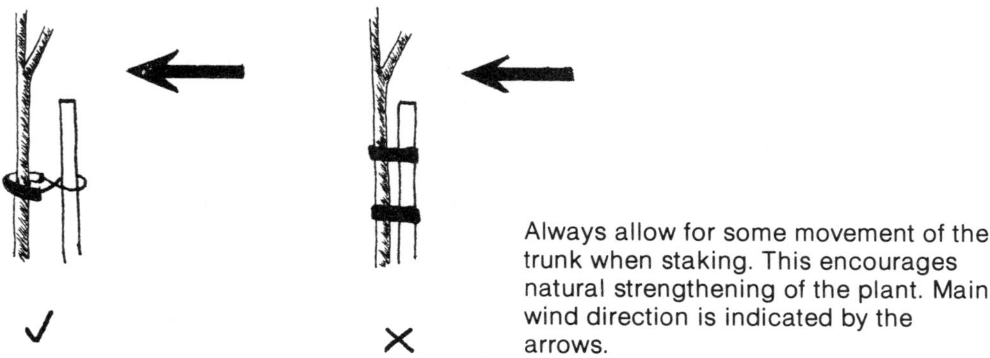

Always allow for some movement of the trunk when staking. This encourages natural strengthening of the plant. Main wind direction is indicated by the arrows.

For large plants, multiple staking using 2, 3 or 4 stakes may be desirable. See illustration.

Check regularly to ensure that the ties are not causing damage to the trunk of the plant.

After allowing a period for the development of the staked plant, it should be possible gradually to loosen the ties in preparation for their eventual removal.

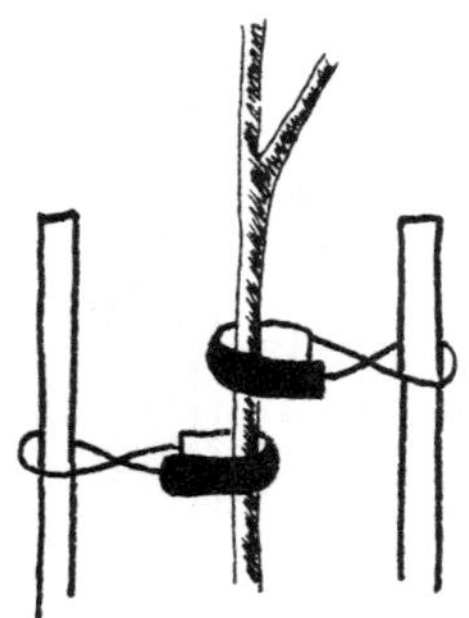

Multiple staking, using two stakes.

THE CONSTRUCTION AND USE OF PLANT GUARDS

Plant guards and shelters are needed, from time to time, for a variety of different reasons. These include protection from climatic elements, such as wind, sun and frost, and from creatures like rabbits, kangaroos, possums and farm animals.

1. PROTECTION AGAINST CLIMATIC ELEMENTS

In almost all cases where plants need protection against climatic extremes partial screening only is recommended. In regard to wind protection it is highly desirable that trees and shrubs be exposed to some degree of wind from an early age. This encourages natural strengthening of the trunk and root system so that the plant will be able to cope when it eventually outgrows the screen, or the shelter is removed.

Partial screens consisting of wooden slats or tea-tree stakes with gaps between each piece will usually provide the protection needed. In coastal areas where winds are salt-laden a screen covered in shadecloth or hessian will give added protection, whilst still allowing air movement around the plant.

One of the best long-term screens in areas of strong winds can be provided through the planting of windbreak plants. Further information will be found in Chapter 16.

If the plants being grown in your garden are all species suited to your area, protection from the summer sun will only be necessary immediately after planting. However, protection is desirable if new plants have been purchased from a supermarket or other place where they have been indoors for some time. Plants which have been grown outside in fairly heavy shade may also be affected adversely by sudden exposure to hot sun. In these cases a short period of 'hardening off' is desirable, before the plant is planted into the garden. Place the pot in a relatively sheltered location, with dappled shade or sun for only a few hours each day, to allow it to adjust gradually to the change of situation.

For shading of young plants in the garden the use of 3 or 4 stakes, or a moveable frame, covered with shadecloth is recommended. This guard can be placed over a selected plant when necessary, and gradually removed for a longer period each day until the plant has no further need for protection.

Frames for frost protection can be similar in construction to those used as sun guards. Shadecloth or hessian has proved very useful in protecting plants from frost, and in farming areas hessian bags can be recycled for use in this way.

Plastic is not recommended as a screening material for protection against sun or frost. Coloured plastic will prevent adequate light from reaching the plant, and new growth can be severely burnt by the sun's rays shining through clear plastic.

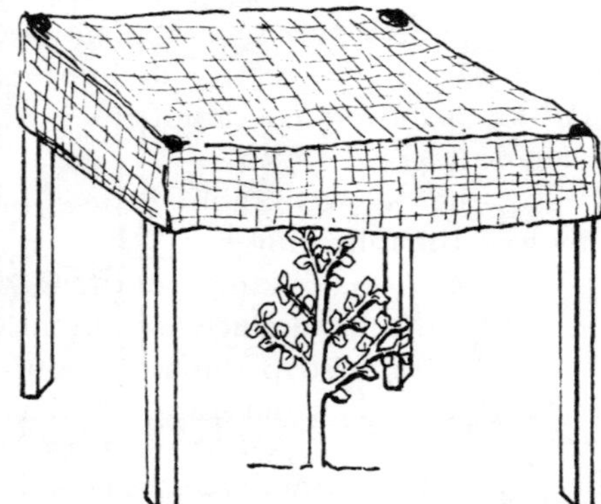

A frost shelter constructed of garden stakes with a covering of shadecloth or hessian.

2. PROTECTION AGAINST ANIMALS

The most pressing need to protect plants from damage caused by animals is in rural areas, although protection against dogs, cats and, in some areas, possums may also be needed in suburban gardens. Guards can also provide shelter for plants from damage caused by children during their play.

In Australia the introduced rabbit possibly causes the most damage to young plants. Individual rabbit guards for young plants can be readily constructed by using wire netting with holes of around 2 to 4 cm diameter. Cut a length of netting

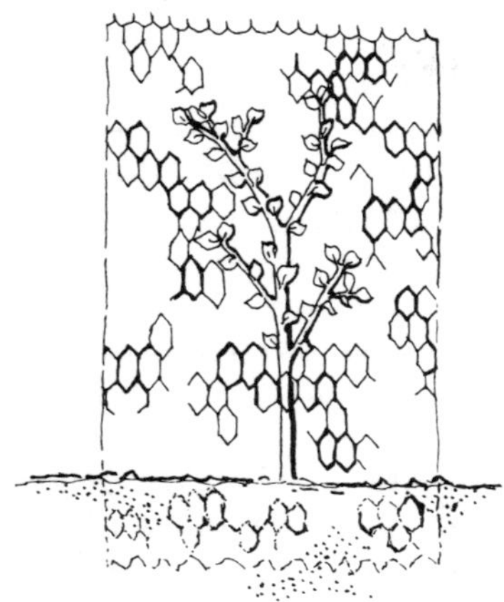

Rabbit guard formed by a circle of wire mesh. It is partly buried into the soil to prevent movement.

about 60 cm long. Roll it into a tube so that the sharp, cut ends are at the top and bottom. Secure at the top and bottom by using the ends of the wire and use a piece of tie wire to fasten in the centre. Position the guard around the plant at the time of planting and bury the base around 6 to 10 cm deep, making sure it is secure. As the plant grows, check it regularly to make sure that branches have not grown out through the wire mesh, or it will be necessary to cut either the plant or the guard later when you want to remove the guard. Guards should be removed when plants have become established. They can be re-used for later plantings.

In areas where several plants are being planted, a rabbit-proof fence can be erected to give protection to the whole area. Ensure that the fence is secure at all points, as if even one rabbit enters at the weakest point the results will be devastating.

Other forms of rabbit protection which have been known to be effective include the following—

1. For small plants, cut the top and bottom from a cardboard milk or juice carton and place around the plant in the same manner as a wire guard.
2. Wrap a strip of plastic around the stem to prevent de-barking.
3. Use deterrent sprays, etc., as mentioned on page 90 in Chapter 12.

In many cases wire rabbit guards, as described, will be adequate to protect plants from the browsing of kangaroos and wallabies. Once plants have grown to the height of the guards, the eating of new growth does not usually harm them but acts as a form of pruning and, whilst plants may not grow quickly to their full height due to repeated eating, they nevertheless survive and become very bushy in habit. One of the main problems is that the kangaroos will often land on the guards as they bound along so that the wire netting becomes crushed around the plant. Checks should be made from time to time so that the crushed guards can be straightened again to allow normal plant growth.

One method of establishing plants in areas where they are threatened by animals is to endeavour to select species which are not popular as fodder plants.

See Chapter 12 under paragraph 16, 'Rabbits, Possums and other Plant Eaters'. It is, of course, also important to choose plants suitable for your particular climatic region. Species which fulfil both these requirements will differ from area to area and will also vary according to which native, domestic or feral animals are in the district. Undoubtedly some of the best advice you can get will be 'local knowledge', usually available from those people in your area who have already grown young plants and who have first-hand knowledge of successes and failures in this regard.

Against animals such as cattle, goats, horses and sheep, larger and considerably stronger guards will be necessary for the provision of adequate protection to plants. Individual guards can be constructed of various materials, many of which re-cycle items already on hand on farm properties.

A truck or tractor tyre can be used as the base support for a plant guard, the upper section of which can be made from steel fence posts and barbed wire.

Old 200 litre (or 44 gallon) petrol drums, with both the top and bottom removed, make satisfactory guards for young plants. If large animals such as cattle or horses are on the property, the drums will need to be supported by metal stakes to prevent their being pushed away.

In some cases a permanent fence or an electrified fence will provide the best results.

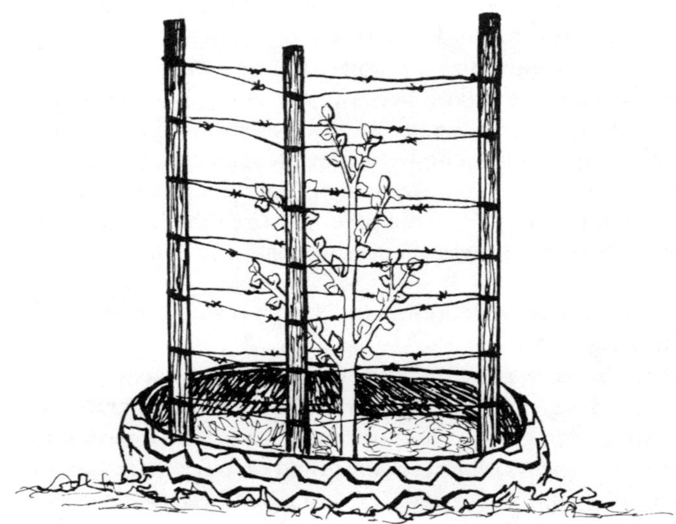

Animal guard around young plant.

9—*Pruning*

Pruning is an aspect of plant maintenance which tends to worry many inexperienced gardeners. Others who have been cultivating plants for a longer period are often quite happy to take a snip off here and there, knowing that the plants will generally respond very favourably and light pruning is unlikely to cause any greater damage than perhaps the loss of a few flower buds if we have chosen the wrong time of year.

In the Australian bush, plants receive regular pruning from native animals such as kangaroos, wallabies, koalas and possums, as well as from introduced rabbits and other animals. Chewing insects and caterpillars also prune plants by removing new growth tips, or even whole sections of foliage.

WHY PRUNE?

Nearly all our native plants respond favourably to regular light pruning, starting at a very early age.

In our gardens we may wish to prune plants for a variety of reasons.

1. TO CONTROL GROWTH

A plant may be spreading further than desired or growing too tall. We may want to make a bushier plant, perhaps to serve as a windbreak or screening plant.

Alternatively, we may wish to prune away the lower branches on a tree or shrub to allow more space or light below or to provide a view through the main trunk or trunks.

2. TO PROMOTE HEALTHY GROWTH AND PERHAPS EXTEND THE LIFE OF A PLANT

Pruning can increase plant vigour and assist in maintaining healthy, disease-free plants. Some species which tend to be short-lived in cultivation can be maintained for a much longer period by regular pruning. Good examples include species of *Boronia*, *Prostanthera* and *Westringia.*

3. TO REMOVE DEAD OR DISEASED SECTIONS OF A PLANT OR TO REPAIR GROWTH DAMAGED BY PESTS, WINDS OR FROSTS

The removal of dead branches will allow for improved plant growth and the pruning of any damaged sections will prevent the spread of diseases. In the case of frost-damaged plants, pruning should not be undertaken until the winter season is over. As new growth normally follows after pruning, further damage could be caused by late frosts if you prune too early.

4. TO PROMOTE BETTER FLOWERING AND/OR FRUIT PRODUCTION
Pruning can help to direct growth into those sections of the plant which bear flowers or fruits.

5. TO COUNTERACT DAMAGE TO THE ROOT SYSTEM OR PREPARE A PLANT FOR TRANSPLANTING
By decreasing the amount of foliage on the plant, the stress placed upon the root system will be similarly reduced.

6. TO PROVIDE CUT FLOWERS OR MATERIAL FOR PROPAGATION BY CUTTINGS
The cutting of plant material for these purposes will have a twofold benefit if the pruning is undertaken with regard to the general improvement of the plant.

WHEN TO PRUNE

The time for pruning evergreen shrubs and trees is after the main flowering or when fruit production is finished. By pruning at other times you may be removing the branches that will provide flowers in the coming season.

The time during which you choose to prune plants will depend to some extent on personal preference. For example, in the case of the NSW Waratah (*Telopea speciosissima*) plants should be pruned by cutting the flowers or flower-stems immediately after flowering has finished to obtain maximum stem growth for blooms in the following year. If, however, you wish to collect seed for subsequent propagation, you may be prepared to accept a reduced number of blooms next year and delay pruning until the seed has ripened, which takes several months.

As mentioned in 'Why Prune?', paragraph 3, the pruning of plants in frost-prone areas is best undertaken in spring-summer, after the conclusion of the cold winter period.

If the purpose of the pruning is to remove broken or diseased growth, it should be done as soon as the damage is noticed.

PRUNING TOOLS

Clean, sharp secateurs or pruning saws are necessary if the best results are to be obtained with minimum damage to the plant. Tools which are not clean can promote the spread of plant diseases and blunt tools can damage the sap wood, thus leading to the entry of disease.

After any diseased material has been removed, the tools should be dipped in a disinfectant before being used to cut other healthy sections of the plant.

It is also desirable that any stools or ladders you use should be sturdy and reliable to avoid injury to yourself or damage to plants by falling against them.

METHODS OF PRUNING

1. TIP PRUNING
This method of pruning is widely used. It is highly recommended for small to medium shrubs and involves simply pinching out the growth tip at the end of a

stem or branch. Side or lateral branchlets then develop from the leaf axils to provide a bushier plant.

Tip pruning can be carried out from the time when plants are around 10 to 20 cm tall and at any time of the year.

Tip pruning. By pinching or cutting out the tip growth of a branch the future growth will be diverted to lateral or side growth.

2. GENERAL LIGHT PRUNING OF SMALL TO MEDIUM SHRUBS

Cuts should always be made just above a bud from which new growth will develop. The cut should be made at an angle which will allow any excess water to run away from, rather than towards, the developing bud.

Generally the bud selected for the production of new growth should be pointing towards the outer area of the plant. If an inside bud is chosen, the new growth will be directed inwards and very dense and possibly congested growth will result. In some circumstances this may be desired, but it is not generally the case.

Pruning to develop growth from outside buds.

Begin any pruning by first removing dead or damaged material. Any diseased branches should be burnt and the tools should be dipped in a disinfectant before they are used again.

You can then proceed with pruning the plant with a view to achieving the desired shape.

If any branches are to be completely removed, they should be cut as close as possible to the main stem. A poorly pruned plant with sections of stem protruding is both unattractive and dangerous. For treatment of cut stems over 2 cm in diameter, see paragraph 4.

Do not burn prunings unless they are diseased. The material can be used for propagation by cuttings, or the leaves can be added to the compost bin and pruned stems cut or broken up and used as a garden mulch.

3. HARD PRUNING OF SMALL TO MEDIUM SHRUBS

Some Australian plants respond well to hard pruning, i.e. the removal of one-half or more of the foliage. For example, three plant species, all well known in the cut flower trade, and farmed for this purpose, are *Boronia megastigma* (Brown Boronia), *Telopea speciosissima* (NSW Waratah) and *Thryptomene calycina* (Grampians Thryptomene). These plants have been cut back severely over a number of years and have proved to respond very well to this treatment.

Other plants which are known to respond well to hard pruning include several species of *Boronia*, some *Grevillea* including *G.* 'Poorinda Constance', *G.* 'Poorinda Queen' and *G. rosmarinifolia* which can be used as hedge plants, and most of the *Prostanthera* or Mint Bushes.

Unless plants are known to tolerate harsh pruning, it is wise to cut back only one section of the plant per season, until the desired size or shape has been reached.

4. PRUNING OF LARGE SHRUBS OR TREES

The pruning and shaping of plants which will become fairly large at maturity must be undertaken with great care. This applies from even the early stages of plant development. Large shrubs and trees which have been the subject of poor maintenance can be both unsightly and dangerous.

If it becomes necessary to prune or remove a large tree in a built-up area, it is generally best to get professional help from a tree surgeon.

It is frequently necessary, for a variety of reasons, to remove one or two large branches from well-developed plants. In these cases, do not attempt to make the cut near to the main trunk. It will be easier to trim back the stub later. Any cuts should, if possible, be made at an angle which will ensure that water will run off the surface, rather than lie on the cut area and maybe lead to fungal disease.

(a) If the branch is large and likely to cause damage when it falls after cutting, tie a rope around it then throw the loose end over a higher branch. Enlist the help of someone else in the family, a friend or a neighbour, to hold the rope in order that the branch may be gently lowered to the ground in the position you wish after cutting. Make sure your helper is not likely to be pulled off his/her feet by the weight of the branch and that the branch is not likely to injure anyone by swinging around when cut.

(b) Make a shallow cut on the underside of the branch to be removed a little closer to the trunk than where you will be making the main cut. This will prevent bark from the branch tearing and causing damage to bark on the trunk.

(c) Remove the branch, leaving a stub of at least 30 cm protruding from the trunk.

(d) When a large branch has been cut through, your friend can slowly lower it to the ground in the place you have chosen. He/she may need help to guide it to the resting place as it is lowered.

14 *Above:* This form of *Correa reflexa* occurs in the Grampians, Victoria.

15 *Below: Lambertia formosa* is known as Mountain Devil, because of the unusual shape of its woody fruits.

16 *Right: Anigozanthos flavidus*, the Tall Kangaroo Paw has a variety of colour forms, with flowers on stems to 3 m tall.

18 *Above: Conostylis aculeata* from Western Australia forms an attractive small clump, with yellow flower-heads produced during August-February.

19 *Top right: Eremophila glabra* is an extremely variable species with many forms in cultivation. All prefer a warm, well-drained situation. The species occurs in all mainland states, with the form illustrated here being from coastal areas of Western Australia.

22 *Right:* A plant of *Lechenaultia formosa* tipped from the pot just prior to planting. Note the new sucker growth which has developed near the side of the pot.

Opposite:
17 *Top left: Banksia baxteri* is grown commercially for cut-flower production. The foliage is also a decorative feature of this large, bushy shrub.

20 *Bottom left:* The flowers of *Micromyrtus ciliata* are initially white, then deepen to red. Plants grow to around 1 m high, and flower over a long period.

21 *Bottom right:* An attractive yellow and red form of *Lechenaultia formosa.* There are many forms of this dwarf shrub, all with very colourful flowers.

23 Immediately after planting all plants should be watered thoroughly. Here *Dampiera linearis* has just been added to an established garden area.

24 A drip irrigation system being used to water stock plants in a nursery. The pot on the right-hand side also has a layer of mulch fabric to prevent germination of weed seeds.

25 An efficient, low pressure watering system, to which spray nozzles can be added at desired intervals.

(e) The stub can then be cut off without any damage to the trunk, which could have resulted from the weight of the branch pulling away. Again cut the underside of the stub first to prevent stripping of bark.

(f) Paint the cut area with a wood sealant. There are several products available in nurseries and stores and their use is recommended for any cuts of over 2 cm diameter. The sealant will provide a temporary 'skin' or bark substitute for the cut area. It will assist in the healing process, as well as preventing the entry of disease through the exposed tissue. Should you be unable to obtain a wood sealant, plastic paint or paving paint provides a suitable alternative.

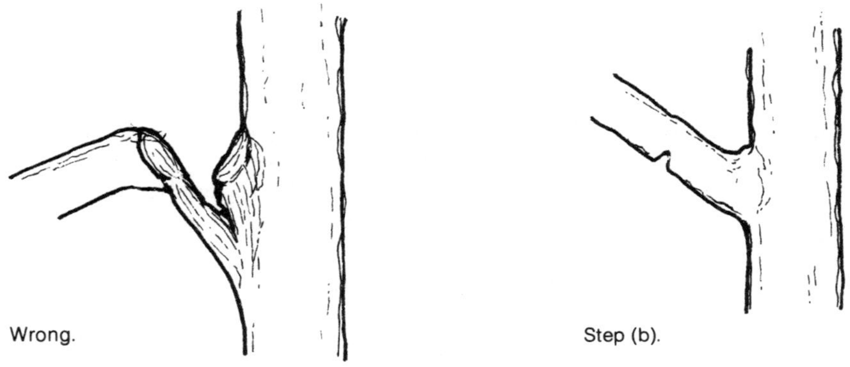

Ripping of bark during pruning can be avoided, as shown in these diagrams.

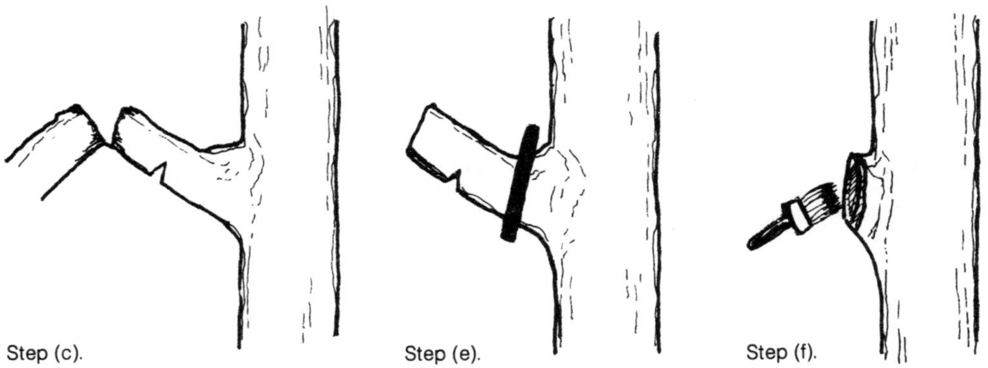

10—Protecting Plants from Frost Damage

Many Australian plant species are frost-resistant and are therefore unlikely to suffer any major damage from severe frost. Species from altitudes higher than 1000 m come into this category, along with others with a high degree of tolerance.

Some species such as *Eucalyptus citriodora* (the Lemon-scented Gum) are frost-tender in their initial stages of growth, but become more hardy as they mature.

Plants which are known to be frost-tender should, if possible, be planted out after the frost season has finished. This will allow them as long a time as possible to become established before the following winter.

Species such as the Australian Rhododendron (*Rhododendron lochae*) from tropical Queensland will always require protection from severe frost. These plants should be grown in a sheltered place or in containers which can be moved to sheltered positions during the frost season. Temporary shelters can be erected around small, frost-tender species. See Chapter 8.

Care should be exercised when mulching in frost-prone regions. Organic mulches can hold considerable amounts of moisture, which freeze when temperatures drop below zero and cause even more damage. Research has shown that bare, uncultivated earth often provides the most favourable conditions for plant survival in areas of severe frost.

CARE OF FROST-AFFECTED PLANTS

If plants have been burnt by frost, they should be left without pruning until the cold season is over. Give them shelter to avoid further damage to the remaining foliage and bark.

Cold, frosty nights are frequently associated with warm, sunny days. Early pruning of the plants in late winter-early spring is likely to encourage new growth, which in turn will be burnt by subsequent frosts.

After the last likely frost of the year, frost-affected plants should be pruned back to where the wood is green. New growth will then follow.

A SELECTION OF FROST-HARDY SPECIES

There are many, many Australian plants which could be included in this chart. It is a selection only and lists plants which have proved to be tolerant of a wide range of conditions in cultivation. They are also species that are readily obtainable from most native plant nurseries. Considerable research into frost-tolerant Australian plants has been carried out at the National Botanic Gardens in Canberra, where severe winter frosts are experienced.

Chart 7 — A selection of frost-hardy plants

(a) Groundcovers and plants to around 1 m high: A selection of 20 species

Plant Name	Height x width	Brief comment — for further description see Section 2
Acacia aculeatissima	Prostrate to 1.5 m x 1-2 m	Has short, sharp foliage and yellow flower-heads.
Acacia cultriformis 'Austraflora Cascade'	0.3 m x 2-4 m	A low, spreading wattle with bright yellow flower-spikes.
Baeckea ramosissima	0.3-1 m x 0.3-1.5 m	Variable species with small leaves and white to pink flowers.
Bauera rubioides	0.2-3 m x 1-3 m	Has white to pink flowers for most of year.
Correa decumbens	0.2-1 m x 1-3 m	Narrow tubular flowers are red with green tips.
Correa 'Dusky Bells'	0.5 m x 2-3 m	Has bright green leaves and pink, bell-shaped flowers.
Grevillea capitellata	Prostrate to 1 m x 0.7-2 m	Several forms grown. Has clusters of dark red flowers.
Grevillea confertifolia	Prostrate to 0.5 m x 3 m	Has terminal heads of mauve to pink flowers.
Grevillea diminuta	0.5-1 m x 1-2 m	Low, spreading shrub with clusters of small red flowers.
Grevillea laurifolia	Prostrate x 2-4 m	Groundcover with dark red toothbrush flower-heads.
Helichrysum semipapposum	0.2-1 m x 0.5-1.5 m	Has greyish foliage and golden-yellow flower-heads.
Micromyrtus ciliata	0.1-1 m x 1-2 m	Profuse, small white flowers turn red as they age.
Prostanthera aspalathoides	0.5m x 0.3-1 m	Tubular flowers are red, orange or yellow.
Pultenaea humilis	0.2-0.4 m x 0.5-1 m	Has heads of mainly orange pea-flowers.
Pultenaea pedunculata	0.5 m x 1-2 m	Has profuse pea-flowers. Several colour forms available.
Scleranthus biflorus	0.1-0.3 m x 0.5-1 m	A light green, firm, moss-like plant.
Stylidium graminifolium	0.1-0.2 m x 0.2-0.3 m	Tufting plant with pink flowers on stems to 1 m.
Tetratheca ciliata	0.2-0.5 m x 0.5-1 m	Has pendant, mauve-pink or white flowers.
Tetratheca thymifolia	0.5-1 m x 0.5-1 m	Has pendant, mauve-pink or white flowers.
Wahlenbergia gloriosa	Prostrate x 0.5-1 m	Has deep blue-purple flowers on slender stems.

Bauera rubioides.

Chart 7 — A selection of frost-hardy plants

(b) Medium shrubs around 1-4 m high: A selection of 20 species

Plant Name	Height x width	Brief comment — for further description see Section 2
Acacia flexifolia	1-2 m x 1-2 m	Has grey-green foliage and globular yellow flower-heads.
Atriplex nummularia	1-3 m x 2-4 m	A dense shrub with bluish-grey foliage.
Baeckea virgata	0.2-6 m x 2-3 m	Several forms grown. Has showy, small white flowers.
Boronia megastigma	1-3 m x 1-2 m	Well known and highly fragrant Brown Boronia.
Boronia pinnata	1-2 m x 1-2 m	Has bright pink, open-petalled flowers.
Callistemon brachyandrus	1-5 m x 1-3 m	Bottlebrush flowers are orange-red, tipped with gold.
Calothamnus gilesii	2-4 m x 2-4 m	Leaves are pointed. Flowers bright red with gold tips.
Calytrix tetragona	1-2 m x 1-2 m	Has white to pink, starry, open-petalled flowers.
Cassia artemisioides	1-2 m x 1 m	Has silvery foliage and yellow bell-like flowers.
Correa baeuerlenii	1-2 m x 2-3 m	Compact, bushy shrub with green tubular flowers.
Correa 'Mannii'	1-2.5 m x 1-2 m	Bell-shaped flowers are red with pale pink interior.
Correa pulchella	Prostrate to 1.5 m x 1-3 m	Bell-shaped flowers usually in various shades of orange-pink.
Dodonaea boroniifolia	0.5-2 m x 0.7-2 m	Has a showy display of green, pink or red hops.
Epacris impressa	0.3-2.5 m x 0.2-1 m	Has tubular, white, pink or red flowers.
Grevillea buxifolia	2-3 m x 2 m	New leaves are rusty. Flowers grey and brown.
Hovea lanceolata	1-2 m x 1 m	Has blue to purple pea-flowers.
Melaleuca squamea	1-3 m x 1-1.5 m	Fairly upright plant with mauve flower-heads.
Olearia floribunda	1-1.5 m x 0.5-1 m	Has showy, small, white to bluish daisy flowers.
Olearia phlogopappa	1.5-2.5 m x 1-2 m	Daisy flowers can be white, pink, blue or purple.
Prostanthera melissifolia	1.5-3 m x 1-2 m	Has highly aromatic foliage and lilac or sometimes pink flowers.

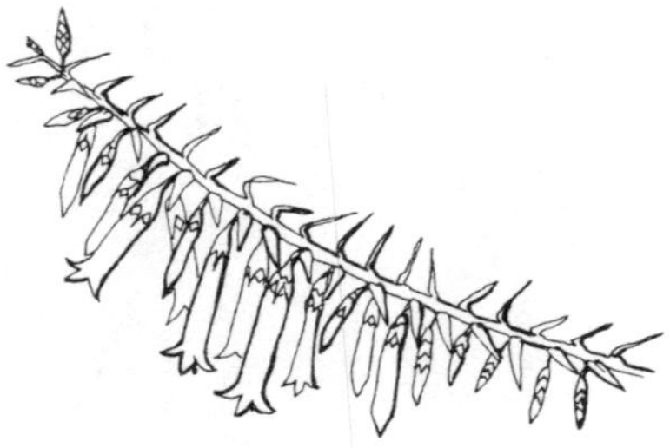

Epacris impressa.

Chart 7 — A selection of frost-hardy plants

(c) Tall shrubs or trees over 4 m high: A selection of 20 species

Plant Name	Height x width	Brief comment — for further description see Section 2
Acacia baileyana	5-8 m x 5-8 m	Has bluish, ferny leaves and profuse bright yellow flower-heads.
Acacia floribunda	4-8 m x 4-6 m	This wattle has pale yellow, rod-like flower-heads.
Acacia howittii	4-8 m x 3-6 m	Has pendulous branches and pale yellow flower-heads.
Acacia prominens	5-20 m x 4-15 m	Tall shrub to medium tree with lemon-yellow flower-heads.
Acacia spectabilis	3-5 m x 2-3 m	Has an attractive trunk and bright golden flower-heads.
Acacia vestita	3-6 m x 3-5 m	Foliage is soft and grey-green. Flowers yellow.
Allocasuarina torulosa	8-25 m x 5-10 m	An ornamental she-oak with reddish to almost black foliage.
Eucalyptus crenulata	6-15 m x 5-10 m	Has grey-green foliage and clusters of white to cream flowers.
Eucalyptus kitsoniana	3-10 m x 3-8 m	A small mallee species with clusters of cream flowers.
Eucalyptus nicholii	8-15 m x 5-10 m	Has narrow leaves and often pendulous growth. Flowers cream.
Eucalyptus pulverulenta	6-8 m x 5-8 m	Foliage is silvery. Flowers cream-white.
Eucalyptus scoparia	9-12 m x 5-8 m	Bark is smooth. Leaves narrow and pendulous. Flowers cream-white.
Eucalyptus stricta	5-12 m x 4-12 m	Has an attractive trunk and cream flowers.
Eucalyptus woodwardii	6-15 m x 3-8 m	Has showy clusters of bright yellow flowers.
Grevillea barklyana	5-8 m x 3-6 m	Has large, lobed leaves and pink toothbrush flower-heads.
Leptospermum phylicoides	3-6 m x 2-4 m	White, tea-tree flowers provide a showy display.
Melaleuca armillaris	4-8 m x 3-6 m	Foliage is dense, with narrow leaves. Flower-spikes cream.
Nothofagus cunninghamii	5-15 m x 3-6 m	Has shiny, oval, leaves with reddish new growth.
Prostanthera lasianthos	2-6 m x 2-3 m	Dark green, aromatic foliage. Mainly white flowers.
Telopea oreades	3-5 m x 2-4 m	Gippsland Waratah. Has large, red flower-heads.

11—Weeds and Weed Control

In some gardens weeds present very little problem and these lucky gardeners may simply turn to another chapter, instead of reading on here. Unfortunately, however, in other areas weeds present a major headache or worse.

Weeds can drain much of the pleasure from the enjoyable pastime of gardening and hours and hours of drudgery may be spent in their eradication. There are fortunately some valuable tips which will help solve the problems created by garden weeds.

It helps if we can tackle the problem of weed eradication in a positive manner, rather than being negative. The manual removal of weeds can be a source of considerable satisfaction and it also gives us the opportunity to come into very close contact with our garden.

Often during weeding we notice a variety of little things which may otherwise have been overlooked. They may be new flower-buds on a plant which has not previously bloomed, some seedlings of garden plants which have germinated in the garden, or perhaps some evidence to indicate pests or diseases which need attention. Frequently, in a native garden our weeding will be interrupted by the presence of butterflies, or honeyeaters and other delightful small birds. In these situations weeding can take very much longer than it should, but it can also be infinitely more enjoyable than simply pulling out weeds.

WHAT IS A WEED?

Basically a weed is the term used for a plant which is growing where we do not wish it to grow.

Some of the plants described in this chapter are in fact very useful species. Clover, for example, is a valuable pasture herb, and who has not enjoyed the delightful taste of fresh, ripe blackberries?

Weeds are usually plants which can adapt very well to a range of situations and therefore do not simply remain growing where they have been planted. Instead they layer, sucker or self-seed freely, and thus become problem plants.

RECOGNISING PROBLEM WEEDS

One of the major steps in weed control is being able to recognise the 'worst' of the weed species. If we can do this we can try to make sure that they don't enter our garden through being carried in in plant pots, or by any other means. If we do happen to have a 'monster weed' in the garden it is only by recognising the species and understanding its main method of spreading that we can hope to be effective in its control.

Some problem weeds such as Couch, Oxalis and Sorrel grow very successfully from even small pieces of root in the soil. It takes little imagination to realise what we are doing when we cultivate an area, or even rotary hoe the soil, in an effort to eliminate these weeds. We merely distribute through a wider area the weed we were trying to wipe out! Had we recognised the weed species before we set to work, our actions would undoubtedly have been different.

The following paragraphs are devoted to the identification and treatment of some of the most common and persistent weeds which exist in south-eastern Australia.

SOME COMMON WEEDS IN AUSTRALIAN GARDENS

The weeds described in this section have been listed in the alphabetical order of their most frequently used common names. This method of presentation has been used because it is by these names that the plants are best known.

Not all the weeds listed will cause problems in all areas — fortunately — however, most gardeners will recognise at least some of the plants described.

1. BLACKBERRY *(Rubus fruticosus)*

This prickly, trailing plant is well known to most Australians and can form dense impenetrable thickets to 3 to 4 m high. It was introduced to Australia during the nineteenth century, primarily for the succulent black fruits produced during late summer and autumn. There are in fact now several different species or forms of European blackberries growing wild in Australia. The leaves have 3 to 5 leaflets with finely serrated margins. The whitish pink flowers have 5 petals.

Rubus fruticosus is a proclaimed noxious weed throughout Australia. Seeds are spread by birds, and new plants also develop from suckers, or layering of branches which touch the ground.

Effective control has been achieved through use of the chemical 2,4,5-T, but suspected problems to human health have led to the suspension of the use of this spray. A fungal disease known as blackberry rust is now causing damage to the plants in some areas and it is suggested that, where there are large areas of blackberry to be controlled, your state Department of Agriculture should be contacted for advice regarding latest methods of eradication.

For small infestations of blackberry within a garden, it is easiest to tackle the problem as soon as possible by digging out even the smallest plants. Burning and slashing will help to eliminate the prickly foliage and enable you to get to the root area, but neither of these methods provides any major degree of eradication.

(x .6)

2. BONESEED (*Chrysanthemoides monilifera*)

This is an erect or bushy shrub of 1 to 3 m high native to South Africa. The leaves are dull green and 5 to 7 cm long. It is quite showy when in flower during late winter and spring, when bright yellow daisy-like flower-heads of around 2.5 cm diameter are produced.

The flowers are followed by greenish to black, globular, fleshy fruits, and a single plant will produce a large number of viable seeds. Seed commonly germinates in autumn and plants grow rapidly to maturity.

Boneseed competes vigorously with native vegetation and presents a real threat to bushland areas.

These plants have relatively shallow root systems and can therefore be pulled up fairly easily. Chopping or other cutting of the shrubs is not recommended, as the plant can shoot from the base.

(x .4)

3. CAPEWEED (*Arctotheca calendula*)
This is a widespread and showy, usually prostrate herbaceous weed introduced from South Africa. It may be best known for its use by children in the making of daisy-chains.

It is common in the pasture lands of many regions and can be seen covering entire paddocks with bright gold. It also grows along roadsides and in some garden areas.

The lobed leaves develop mainly from the base of the plant although some may be on the soft stems. The undersurface is covered in whitish hairs.

The flower-heads of around 5 cm diameter are daisy-like, with a black centre. There is one row of yellow petal-like florets, each of which has dark blackish veins on the underside.

Plants develop from a tap-root and should be pulled or dug up while small. Mature plants are often resistant to weedicides.

(x .5)

4. CLOVER (*Trifolium spp.*)
Clover is a widely cultivated and valuable pasture herb. It can also be a problem weed in areas where its growth is not desired.

There are several different species of *Trifolium*, the most common being the White Clover (*Trifolium repens*). It is a perennial plant able to self-layer by forming roots at the leaf-nodes when the stems touch the ground.

The leaves are stalked and nearly always have 3 leaflets. Occasionally a '4-leaved clover' can be found. There is commonly a white crescent or V-marking near the base of each leaf. The small flowers are white, or tinged with pink, and are produced in globular heads.

Digging will provide an effective means of control in small garden areas. The use of ammonium sulphate or nitrogen fertilisers can be of assistance.

(x 1)

5. COUCH GRASS (*Cynodon dactylon*)
This hardy grass is native to many areas of the world and is widespread in Australia. It is widely used as a lawn grass and is extremely useful for this purpose. It can also be planted to control soil erosion.

This species has underground rhizomes and, as new plants can develop from even relatively small pieces, cultivation can cause the number of plants to increase, rather than achieve control. Plants will also self-layer from nodes on the creeping, wiry stems, or can develop from the seed produced.

Individual plants should be removed from garden beds or pathways as soon as noticed. Small infestations are easily removed by digging, as long as the stems are followed to the end. Spraying with Zero or Roundup is also helpful.

(x .5)

6. DOCK (*Rumex spp.*)
There are several species of *Rumex* classifid as weeds in Australia including *R. bidens* (Mud Dock), *R. brownii* (Swamp Dock), *R. conglomeratus* (Clustered Dock), *R. crispus* (Curled Dock), *R. dumosus* (Wiry Dock), *R. obtusifolius* (Broad-leaved Dock) and *R. pulcher* (Red Dock).

The Curled Dock (as illustrated) is an erect herb with leaves of around 15 to 20 cm long. Numerous small flowers are produced on stems which grow to around 1 m tall and these are followed by dry, brown-winged fruits crowded along the stems.

Most Docks grow from long, thin tap roots and these must be removed completely if you are removing the plants by hand. Spraying with Zero or Roundup has also proved effective. Generally these plants will be more prolific if an area is constantly moist, or poorly drained.

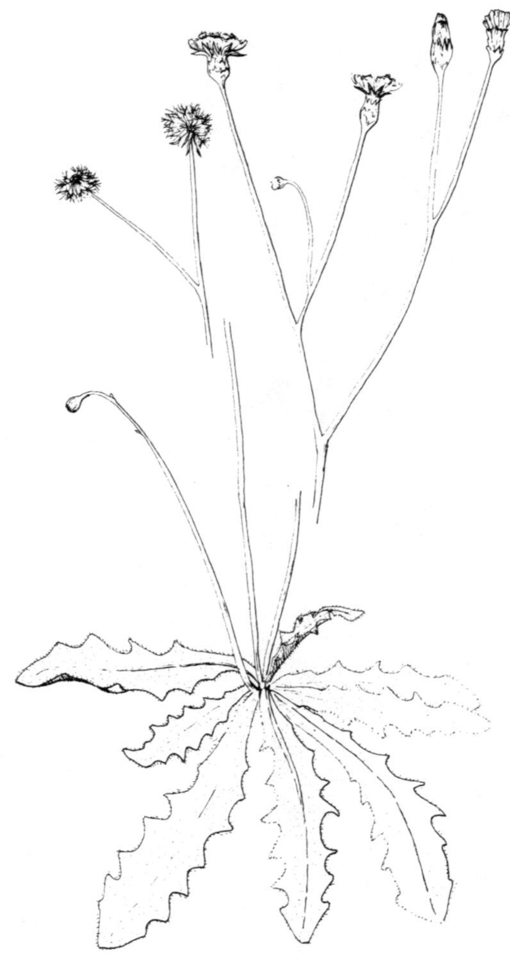

(x .4)

7. FLATWEED (*Hypochoeris spp.*)

There are several species of *Hypochoeris* weeds in Australia. They originated from Europe and Northern Africa.

Some *Hypochoeris* are known as Cat's Ear or Smooth Cat's Ear and the common name of Dandelion is also sometimes incorrectly used for *Hypochoeris* species, whereas it correctly applies to a very similar plant, *Taraxacum officinale.* Whilst Flatweeds have branched flowering stems, the flowering stem of a Dandelion is unbranched.

These herbs can be annual (*H. glabra*), or perennial (*H. radicata*), with basal rosettes of leaves and flowering stems of up to 40 cm high. The flowers are usually bright yellow with numerous rows of overlapping petal-like florets.

A tuft of fine whitish hairs is attached to each seed, thus allowing very efficient wind distribution.

Plants develop from thickish tap roots and these can usually be removed fairly easily if the soil is moist. It is wise to do this before the seeds begin to develop.

If necessary, sprays such as Zero or Roundup can be used.

(x 1)

8. FLICKWEED or COMMON BITTERCRESS (*Cardamine hirsuta*)
This species is a fairly common weed in Australian plant nurseries and gardens. It is a relatively small plant growing to around 30 cm tall, but it can develop, flower and seed extremely quickly. The leaves are soft with scattered hairs and the leaflets are 2 to 10 mm wide. Some forms are more hairy than others. The whitish flowers are only around 2 mm long, but the narrow fruits are up to 25 mm in length and contain many seeds, which are dispersed with great vigour on ripening.

Plants have been known to complete their growth cycle, including the setting of seed, before fully emerging through a thick layer of gravel mulch. It is therefore important to remove any small plants immediately they are noticed. Removal by hand is not difficult, but a constant lookout must be maintained if the weed is to be eradicated.

Contact sprays of paraquat/diquat can be used with success if desired.

(x .7)

9. HAIRY WILLOW-HERB (*Epilobium cinereum*)

This small herb is also known under the common name of Epilobium.

It is an upright species and can grow to almost 1 m in height. The stems and soft green leaves sometimes have reddish tonings, and the leaves have finely toothed margins. Plants mature very quickly and can begin producing viable seeds when only 5 to 10 cm high. The small 4-petalled flowers are pink. These are followed by elongated pod-like capsules. Within hours of maturing the capsule begins to split in four from the tip. As the segments curl back large numbers of tiny seeds are released, each with a tuft of hairs to assist distribution.

Because of its very efficient seed production it is recommended that plants be removed as soon as possible after they are first noticed. This can be done fairly easily, particularly if the plants are small. Any plants bearing capsules should be burnt, as the seed can be released after picking.

This is now a relatively common weed in many plant nurseries and gardeners should be on the lookout for any seed germination in pots recently purchased.

Other species of *Epilobium* are also troublesome weeds in many gardens, e.g. *E. billardierianum* which also now includes *E. glabellum.* This species has smooth leaves and can hybridise with the hairy *E. cinereum.*

10. KIKUYU GRASS (*Peninsetum clandestinum*)
This is a robust, perennial grass, native to East Africa. It is hardy, drought-resistant, and useful as a pasture and lawn plant.

The nodes along the stem are close together and, as plants root freely from these points, they frequently spread to become a problem. New plants also develop from the underground rhizomes and can spread under brick paving or cement pathways.

Successful hand removal of plants is extremely difficult, unless there are just a few plants in the area. It may be necessary to use herbicides such as Zero or Roundup in badly infested areas.

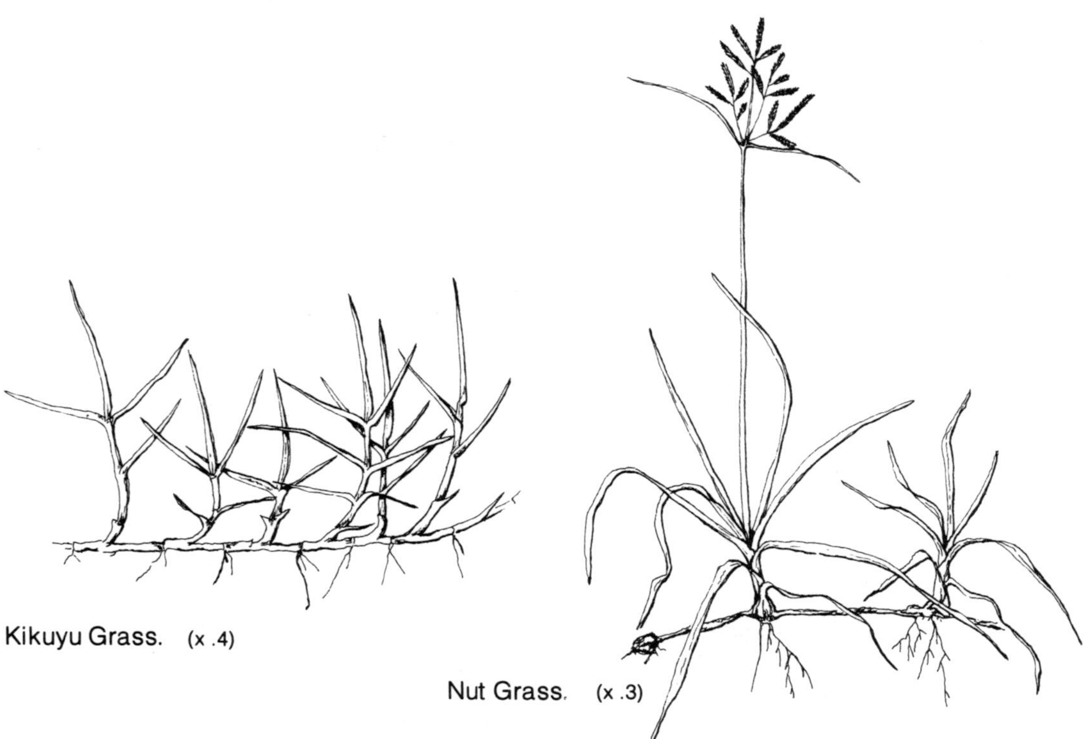

Kikuyu Grass. (x .4)

Nut Grass. (x .3)

11. NUT GRASS (*Cyperus rotundus*)
This grass-like sedge occurs throughout most of the world and is regarded as a highly significant agricultural weed.

Plants have deep root systems which produce tubers or 'nuts' at frequent intervals. Each tuber is capable of producing a new plant and it is this feature which makes the plants difficult to eradicate. The tubers are edible and were used as a source of food by the Aborigines.

Plants grow to around 75 cm high. The flowers are insignificant and are borne in reddish to brown spikelets.

As this species is very difficult to eradicate once established, it is important to prevent its introduction into garden areas, or to remove the plants as soon as they are noticed. It should be remembered that the roots can extend to considerable depths. Regular cultivation, every three weeks, maintained for a period of 2 years is reported to have eliminated this weed.

12. ONION GRASS (*Romulea longifolia*)
This is a small, perennial plant which grows from an underground corm. The narrow leaves develop from ground level and up to 4 flower-stems develop from each corm. The attractive, open-petalled flowers are mauve-purple with a yellow centre. Seeds are produced in a leathery capsule of 5 to 10 mm long, which splits to release the seeds when ripe. The immature capsules and the whole plants are sometimes known by the common name of Plum Puddings.

Control can be achieved by digging up the corms after growth has commenced in autumn, or by spot treatment with amitrole in early spring just prior to flowering.

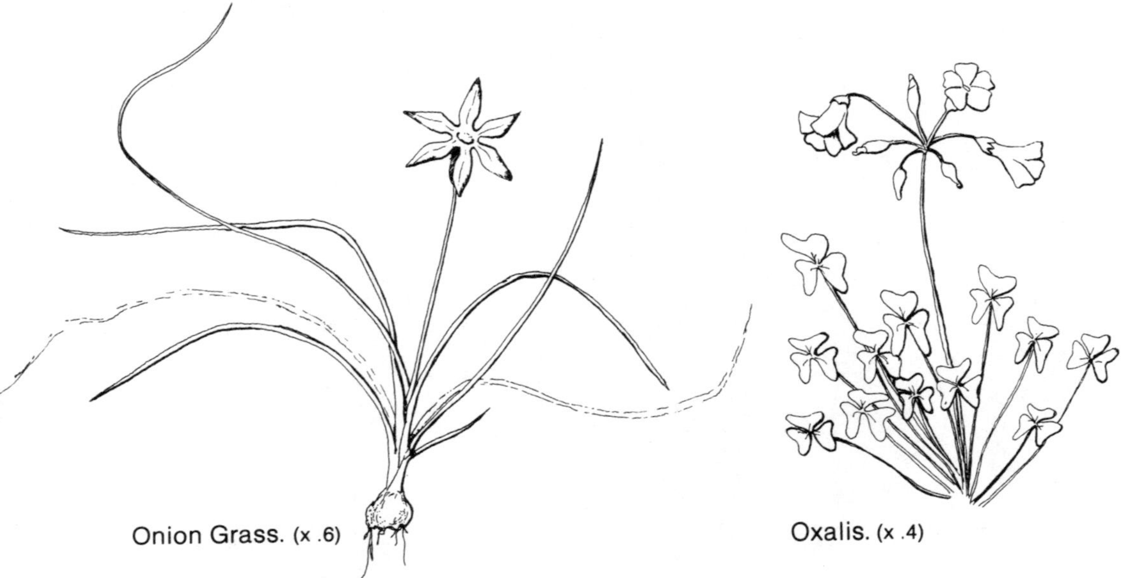

Onion Grass. (x .6)

Oxalis. (x .4)

13. OXALIS or SOURSOB (*Oxalis spp.*)
Oxalis is a large genus with worldwide distribution, including some native Australian species. Those species which present a significant weed problem in Australia include *O. articulata* (Wood Sorrel), *O. corniculata* (Yellow Wood Sorrel or Creeping Oxalis), *O. latifolia* (Oxalis), *O. pes-caprae* (Soursob) and *O. purpurea* (Large-flower Wood Sorrel).

The leaves are clover-like, with 3 leaflets, and flowers are usually produced on slender stems above the foliage.

Many species are quite decorative in flower, with colours of white, yellows, pinks and mauves. Some were in fact introduced to cultivation because of the attractive flowers.

Some species spread by seeds which are produced in cylindrical capsules and these can often be controlled effectively by weeding out the plants prior to seeding. Others, such as *O. pes-caprae*, can spread very efficiently from parts of the fleshy root system. In these cases eradication by hand weeding is often very difficult; however, the time recommended for this method is when plants are at flower-bud stage.

Sprays with amitrole or glyphosate (Zero, Roundup) have proved useful.

(x .6)

14. PASPALUM (*Paspalum dilatatum*)

Paspalum was introduced to Australia from South America as a pasture grass, but it has now become a weed in many regions and thrives in garden lawns.

It is a robust grass, which can grow to 1 m in height. It is possibly mainly recognised by the long spikelets of small greenish flowers which are sticky to touch or brush against. They are therefore unpopular with those walking through the grass during summer.

Individual plants can be removed by hand or with the use of a small fork or weed lifter.

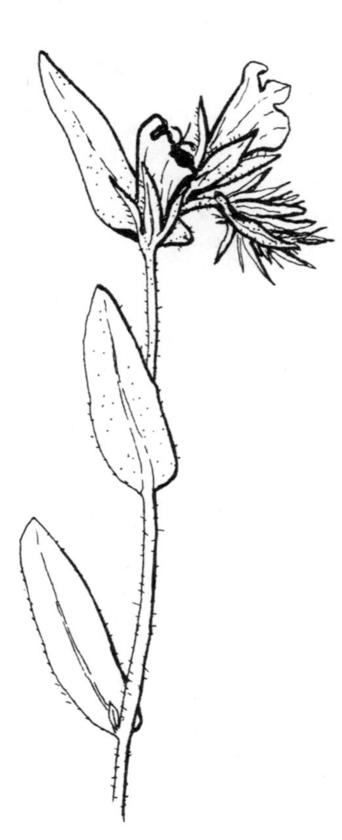

(a) Flowers and foliage. (x 1)

(b) A typical flowering stem with numerous spent flowers. (x 1)

15. PATERSON'S CURSE or SALVATION JANE (*Echium plantagineum*)
This is an annual or biennial herb of 0.5 to 1 m high. It has a basal rosette of hairy ovate leaves, with narrower leaves on the upright stems. The flowers are shaped like a curved trumpet and are commonly bright purple or in paler shades to light pink. They provide a very showy display in spring to summer and plants can cover extensive areas in regions such as the Flinders Ranges, SA. The fruits are made up of 4 nutlets.

In areas where this species has not become widespread plants should be removed and destroyed before seeding can occur. In some regions, with large infestations covering many hundreds of acres, major control measures have received some opposition because the species is excellent for honey production when in flower. Advice regarding major control programmes can be obtained from offices of the Department of Agriculture.

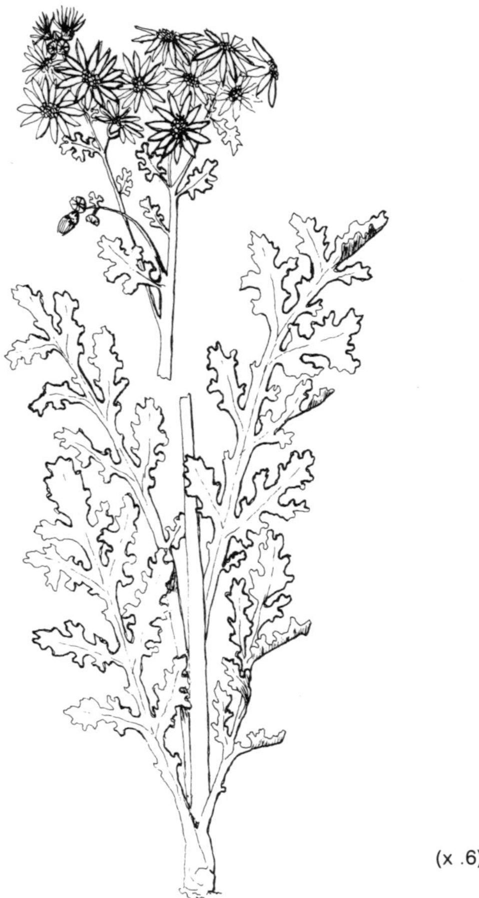

(x .6)

16. RAGWORT (*Senecio jacobaea*)
This perennial herb is a declared noxious weed in areas of Western Australia, South Australia, Victoria, Tasmania and New South Wales. It presents serious problems in grazing country, as it is poisonous to cattle and horses, both when fresh and when contained in dry hay. Sheep can also be adversely affected, although usually to a lesser extent.

Plants grow to around 1 m high, with single or multiple stems arising from a strong rootstock. The leaves are deeply divided and after seed germination they form a rosette at ground level. Further stalkless leaves develop on the upright stems as plants mature.

The bright yellow flowers are open-petalled and daisy-like. Flowering period is in summer to autumn and, as a single plant can produce several thousand viable seeds, it is important to remove and destroy plants before they reach this stage.

Although this weed is more troublesome in farmlands and wastelands than in gardens, it is important that any that do occur in gardens should be destroyed to prevent their spread into adjacent areas.

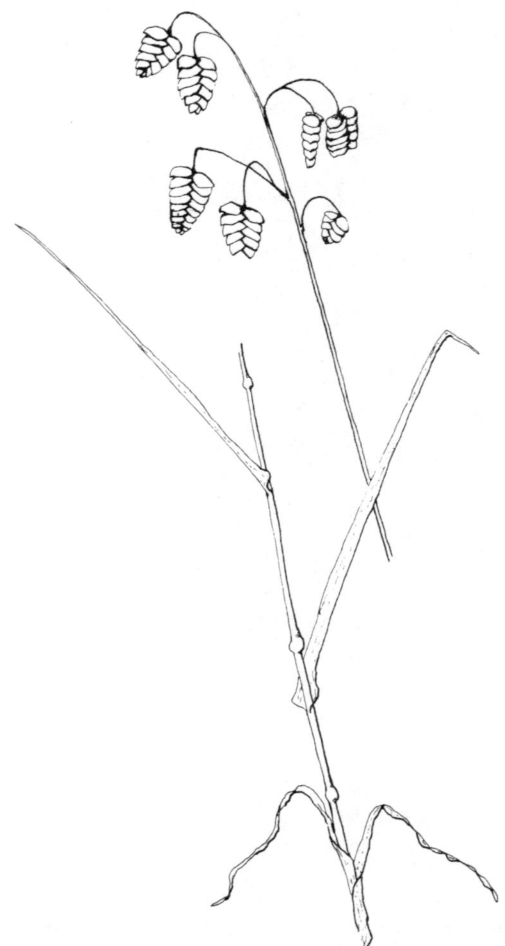

(x .6)

17. SHIVERY GRASS (*Briza minor*)
This species is closely related to *Briza maxima* (Quaking Grass). Both are annual grasses, native to Europe, and now widespread throughout temperate Australia.

B. minor grows to around 30 cm high and has numerous, pale green spikelets of 3 to 5 mm long. *B. maxima* is a larger plant, growing to around 60 cm in height. The spikelets can be 10 to 20 mm long.

Both are relatively common garden weeds. They often present no major problem and some people regard them as a decorative garden grass. They can however spread rapidly in native vegetation and compete vigorously with it. Plants can be readily removed by hand weeding.

(x .5)

18. SORREL (*Rumex angiocarpus* and *R. acetosella*)
These are vigorous herbs, highly efficient at invading garden areas. They are difficult to control because of their spreading root systems, which can send up suckers from even small sections broken during cultivation. Plants also self-layer from nodes along the prostrate stems.

The lobed leaves are on long leaf-stems, and are shaped somewhat like arrow-heads. Small, reddish or yellowish flowers are produced in clusters on the upright stems and these are followed by small 3-sided nuts.

Regular cultivation and removal of the plants will provide some degree of control, although every effort must be made to try and follow the slender creeping roots. Success has also been achieved through the use of herbicides that contain dicamba or glyphosate.

Sorrel develops best in acid soils and can be controlled to some extent by applying ground limestone to the affected areas, but caution is needed as an overdose may have a detrimental effect on existing garden plants.

With this species, as with many other garden weeds, prevention is easier than cure and all efforts should be made to avoid introducing this plant into the garden in the first place.

There are several other species of the genus *Rumex*, some of which have the common name of Dock.

(x 1)

19. STINKWORT (*Dittrichia graveolens*)

This species, previously known as *Inula graveolens*, is an erect plant, growing 0.5 to 1 m in height. It is covered with glandular hairs, which make the plant sticky and strong-smelling.

Small yellow flowers are produced in autumn and these are followed by seeds, each of which is attached to a tuft of barbed bristles.

Illness and death to animals can result from inhaling or eating the barbed bristles and, as plants can seed prolifically, they can be a major pest in rural areas.

Plants can be readily pulled up and burnt or very young seedlings can be destroyed by using a weedicide spray.

(x 1)

20. THISTLES

Thistles are members of the very large, worldwide, Compositae family, which has over 14 000 species.

There are many different genera with plants commonly known as Thistles and a large number of these are declared weeds. The genera include *Carduus, Carthamus, Centaurea, Cirsium, Cynara, Onopordum, Scolymus, Silybum* and *Sonchus.* Fortunately many are confined to particular regions.

Plants frequently develop from a tap root and the leaves are commonly lobed or divided. In some species they are prickly.

The flowers are mainly mauve-pink or yellow and these are followed by numerous seeds, each attached to stiff hairs or bristles. Thus the seeds are ideally suited to wind distribution and plants are spread in this way.

Young seedlings can be controlled by cultivation during warm to hot weather. Older plants can often be pulled successfully from moist soils, or they can be dug out with a fork or mattock, etc. Burning of the flower-heads is recommended to avoid spreading the seed.

(x .5)

21. WANDERING JEW (*Tradescantia albiflora* and *T. fluminensis*)
Wandering Jew is the name given to these two very similar trailing plants which root readily from stem nodes. They are hardy plants for gardens, containers or hanging baskets and are often grown as indoor plants. The leaves of *T. albiflora* are commonly green underneath, while in *T. fluminensis* the undersurface is reddish. Small, white, 3-petalled flowers are produced in spring and summer.

Plants can spread rapidly to become invasive in the garden. They are best controlled through removal by hand and regular cultivation. New plants can develop from small segments of the parent plant.

(x .5)

22. WINTER GRASS (*Poa annua*)
This annual weed grows widely throughout temperate regions of Australia. It is common in gardens and lawns and on pathways. It is known also by the names of Path Grass and Meadow Grass.

Plants can be prostrate or up to around 30 cm in height. The leaves are narrow and 10 to 15 cm long. The green spikes are 3 to 10-flowered and sometimes tinged with red or purple.

Regular hand weeding or cultivating will eliminate plants. As a last resort, dense areas can be sprayed with specified chemicals available for this purpose.

OTHER WEEDS

There are also, unfortunately, many other weeds not illustrated here, which occur in garden areas. To cover the list fully would require a separate book and in fact several publications are obtainable for those wishing to continue research in this area. (See Bibliography.)

As mentioned earlier, some plants generally regarded as weeds in our gardens are actually lawn and pasture grasses and very useful plants in their correct situations, e.g. Clover and Couch. Larger plants such as *Genista* and *Sarothamnus* species, commonly known as English Brooms, are very showy and are cultivated for their ornamental value. They have, however, become weeds in some areas. The best example of a plant run wild is undoubtedly the Blackberry (*Rubus fruticosus*), which was originally introduced to Australia as a food plant and adapted so well to the climate in many areas that inpenetrable thickets were created.

It is important that we should always be aware of the possibility of introducing plants which can spread rampantly to the detriment of the surrounding area. Often we may feel that although this happened following early white settlement of Australia, it is no longer possible. This is in fact far from correct.

One comparatively recent example is the highly ornamental Pampas Grass (*Cortaderia selloana*). There are many areas in Victoria at least where these plants can be seen to be thriving, with numerous new plants developing nearby from germinating seed. In vacant land or bushland adjacent to domestic gardens this grass is becoming extremely invasive.

Even in the area of our own native plants, species which have been introduced to one area from another have been found to adapt extremely well and dominate to the detriment of indigenous plants. *Acacia baileyana*, the very showy Cootamundra Wattle, and *Pittosporum undulatum* are two such species. There are others also.

HERBICIDES OR WEEDICIDES AND THEIR USE

Generally, herbicides should be used only as a last resort in the control of weed infestations. Regular manual control can be highly effective with most weeds, especially if it is done before the weeds reach flowering and seeding stages.

The use of mulching materials and dense growing groundcovers can also help to control the spread of most weeds, but of course there are always exceptions, such as Couch, Kikuyu and Sorrel.

Herbicides are chemicals and they will all affect the environment to a degree. Some have long-lasting and very detrimental effects, while the effects of others are minimal.

Some herbicides can affect human health as well as weeds, and it is therefore best to treat them as being toxic. Always wear protective clothing such as gloves when using herbicides. If sprays are used, full protective cover including goggles may be desirable. Never spray with a herbicide on a windy day. Always wash thoroughly after using any herbicide.

A very important aspect of herbicide use is the manner in which the chemicals are applied to the weeds. Efforts should be made to ensure that the chemicals are applied only to the plants you want to eradicate. If herbicides are sprayed on to other plants nearby, or allowed to spread along the soil to other plants, there may be long-reaching effects, detrimental to future plant growth.

Garden 'wands' are now widely available in nurseries and stores, and these help in the efficient use of herbicides. If used properly, they result in minimal damage to the environment.

Knock-down sprays such as glyphosate are not selective and will affect any green part of a plant. The application of glyphosate and similar products over large, weed-infested areas can have startling results. The weed growth may be killed, but unless the area is prepared for planting immediately there will often be rapid germination of weed seedlings. These can develop with even more vigour than the weeds which were sprayed. There is evidence that as some herbicides break down they form fertilisers which in turn stimulate vigorous new weed growth. A common side-effect of regular spraying with glyphosate or diquat/paraquat is a dense covering of moss.

SOME TRADE NAMES OF COMMONLY USED HERBICIDES

The following is a small selection of the herbicides currently obtainable. It is *not* a listing of recommended products. Always read thoroughly the labels and instructions before purchasing or using any product. If you are still unsure of the effects which the chemical is likely to produce, discuss the product with staff at the nursery or store. It is much better to discover exactly what you are using and how it will affect your garden, and maybe your own health, than to find out this information later.

Active Ingredient	*Trade Name*
amitrole	V-4 Weed-A-Way
dicamba	Dicambamine
dicamba and MCPA	Hortico Broadleaf Selective Weedkiller; Selleys Tumbleweed Selective Lawn Killer
diquat and paraquat	CRC Tryquat Granules; ICI Tryquat; ICI Weedex Granules
glyphosate	V7 Comkil; Roundup; Zero Weedspray

THE 'BRADLEY METHOD' OF WEED CONTROL

This is the term commonly used to describe a method of manual weed control established by the late Joan Bradley of Sydney, NSW. For around twenty years she and her sister were actively involved in weed control in the Sydney area. They were helped by a group of dedicated environmental workers.

Although their method was developed primarily for areas of natural bushland, it is nevertheless of interest when considering weed control in general. Readers who own property adjacent to bushland reserves, or whose property includes some areas of natural vegetation, may find the method of value.

Initially this group worked on conventional weed control, but in subsequent years their work was along new lines and the success of their labours has gained wide acceptance of the methods used.

The basis of the 'Bradley Method' is that weeds are removed manually, with minimum disturbance to the soil or environment in general. It was found that more vigorous methods of weed removal often resulted in re-growth of the same species, or germination of other quick-growing weeds in the newly disturbed topsoil.

GENERAL PRINCIPLES OF THE 'BRADLEY METHOD'

1. Work from good areas towards bad ones

Start where there are few weeds only and gradually work towards the badly infested areas. Better regeneration follows if work is commenced where the growth of native species is strongest.

2. Allow regeneration to dictate the rate of clearing

Regeneration slows down as the weeds get thicker and the weeding rate must be reduced to match. Never over-clear! If you do you will pay for it next season, pulling up hundreds of weed seedlings which would never have had a chance to grow if you had kept them smothered, first by their parent plants and then by regenerating native species.

If you have a lot of helpers, spread them out to weed small amounts in many places. The total area they weed will be just as great as if you had concentrated your efforts in one place and the regeneration rate will be very much greater.

3. Disturb the soil as little as possible

Never use a heavy tool when you can use a light one or hand pull weeds without using any tool at all.

4. Sweep back the surface mulch

However carefully you weed you cannot avoid disturbing some ground litter and exposing some soil. Repair the damage as you go. Bare soil will encourage the development of weed seedlings.

5. Mulch with the weeds themselves

Burning weeds or carting them out of the bush is often worse than unnecessary; it is wasteful. Keep everything you possibly can and add to the mulch. Materials unsuitable for mulch will need to be carried away. These include bulbs and tubers of weeds, plants that root at every node (e.g. Couch grass) and free-seeding plants with ripe seed.

As mentioned earlier in this chapter, being able to recognise the main weeds in your area and their methods of spreading, will be of considerable assistance when you seek to eradicate them.

6. Watch where you put your feet

Any native plants you tread on will get a set-back. See that your own feet don't undo any of the good you are doing by weeding.

The success of the 'Bradley Method' of weed control has been proved in several areas and the principles involved are certainly worthy of trial. For further details see Bibliography.

12—*Pests, Diseases and Nutritional Disorders*

GARDEN PESTS

Australian plants, like all others in their natural environment, are an important part of the food chain and ecological balance of an area. Leaves, stems and roots provide food for insects, caterpillars and other creatures large or small. Flowers, fruits and seeds extend the food supply further and many birds rely on these for their survival. Birds are also attracted to the plants as they seek out insects and caterpillars as part of their diet. Thus the food chain continues and a degree of ecological balance is maintained.

This is all very well in the bush, we may say, but our attitude often changes dramatically when we see evidence of this food chain in our gardens. Caterpillars, grubs, beetles — help! We've got garden pests!

We usually don't like to see treasured garden plants defoliated or disfigured.

Generally, however, Australian native plants can withstand the majority of attacks by insects, without any need for treatment. The eating of young growth provides a form of 'tip pruning' and bushier growth results.

It is frequently possible simply to remove some of the individual pests and squash them underfoot or prune away a badly infested branch and burn it. Other control methods are detailed later in this chapter.

If we are growing fruit trees, however, it is important that we provide adequate maintenance to ensure that we don't simply create a breeding ground for pests which will then spread to neighbouring trees or orchards. A similar situation exists in regard to vegetables and other agricultural crops.

PLANT DISEASES AND NUTRITIONAL DISORDERS

These two topics have been grouped together, as it is not always easy to distinguish them by simply looking at a plant which appears to be unhealthy.

The easiest way of controlling plant disease is to maintain healthy and vigorous plants. Thus, they are better able to cope with any problems, in the same way that a healthy and active person can usually overcome human ailments more readily than someone who is unwell at the time of the attack.

If soil preparation, drainage, selection of healthy plants and watering and fertilising procedures have been followed correctly, major disease problems in the native garden will rarely if ever occur.

Probably, however, you will not be reading this chapter unless you do have a problem.

If a plant dies, it should be removed as soon as possible. Look closely to see if there are any indications of the cause of death. If it seems that it is the result of plant disease, the affected material should be burnt to avoid spreading the problem.

Similarly, dead branches or sections of plants should also be removed, checked for any evidence of disease and burnt if they seem diseased.

Methods of treatment to combat diseases are found later in this chapter, listed under particular plant problems.

The main diseases associated with Australian plants are those involving fungi (including moulds and wood rot) and viruses.

Nutritional disorders arise either from deficiencies or excesses of elements in the soil, or in potting mixes in the case of container-grown plants.

In order to correct a nutritional disorder we must be able to recognise the symptoms in the first place. Fortunately we have today the benefit of many years of research into the development of balanced fertilisers. Nutritional disorders are therefore not as common in the home garden now, as in previous times. We should nevertheless endeavour to find out the cause of any problem, as an incorrect or excessive use of fertilisers can and does cause imbalance to occur.

OTHER PROBLEMS

Not all plant deaths in a garden are the result of pests or diseases. Undoubtedly many more plants die from excessive dryness, over-watering, or damage caused by wind, frost or other climatic extremes.

In the event of a plant dying it is wise to check out these factors first, before taking any hasty steps to combat pests or diseases.

PLANT PROBLEM CHECK LIST

Generally, as gardeners, we don't make a point of becoming familiar with all possible pests and diseases of plants. We become interested mainly when it is our plants that are suffering some form of attack.

Therefore this Plant Problem Check List outlines the symptoms which may occur in a garden and their possible causes.

If the problem involves garden pests, from here we can then read further to find out how to recognise some of the creatures involved, and to discover methods of handling the situation.

1. THE WHOLE PLANT SUDDENLY DIES

(a) Main stem may have been broken by wind, dogs, balls thrown or kicked during play, etc.

(b) Base of stem may have collar rot.

(c) Check for evidence of borers in the main stem. There may be a small hole surrounded by sawdust or webbing.

(d) Root system may have become twisted or knotted following poor potting-on at an early age.

(e) Check for excessive dryness or waterlogging of the root system.

(f) The roots, or the base of the trunk, may have been attacked by root borer grubs. This is sometimes seen as ringbarking of the lower trunk.
(g) Root system may be affected by Armillaria Root Rot, or *Phytophthora cinnamomi* (the Cinnamon Fungus).

2. ONE STEM OF A PLANT DIES
(a) Check to see if the stem has been broken by accident.
(b) Look for evidence of borers in the stem (see 1(c)).
(c) Check for any area of disease, perhaps caused by earlier damage to the bark or by poor pruning.
(d) If a plant continues to die, one branch at a time, it is likely that the root system is being damaged, possibly by a fungal disease.

3. A PLANT LOSES ITS LEAVES
(a) The plant may be deciduous. This isn't such a silly idea, as some Australian plants *are* deciduous, e.g. *Melia azederach* (the White Cedar).
(b) The plant may have suffered recent damage from frost or other climatic conditions, e.g. salt spray on a species not suited to coastal conditions.
(c) The plant may be under stress from extreme dryness or from possible root damage.
(d) The leaves may have suffered a major attack from leaf-eating or sucking insects, or caterpillars. There may be no creatures to be seen if they have moved on elsewhere. If stems and trunk are still alive, the plant is likely to re-shoot in due course.
(e) The plant may be suffering from an excessive application of fertiliser.

4. LEAVES REMAIN ON THE PLANT, BUT ARE DRY AND BROWN OR SKELETONISED
(a) Drying of leaves can be caused by frost, sun-scorching or dehydration.
(b) Dry or skeletonised leaves can also indicate attack by sucking insects, e.g. aphids, scale, lerps and mealy bugs.

5. LEAVES ARE PARTIALLY GREEN, WITH DRY BROWN BLOTCHES
(a) See 4(b) above, re sucking insects.
(b) This can be a symptom of several fungal diseases, known generally as leaf spots.
(c) High levels of air pollution or salt-laden winds may be affecting the plant.
(d) The spotting may be caused by mineral imbalance (see also Chapter 7, 'Fertilising').

6. LEAVES HAVE BLISTERED SURFACES, TUNNEL MARKS OR SKELETONISING
This is generally the result of leaf miners, which are the larvae of small moths, flies or beetles.

7. LEAVES ARE PARTIALLY EATEN
Damage is usually caused by one or more of the many common biting and chewing creatures. Main offenders are caterpillars, beetles and grasshoppers; or slugs and snails if near ground level.

This *Eucalyptus* is growing in a coastal situation and the dry brown areas on the leaves are the result of exposure to salt-laden winds.

The leaf-chewing Painted Apple Moth caterpillar on *Hardenbergia violacea.*

8. LEAVES ARE ROLLED OR WEBBED TOGETHER

Identification is often made easy here, as the creatures may be 'in residence' within the leafy hideaway. Species which make shelters of this nature include some caterpillars, thrips, ants, spiders and sometimes crickets. Some also feed on surrounding foliage.

9. LEAVES, STEMS OR SPENT FLOWERS HAVE HARD PIMPLES, BUMPS OR OTHER SWELLINGS

These swellings are known as galls and are discussed on page 85.

Leaf galls on a *Eucalyptus* leaf.

10. DEPOSITS OF STICKY 'HONEYDEW' SUBSTANCE ON STEMS AND BRANCHLETS

This substance is deposited by small sucking insects such as aphids and lerps. See also 11 and 12.

11. STEMS AND FOLIAGE COVERED WITH A BLACK, SOOTY MATERIAL

This is known as Sooty Mould. It grows on the 'honeydew' secreted by small sucking insects, such as scale, and is usually an indication of their presence.

12. LARGE NUMBERS OF ANTS ON STEMS AND FOLIAGE

Ants frequently come to feed on the 'honeydew' of aphids and lerps, etc. The ants rarely cause plant damage, but they do indicate the presence of the sap-sucking insects.

13. PLANTS, AND NEW GROWTH, IN PARTICULAR, COVERED IN A WHITE, POWDERY MATERIAL

(a) This can indicate the presence of Powdery Mildew, a fungal disease with masses of white, powdery spores.

(b) In some plants a white 'bloom' is natural on leaves, branchlets, buds and fruits, e.g. *Eucalyptus caesia.*

26 A strong wire tie is here being used to manipulate the shape of a young *Hymenosporum flavum*. Note the section of garden hose used to avoid damage to the trunk.

27 Pruning a plant of *Grevillea banksii* to encourage growth from an outside bud.

28 Young *Eucalyptus* plants being watered through the use of recycled plastic soft drink bottles fitted with 'Aquaspikes'.

35 *Top left:* The Grass Trigger-plant, *Stylidium graminifolium* is a tufting plant, with pale to dark pink flowers produced during late spring to summer. This form, with short flower-stems, is from sub-alpine areas.

36 *Above:* These leaf galls (upper right hand side) mimic with fascinating accuracy the seed capsules of this eucalypt.

37 *Left:* Eriococcid galls have varied and interesting shapes.

14. VISIBLE MOULDS OR FUNGAL GROWTH ON PLANTS

It is usually not important for the home gardener to be able to identify the various moulds and fungi found growing on plants. Details regarding treatment of affected areas follow later in this chapter.

15. YELLOWING, REDDENING OR BROWNING OF LEAVES ON EVERGREEN PLANTS

(a) Such colouration of new growth is natural on many species.
(b) All leaves have a limited life span. In evergreen plants they do not all fall in the one season. Many leaves attain colouration prior to falling.
(c) Variegated forms do develop within some species.
(d) Colouration of foliage can be an indication of mineral deficiency. In these cases yellowing or reddening is common around the leaf margins, or as blotching on the leaf surfaces.

16. LEAVES, BRANCHLETS, BUDS, FLOWERS AND FRUITS BROKEN OR EATEN

Young plants are commonly attacked by rabbits or possums, particularly in rural or outer-suburban areas, or in gardens adjacent to bushland. Birds such as blackbirds will also snap the tops off young plants.

Rabbits and possums can continue to cause damage to older plants, by eating foliage and chewing or scratching bark.

CONTROL AND CORRECTION OF PROBLEMS

1. LEAF-CHEWING PESTS

These include beetles, caterpillars and grubs, grasshoppers, locusts and stick insects, also slugs and snails.

The growing of plants which will encourage native birds to a garden will assist greatly in the control of these pests. Generally, plants can cope with most attacks, but if infestation is severe you may feel it is necessary to provide some assistance.

Flying insects are difficult to eradicate. It is easier to locate and destroy either the eggs or the insects at caterpillar stage. This can be done by squashing or burning them, or if necessary by use of a contact spray. Sprays made from pyrethrum are usually effective, as well as being safe to use. Sprays which combine garlic and pyrethrum, or eucalyptus oil and pyrethrum can provide a deterrent, as well as a means of control.

Traps can be set to assist in the capture of these pests. One such method is the use of a broad strip of cloth tied around the lower trunk of the plant. Several insect species will tend to congregate in the cloth and can then be easily removed and destroyed.

For the protection of young plants in areas of severe infestations, thin nylon pantihose can be used. The body section of the pantihose should be tied loosely around the plant as illustrated. Sunshine, moisture and air will be able to filter through, and the plant will be protected from insect predators as it becomes established during its first year. At the end of the year the stocking should be cut away, rather than pulled off, to avoid damage to the plant. Choose a time for removal when temperatures are mild, to allow the foliage to become gradually hardened.

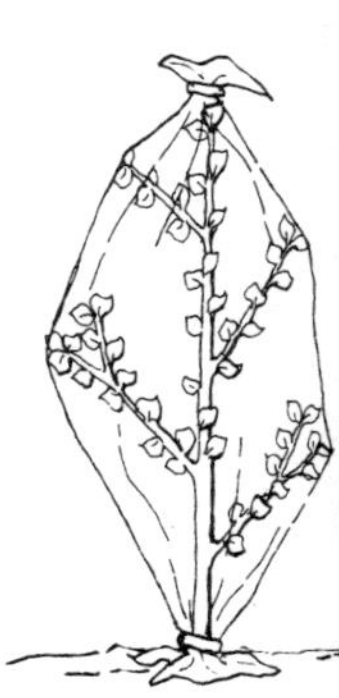

Slugs and snails can often be located around favourite plants in the garden.

A number of different snail bait preparations are available through nurseries to assist in controlling these creatures.

SOME TRADE NAMES OF COMMONLY USED PESTICIDES

The following is a listing of some of the pesticides currently obtainable. Highly toxic sprays are not recommended, and have therefore not been included.

Always read the labels and instructions thoroughly before purchasing or using any pesticide. If you are still unsure of its effects, discuss this with staff at the nursery or store.

Very young plants can suffer damage from applications of sprays, and this is often accentuated if spraying is done during hot weather (25° Centigrade plus).

Relatively Safe Sprays

Active Ingredients	*Trade Name*
Ammoniated Soap	Clensel
Bachillus thuringiensis	Dipel
Eucalyptus oil	Eucalyptus spray
Garlic	Garlic spray
Pyrethrum	Garden Pest Eradicator; Pyrethrum; Selleys Insect Killer
Rotenone	Derris Dust
White Oil emulsion	White Oil

Less-safe Sprays

Active Ingredients	*Trade Name*
Carbaryl	Carbaryl; Hortico Plant and Pest Insecticide
Lead Arsenate	Lead Arsenate
Maldison	Malathion
Nicotine Sulphate	Nicotine Sulphate

2. LEAF-SUCKING PESTS

This group includes aphids, bugs, leaf hoppers, lerps and scale insects plus other small creatures. Control as for 1 is effective, if the pests can be located and destroyed.

Contact sprays, which kill the creatures actually sprayed, can be effective for aphids, bugs and leaf hoppers, whilst White Oil will control lerps and scale. Ladybird beetles also provide an excellent form of natural control by feeding on these garden pests.

3. BORERS

Stem borers can usually be detected by little patches of sawdust or webbing on the branch of a plant. If wiped away, the telltale hole of the borer is revealed.

Boring insects are commonly beetles, weevils or wood moths. In some species it is the larvae which tunnel into the timber, whilst in others the adults also contribute to plant damage in this way.

Stem borers can be controlled by squirting a mild contact insecticide (e.g. a pyrethrum spray) into the hole, then plugging the outlet with clay or a similar

Evidence of a borer. A round hole in the stem, surrounded by sawdust-covered webbing.

substance. A squirt of kerosene will usually cause larvae to leave the hole and they can then be destroyed. In some borer holes the larvae can be squashed by use of a long piece of wire.

In cases of severe infestation it may be desirable to prune away affected sections of the plant and burn the wood containing the borers.

Where borer holes exist without any sawdust or webbing being present, it usually means that the culprit has moved elsewhere.

4. GALLS

Galls are commonly caused by small insects, including wasps and flies, which lay their eggs just below the surface of a stem or leaf, or in flowers such as those of Wattles.

The plant responds by producing a swelling. This becomes an ideal habitat for the hatching larva, which then feeds and pupates within the gall. The gall also provides the creature with effective protection from predators or contact sprays.

There are many different types of galls, some of which are extremely interesting. The casuarina gall, for example, resembles closely the distinctive shape of the *Casuarina* fruit. Other galls have similarly interesting formations. Some are not uncommonly mistaken for seeds and planted — without any success in germination of course.

Galls can be removed by picking or cutting away the affected sections of the plant. If the larvae are still inside the galls the affected material can be burnt. Removal does not achieve any real purpose if the larvae have already hatched.

As mentioned earlier, contact spraying is ineffective. The use of a systemic spray, which is absorbed through the sap flow of the plant, can offer control, but only in rare cases is this necessary. If you do use one of these sprays follow the instructions carefully. They can be dangerous.

On some *Acacia* species there are galls which are not a result of insect attack, but rather of a fungus, *Uromycladium.*

5. LEAF MINERS

The term leaf miner commonly refers to a range of insect larvae, which feed and tunnel through the inner leaf tissue below the surface of the leaf. As is the case with galls, the creatures causing the damage are shielded from contact sprays by plant tissue.

Apart from the unattractive foliage which results, these pests cause little or no permanent damage. If you notice them whilst they are still in the leaves, the affected parts of the plant can be removed and burnt.

Systemic insecticides, which are absorbed through the sap flow of the plant, will provide a means of control if other methods prove ineffective. These sprays can be dangerous and care must be exercised to ensure the safety of the user.

6. WEBBING CATERPILLARS AND SPIDERS

The caterpillars of some moths and other insects work together in groups to form nests of leaves and twigs bound together with webbing. These can become quite large and unattractive.

Nests can be removed and burnt if desired, but care should be taken to avoid skin contact with the nest or the caterpillars, as many of these species have hairs which cause irritation to the skin.

Some spiders form small nests of leaves in which to lay their eggs and for use as a place of shelter. Spiders help to control many of the small insect pests and therefore it is in the interest of the garden in general that they be allowed to remain in the leaves if possible. Individual nests which may appear unsightly can be removed and transferred to a more convenient location if desired.

Many spiders are venomous, although few present any real danger to humans. It is nevertheless wise to avoid any skin contact with these creatures.

7. SOOTY MOULD

This is a relatively common fungus disease, which develops on 'honeydew' excreted by sucking insects such as aphids and scale. It covers stems and areas of foliage with a black, sooty substance.

Some plants are more affected by sooty mould than others. The brightly coloured *Leptospermum* hybrids appear to be particularly susceptible.

Generally sooty mould will disappear if the insects which produce the honey-like secretion are removed, see 2, 'Leaf Sucking Pests'. Brushing or wiping stems with cool water to which a mild detergent has been added will also help to remove sooty mould.

8. POWDERY MILDEW

This is another fungal disease. It produces white, powdery spots or a whitish covering on the foliage.

The disease occurs mainly in glasshouses or enclosed areas, but can also attack garden plants in humid weather if there is very little air movement.

Areas affected can be removed and destroyed, and fungicidal sprays such as benomyl are available to control further spread of the disease.

9. LEAF SPOTS

Leaf spots can appear on plants due to minor fungal diseases. The bluish-grey leaves of some *Eucalyptus* species are often affected in this way. If the plant is generally healthy it will be able to withstand this problem and no further treatment will be necessary.

In cases of severe infestation your nurseryman will be able to suggest a suitable spray.

10. MOULDS AND FUNGI

In areas of high humidity moulds may develop on plant species which have come from drier climates and are not totally suited to the conditions of the region in which they are now growing. Frequently the moulds will be seen first on spent flowers or in soft new growth.

Eremophila species, which are found mainly in arid regions of Australia, are particularly susceptible when grown in the high rainfall areas of south-eastern Australia.

Planting in a sunny situation with good air movement is recommended as a means of avoiding mould on plants known to be affected by this problem.

If mould develops, the material affected should be pruned away and burnt. A fungicidal spray can be used to control its spread.

Kangaroo Paws (*Anigozanthos* species) are frequently attacked by a fungus disease which blackens the leaves. It is known as Ink Disease.

One of the species most frequently cultivated, *Anigozanthos flavidus*, is generally resistant to the disease. Several hybrids are now in cultivation with *A. flavidus* as one parent. It is hoped that a wider range of flower colours will soon be available on plants resistant to Ink Disease.

As is the case with most other plant diseases, Kangaroo Paws which are growing vigorously are better able to withstand Ink Disease and therefore the maintenance of healthy vigour is the best method of treatment. Applications of benomyl can also provide effective treatment.

11. COLLAR ROT

This is a fungal disease which affects the base of a plant stem at or around soil level.

Collar rot can occur if plants are planted too deeply when transferred from a container or other position in the garden. Another frequent cause is the practice of placing grass clippings or other organic mulch right against the trunk of a plant. Damage to the base of a plant caused by lawn mowers or grass whippers can also lead to the development of collar rot.

Collar rot is more likely to occur in moist to waterlogged soils than if the area is well drained. Improvement of drainage can therefore assist both in prevention and treatment of collar rot.

Damaged tissue should be removed with a sharp knife and the surrounding area can be painted with a fungicide such as bordeaux paste to assist recovery and regrowth.

12. ROOT WEEVILS

Several species of weevil spend at least part of their life cycles below the surface of the soil, where plant roots form a major part of their diet. If plants are healthy and vigorous they will tolerate the presence of weevils or grubs without any detrimental effect being noticed.

One large grub which does cause noticeable damage to garden plants is the Cockchafer.

Grubs or root weevils will sometimes chew completely around a trunk just below ground level, effectively ringbarking the plant and resulting in its death.

Unfortunately there is no simple and safe treatment for the eradication of root weevils. One complication is the fact that it is not possible to tell at any one time just where the creatures are in the soil. Drenching of the whole soil area with toxic chemicals will certainly kill the weevils, along with all the other desirable creatures which are in the area at the same time. Substances used for this purpose can also be harmful to human health.

The tying of a piece of cloth around a trunk just above ground level (as mentioned in regard to chewing insects) has been used with success for the trapping of root weevils. Repeated attempts at various methods of trapping the insects are certainly recommended in preference to the use of toxic chemicals.

13. ROOT FUNGUS

There are several fungal diseases which attack plant roots. It should again be mentioned that vigorous plants can frequently withstand minor attacks which therefore go unnoticed. Plants which are struggling may be unable to recover and they may die.

(a) Armillaria Root Rot

This is a fairly common and vigorous fungus. It is also known as honey fungus, mushroom root rot, or shoestring fungus. The fungus can be recognised by the clusters of brownish-orange toadstools produced at ground level.

The development of *Armillaria* fungus can be prevented by removing dead stumps and roots from the soil. Treatment of an infected area is not easy and it is suggested that professional advice be sought if the fungus is found to be present.

(b) Phytophthora cinnamomi (the Cinnamon Fungus)

This is a particularly damaging fungal disease. It has been the subject of considerable research in recent years and much has been written regarding it. However, to date no completely effective method of eradicating the problem has been found.

Phytophthora cinnamomi is a water-borne, microscopic fungus which attacks the small feeder roots of a plant. The plant may continue to live for some time, but if placed in a situation of stress, such as in hot or dry weather, it will die almost overnight for no apparent reason.

It is also not easy positively to identify *Phytophthora cinnamomi* without a microscope. If you think your plants may have this disease you should telephone your nearest Department of Agriculture for advice.

Fungicides have been developed to assist in its control and they are constantly being improved as a result of research being carried out in various places, both in Australia and overseas. Instructions on the use of fungicides are given in detail on the containers, and these should be carefully followed.

In regard to *Phytophthora cinnamomi* it can certainly be said that prevention is better than cure. The following recommendations may help to prevent it.

(i) As this is a water-borne fungus, improvement of drainage in the garden is useful in combating attacks and should be given high priority.

(ii) Most plant nurseries now carry out some form of sterilisation or other treatment of potting mixes to eliminate the possibility of spreading the disease. This is highly recommended. As some plant species are resistant to the fungus, it is possible for spore to be present in a pot without affecting the plant it contains.

(iii) Never collect leaf litter, sand, or other material from an area where plants have died for no apparent reason.

(iv) Undertake regular garden maintenance which will promote health and vigour in the plants being grown. Light applications of complete slow-release fertilisers will assist in this regard. Prune and then burn any diseased plant material.

(v) If plants do die for no apparent reason, drench the soil with a fungicide before replanting. Your local nursery should be able to suggest a suitable product for this purpose.

It is not only Australian plants which are affected by the devastating *Phytophthora cinnamomi.* Fruit orchards and other agricultural crops, as well as a wide range of garden ornamentals are highly susceptible.

A number of Australian plant species are known to be resistant to *Phytophthora cinnamomi.* In many cases these are plants which will tolerate high levels of moisture in the soil; however, some species from drier regions also fall into this category. A listing of plants believed to be tolerant of *Phytophthora cinnamomi* is contained in Volume 1 of *The Encyclopaedia of Australian Plants Suitable for Cultivation* (see Bibliography).

14. MINERAL DEFICIENCIES OR EXCESSES

Imbalances in the nutrients available to a plant do from time to time occur. These are often reflected in yellowing of leaves or other symptoms seen in the foliage.

The use of complete fertilisers will usually correct any deficiencies that exist in the soil.

The yellowing of foliage (see 15 under 'Plant Problem Check List' page 83) due to iron deficiency is not uncommon in some Australian plants. This can be corrected by an application of iron chelates, which is readily available from nurseries. (See also Chapter 7.)

Excessive use of fertilisers with a high phosphorus content can have a detrimental effect on plants. This is called phosphorus toxicity. Further details can be found at the end of Chapter 7, 'Fertilising'. Browning of the leaves around the margin can be a symptom of excessive phosphorus. The problem is more likely to occur in container-grown plants than those in garden cultivation.

Excessive soil salt can affect plant growth, particularly in low lying areas where temperatures are often high. As water continually evaporates, salting of the soil increases. This is not a problem which is easily corrected and it requires long-term planning.

There are some Australian plant species which will tolerate high levels of soil salt and these are very useful for problem areas of this kind. A list of species will be found in Chapter 3, Chart 4.

15. AIR POLLUTION

Severe air pollution can be detrimental to plant growth and this is evident in some plantings beside major freeways.

Trials have been carried out in various countries to ascertain those plants which will tolerate high levels of air pollution and several Australian plant species have performed very favourably. One excellent example is the *Callistemon citrinus* (the Crimson Bottlebrush).

If your garden is beside a busy roadway this problem should be borne in mind, so that you can select suitable species. You can find out which species will be suited to your needs by observing those plants growing well on roadsides in your area, or by contacting the road planning authority in your capital city.

16. RABBITS, POSSUMS AND OTHER PLANT EATERS

Whilst rabbits are mainly a problem of rural areas, possums can cause considerable damage in suburban gardens, particularly if there are trees nearby to provide shelter and nest sites.

The most effective method of providing protection against rabbit attacks, particularly for young plants, is through the use of constructed plant guards, see Chapter 8. Rabbits can cause a good deal of damage to young plant growth, but through observation and experiment it is often possible to learn which species are favoured in preference to others, and some may not need the protection of guards. Certain species of *Banksia* have been found to be ignored by rabbits, whilst other plants nearby are devastated.

Rabbits will also ringbark plant trunks, or dig into the soil to eat selected roots such as those of *Allocasuarina, Callitris* and *Casuarina* spp. Guards will help to protect plant roots as well as upper growth.

Deterrent sprays, including garlic spray and the fungicide thiram, can act as repellents against rabbit attacks. Rags soaked in creosote and placed near (but not against) plants have been used with success for rabbits, as also have containers of mothballs hung from the low branches of plants.

A number of possum species are widespread throughout rural and suburban areas of Australia, and flowers, fruits and leaves are commonly regarded as tasty treats by these creatures. Young plants can be protected by wire guards, but it must be remembered that, unlike rabbits, possums can climb.

On larger plants a sheet metal band about 30 cm wide can be placed around the trunk to prevent possums gaining a foothold to climb. Deterrent sprays and mixtures such as those used for rabbits have also been used with success.

If the number of rabbits and/or possums in the garden is relatively few, one of the most successful methods of solving the problem is through the use of a wire possum trap. These traps can be baited with apple, bread and peanut butter, or other suitable foods. The door to the cage shuts when the animal enters and eats. Possums are protected native animals and should not be harmed after trapping. Do not endeavour to handle them as they will scratch when cornered. The possum should be taken in the cage to an area of bushland at least 10 km away and released there, or it will quickly return to its former territory. Information regarding the availability of possum traps can be obtained from State Wildlife Department offices.

Other animals which can cause damage to plants, particularly in rural areas, include kangaroos, wallabies and wombats. Guards can be used to protect young plants (see Chapter 8). With established trees and shrubs the foliage eaten by kangaroos and wallabies is often no more than would be lost through garden pruning. Chapter 8 also includes information about guards to prevent plants being eaten by farm animals.

Relatively minor but annoying damage can be caused by blackbirds and members of the parrot family. Fine netting can be thrown over plants particularly at risk, or these birds can be deterred by a wide range of scarecrow devices.

OTHER GARDEN CREATURES, NOT NECESSARILY PESTS

In this chapter we have looked at the major groups of garden pests. The aim has been to present the information as simply as possible, whilst providing helpful advice. There are, of course, many hundreds of creatures, large to minute, to be found in the average home garden.

Not all garden creatures are pests. Some are in fact quite the opposite and are of great value in the garden. This is one of the reasons why toxic sprays are not always recommended in gardening publications.

Many of the small creatures in our gardens serve a vital role in the pollination of flowers and the subsequent setting of seeds and fruits.

The value of earthworms is widely known. They can eat about half their own body weight in soil or organic matter each day and in doing so they increase soil fertility by mixing organic materials through the soil. Their action allows better penetration of oxygen and water into the soil, and plant roots can also develop more readily in areas where worms are present. Worm casts increase the nutrients available for plant growth.

Ladybird beetles are particularly useful, as their diet includes aphids, psyllids and other small insect pests. There are several different species of ladybird in the family *Coccinellidae.*

Spiders also help to control the numbers of insects commonly regarded as garden pests.

Lacewing insects and Praying Mantids are creatures which eat smaller insects or their eggs.

The major assistance to the gardener in regard to insect control comes, of course, from native birds. This topic is in fact so important that the next chapter has been devoted to 'Encouraging Birds to Your Garden'.

A ladybird beetle will eat up to 50 aphids in a day. (Photograph by courtesy *Your Garden* magazine.)

13—Encouraging Birds to your Garden

Birds play an important role in the balance of nature within a garden.

Most plant species rely on the presence of insects, birds or sometimes other creatures, to transfer pollen from flower to flower. This enables fertilisation and seed production to take place.

Without bird populations in our gardens, the numbers of insects increase dramatically and it is then that we find we must turn to chemical sprays in an effort to reduce the insect numbers. To achieve natural control by encouraging birds to an area is by far the more desirable method.

Many people have been encouraged to grow Australian plants simply by observing the fascinating bird life which exists in native gardens. It is now generally appreciated that the numbers of native honeyeaters in suburban areas have risen very significantly because of an increased number of Australian plants being grown.

There is nothing quite like watching a colourful Eastern Spinebill visiting a Kangaroo Paw flower to gather nectar. Despite the small size of the bird, the flower-stem will bend and sway as the little creature moves around, its long slender beak probing right up into the tubular flowers to where the nectar lies. First into one flower, then into another, it sometimes hovers in almost Hummingbird fashion, until if finally departs. You are left feeling almost as satisfied as that beautiful creature which drank the nectar.

There are three basic requirements to be fulfilled if birds are to be attracted to a garden.

1. Food,
2. Water,
3. Shelter.

We will look at each one in detail.

1. FOOD

The easiest and most satisfactory method of ensuring a constant food supply for the birds is through garden planning and the planting of suitable plants.

Birds in the group known as honeyeaters require a constant supply of nectar throughout the year. These birds range from very small creatures such as the Spinebills to larger honeyeaters including Wattlebirds. In addition to their diet of nectar and pollen, they also eat some of the insects that in turn may have been attracted to the nectar-producing flowers.

Insects form the major part of the diet of birds such as Fantails, Flycatchers, Pardalotes, Robins, Silvereyes and Wrens. The Flycatchers are expert at taking the insects whilst in flight, while others like the small and colourful Pardalotes will clean up infestations of small creatures such as aphids and scale from the flowers and foliage of plants.

Larger insects, grubs and other small creatures are gathered enthusiastically by native birds such as Butcherbirds, Cuckoo Shrikes, Currawongs, Kookaburras, Magpies and Wattlebirds.

Finches, Pigeons and the many Australian Parrots feed primarily on seeds. Their diet does, however, include other items such as insects and in some cases nectar.

It is possible in even a relatively small garden to grow plants which will provide food for birds throughout the year. Small honeyeaters and insect-eating birds will be readily attracted to native plants in flower. Attracting some of the larger birds such as Kookaburras and Parrots is more difficult and can usually be achieved only in areas where there are good stands of large trees.

By growing plants which will attract birds to a garden, a natural source of food supply is ensured. Supplementary feeding is mentioned later in this chapter, but although it allows us the pleasure of bringing birds to a position where they can easily be viewed, it is not nearly as satisfactory as a natural food supply.

The following charts list but a few of the many Australian plants useful in attracting birds to a garden. They are species which have proved to be very adaptable in cultivation and most should be readily available through nurseries. You can choose from these to provide a basic selection of plants with flowers throughout the year, then include additional species as desired.

Kookaburras. (Photograph by courtesy *Your Garden* magazine.)

Chart 8 — Plants which will provide food for native birds

(a) Groundcovers and plants to around 1 m high: A selection of 20 species

Plant Name	Height x width	Brief comment — for further description see Section 2
Anigozanthos flavidus	0.5-1 m x 1 m	Tall kangaroo paw with flowers of several colours on stems to 3 m.
Anigozanthos rufus	0.3-0.75 m x 1 m	Clump-forming kangaroo paw with deep red flowers.
Astroloma ciliatum	0.5-1 m x 1-2 m	Cigar-shaped flowers are red-tipped with greenish-yellow.
Austromyrtus dulcis	0.5-1.5 m x 1-2 m	White flowers are followed by edible black berries.
Blandfordia grandiflora	0.3-0.8 m x 0.2-0.4 m	Has grass-like leaves and yellow to red bell-like flowers.
Brachysema species	Prostrate x 1-2.5 m	Has oval, dark green leaves and red with yellow pea-flowers.
Conostylis bealiana	0.2 m x 0.3 m	A small, tufting plant with yellow to orange tubular flowers.
Correa reflexa	Several forms 0.3-1 m high	Bell-shaped flowers in many different colours.
Darwinia taxifolia ssp. *macrolaena*	0.1-1 m x 1-2 m	Has narrow, grey-green leaves and pink to red flowers.
Eremophila glabra, prostrate forms	Prostrate x 1-2 m	A variable species with yellow or orange-red flowers.
Grevillea alpina, Grampians low form	0.3-0.5 m x 1-2 m	Several forms available. This form has red and yellow flowers.
Grevillea x *gaudichaudii*	0.3 m x 2-5 m	Has attractive reddish foliage and burgundy toothbrush flower-heads.
Grevillia juniperina, low forms	Prostrate x 1-5 m	Variable species with buff, yellow or red flowers.
Grevillea lanigera 'Mt. Tamboritha'	Prostrate x 1-1.5 m	Has clusters of cream and deep pink flowers.
Grevillea rosmarinifolia 'Lara Dwarf'	0.5-1 m x 1-2 m	Has narrow leaves and pink to red with cream flowers.
Grevillea thelemanniana, prostrate forms	Prostrate x 2-3 m	Variable. Leaves green or greyish. Flowers bright red.
Homoranthus darwinioides	0.5-1 m x 0.5-1 m	Compact shrub with bluish-green leaves. Has small, pink, yellow and green flowers.
Kennedia glabrata	Prostrate x 1-2 m	Quick-growing. Has brick-red pea-flowers.
Prostanthera serpyllifolia ssp. *microphylla*	0.3-0.5 m x 1 m	Has small, aromatic leaves and red or bluish-green flowers.
Prostanthera monticola	1 m x 2 m	Tubular flowers are green streaked with purple.

Chart 8 — Plants which will provide food for native birds

(b) Medium shrubs around 1-4 m high: A selection of 20 species

Plant Name	Height x width	Brief comment — for further description see Section 2
Acacia myrtifolia	1-3 m x 2-3 m	Has a profuse display of globular cream-yellow flower-heads.
Callistemon subulatus	2-4 m x 2-4 m	Bottlebrush flower-spikes are deep red.
Calothamnus rupestris	1-3 m x 2-3 m	Has dense, pine-like leaves and pink to red flowers.
Correa glabra	2-3 m x 1-3 m	The tubular flowers are usually pale green.
Correa 'Mannii'	1-2.5 m x 1-2 m	Has red with pale pink bell-shaped flowers.
Darwinia citriodora	1.5 m x 1-2 m	Has grey-green, aromatic foliage and green-red flower-heads.
Epacris longiflora	0.5-2 m x 0.5-2 m	Narrow tubular red and white flowers for most of year.
Grevillea aquifolium	0.2-3 m x 1-4 m	Holly-like leaves. Red and green toothbrush flower-heads.
Grevillea arenaria	1.5-2.5 m x 1.5-2.5 m	Foliage is grey-green. Flowers reddish or yellow-green.
Grevillea hookeriana	2-4 m x 3-4 m	Large shrub with bright red toothbrush flower-heads.
Grevillea jephcottii	2-2.5 m x 1.5-2 m	Has cream to green flowers for most of year.
Grevillea longistyla	2-5 m x 2-4 m	Bushy shrub with attractive foliage and pink to red flowers.
Grevillea miqueliana	2-3 m x 2-4 m	Has clusters of orange-red to bright red flowers.
Grevillea mucronulata	1-2 m x 1.5-2.5 m	A dense shrub with greenish flowers.
Grevillea 'Poorinda Constance'	1.5-3 m x 1.5-3 m	Has clusters of red flowers for most of year.
Grevillea 'Poorinda Queen'	2-4 m x 2-4 m	Has clusters of orange flowers for most of year.
Grevillea rosmarinifolia	2-3 m x 2-4 m	Large shrub with narrow, prickly foliage. Flowers are pink to red with cream.
Melaleuca lateritia	2-4 m x 1.5-3 m	Has narrow leaves and bright orange-red flower-spikes.
Pultenaea gunnii	1-1.5 m x 1-1.5 m	Has a showy display of orange-yellow pea-flowers.
Telopea speciosissima	3-5 m x 2-3 m	NSW Waratah. Has large showy red flower-heads.

Grevillea longistyla.

Chart 8 — Plants which will provide food for native birds

(c) Tall shrubs or trees over 4 m high: A selection of 20 species

Plant Name	Height x width	Brief comment — for further description see Section 2
Acacia pycnantha	3-10 m x 2-6 m	Has large, globular, golden-yellow flower-heads.
Acacia retinodes	3-5 m x 3-6 m	Lemon-yellow flower-heads almost throughout the year.
Acmena smithii	10-20 m x 5-15 m	Has shiny, dark green leaves and showy white to purple fruits.
Angophora costata	10-30 m x 6-15 m	Trunk has decorative, smooth bark. Flowers white to cream.
Banksia ericifolia	3-6 m x 2-5 m	Has small, narrow leaves. Flower-heads mainly orange.
Callistemon 'Harkness'	3-6 m x 2-6 m	Has very showy, bright red flower-spikes.
Callistemon viminalis	1-12 m x 1.5-6 m	Variable species, often weeping. Has red bottlebrush flower-spikes.
Castanospermum australe	10-30 m x 5-12 m	Rainforest tree with attractive foliage and red with yellow flowers.
Eucalyptus caesia	5-10 m x 3-5 m	Buds and fruits are silvery. Flowers pink, tipped with gold.
Eucalyptus conferruminata	5-10 x 4-8 m	Has large clusters of yellow-green flowers.
Eucalyptus leucoxylon, dwarf forms	5-8 m x 5-8 m	Has attractive trunk, and white to deep pink flowers.
Eucalyptus macrandra	5-10 m x 3-6 m	Trunk smooth, brown-grey. Has clusters of yellow-green flowers.
Eucalyptus maculata	15-30 m x 8-15 m	Has spotted trunk and profuse white flowers.
Eucalyptus megacornuta	6-15 m x 5-10 m	Has decorative trunk and clusters of yellow-green flowers.
Eucalyptus polybractea	5-10 m x 3-7 m	Foliage bluish-green. Flowers white to cream.
Eucalyptus sideroxylon	10-20 m x 5-10 m	Bark is black and furrowed. Leaves grey-green. Flowers usually pink.
Eucalyptus torelliana	6-15 m x 4-10 m	Has decorative trunk and large clusters of creamy white flowers.
Grevillea shiressii	3-8 m x 2-5 m	Bushy plant with bluish-green flowers.
Melaleuca hypericifolia	3-6 m x 2-5 m	Has orange-red flower-spikes.
Syzygium coolminianum	5-10 m x 3-5 m	Leaves are shiny, dark green. Has pink to blue-purple fruits.

SUPPLEMENTARY FEEDING

Birds should not be encouraged to rely solely on this type of feeding. A natural source of food is desirable at holiday times, or should you be unable to continue putting out food due to illness.

Constructing a nectar feeder

Nectar feeders are available commercially, or you may care to construct your own. You will need a glass bottle and a small but rigid plastic bowl of similar diameter to the bottle. It is helpful if the bowl has a firmly fitting lid.

(a) Construct a support for the bottle and the bowl, using the illustration as a guide. Make a perching rail for the birds.

(b) Make a hole in the lid of the bowl and fit it over the neck of the bottle. Use tape, glue or wire, etc., to secure the lid after checking it is in the correct position.

(c) Fill the bottle with water. Place the upturned bowl on top. Turn the feeder to its correct position, and place it in the support prepared.

(d) Check the level of the water, adjusting the bottle if necessary, and mark the level on the plastic bowl.

(e) Make 4 to 5 equally spaced feeding holes in the plastic bowl about 0.5 cm above the water level. Holes should only be a few millimetres in diameter. A heated metal skewer or nail can be used.

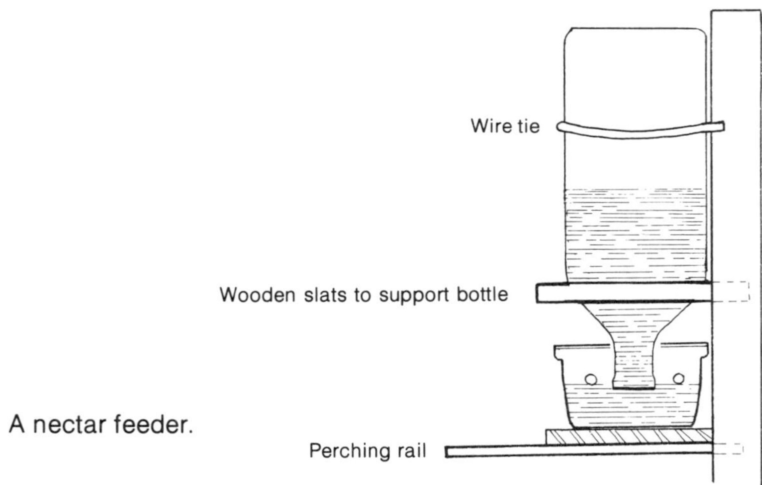

A nectar feeder.

Feeders should not be placed in direct sunshine where the nectar can become heated. Choose a sheltered location and one which is easily visible. Avoid positions near large areas of glass, as birds may be distracted by reflections and hurt themselves by flying into glass windows or doors. Make sure any feeder is beyond any possible access from predators such as domestic cats.

Recipe for bird nectar

1 cup brown sugar
4 cups water
Dissolve the sugar in the water.
1-2 drops of infant vitamin concentrate may be added.

Any nectar not put out immediately should be stored in a refrigerator. Feeder bottles and bowls should be washed thoroughly before refilling.

Bird puddings

A bird pudding can be made by using a mixture of breadcrumbs, bird seed and breakfast cereal. These are combined together in melted dripping and set in a container of suitable size. After the pudding has set it should be tipped out of the bowl. A piece of string can be inserted through the centre like a wick with a large button to hold the pudding at the base. An alternative method of suspending the pudding is to hang it in a mesh bag such as an onion bag.

Food tables

Seed-eating birds such as Finches and Parrots will be attracted to a tray spread with suitable seed.

Sections of hollow logs or pieces of thick bark can make attractive as well as functional tables. They can be positioned on upright stands, or wired to hang from a verandah, pergola or branch of a tree.

Pieces of meat will attract Kookaburras or Magpies and cheese is also considered a delicacy by many birds.

2. WATER

A constant supply of clean, cool water is the second main requirement if birds are to be attracted to an area.

Birds need water for drinking and also for bathing.

You can use a specially constructed birdbath or pool, or simply leave a bowl of suitable size and shape beneath a tap in the garden.

Small containers should not be put where they will get hot on sunny days. It is also important that water containers for birds should never be placed in positions where the birds will become easy prey for domestic cats and other predators.

A pond can be an attractive feature in a garden, as well as providing a source of water for the birds.

In large gardens a pool can provide a most attractive landscape feature. A rock or log placed away from the edge of the pool will create a safe place from which birds can drink or bathe.

You may be surprised at the birds which visit your garden pond. If the area around the water's edge is fairly open to allow good access, your garden bird list could include a number of different water-birds, such as Grebes, Herons and native Ducks.

3. SHELTER

Creating shelter and protection is the third major requirement if native birds are to remain within a garden area.

Provided that the birds have a sense of security, they will feel confident about staying there and even nesting within the garden.

The inclusion of some dense, prickly plants is of considerable value in this regard. A selection of suitable species is included in Chart 9, below.

Small birds can dart into the foliage of dense, prickly plants and the larger birds which may be attacking them will be unable to follow them into the plant. These plants also provide protection against domestic cats.

Cats are a real problem if you are trying to attract birds to a garden in a residential area. It is undesirable for birds to be encouraged into your garden if you own a cat. Cats are by nature hunters and it is only to be expected that they will seek to follow their natural instincts. Even a bell around the cat's neck often gives inadequate warning to the birds.

In a garden of average size which has been planted with some of the main food-producing plants for birds, it is likely that sufficient shelter will be available in these plants.

BIRD NESTING SITES

Birds have a wide variety of preferences and requirements in regard to nesting sites. Small Pardalotes will nest in a pile of soil, sand or sawdust. Other birds rely heavily on hollows of mature or even dead trees. Unfortunately these birds have been forced from many regions by the removal of trees and the elimination of their nesting sites.

There are a number of Australian plants which are excellent nesting sites for birds or supply materials commonly used by native birds in their nest construction. A selection of these is provided in Chart 9.

To increase the number of nest sites in the garden be on the lookout for hollow branches and logs which can be tied in suitable positions within your trees. It may be desirable to close one end of the log with a piece of galvanised iron or other suitable material.

Nesting boxes can also be constructed if desired.

Further information

The subject of attracting birds to the garden is wide enough for a complete book in itself, as will be seen by referring to the Bibliography under 'Landscaping and the Selection of Plants'. The titles listed there are recommended for further information and you can also contact the Bird Observers' Club, P.O. Box 185, Nunawading, Victoria 3131.

Chart 9 — Plants which will provide shelter for birds, also nesting sites and/or nesting materials

A selection of 20 species

Plant Name	Height x width	Brief comment — for further description see Section 2
Acacia inophloia	3-4 m x 3-4 m	Has brown, string-like bark. Flowers yellow.
Acacia ulicifolia var. *brownei*	0.5-1 m x 1-2 m	Foliage is prickly. Flower-heads golden-yellow.
Banksia spinulosa	3-6 m x 2-4 m	A bushy shrub, popular for nesting. Has usually honey-coloured flower-spikes.
Coprosma quadrifida	2-4 m x 1-2 m	Foliage prickly. Has small flowers and bright red fruits.
Dryandra polycephala	1-3 m x 1-2 m	Prickly shrub, popular for nesting. Flower-heads bright yellow.
Dryandra sessilis	2-6 m x 1.5-3.5 m	Foliage prickly. Flower-heads pale yellow.
Eucalyptus camaldulensis	20-40 m x 10-25 m	Large tree often with nesting holes in trunk. Flowers white.
Gahnia sieberiana	2-3 m x 1-2 m	A clumping plant with long, sharp leaves.
Grevillea asparagoides	1-2 m x 1-3 m	Has stiff foliage and bright red flowers. Good nesting plant.
Grevillea juniperina	2-4 m x 2-4 m	Bushy shrub with prickly foliage and orange-red flowers.
Grevillea 'Pink Pearl'	2-4 m x 2-4 m	Large shrub with pointed leaves and pink flowers.
Grevillea tripartita	2-3 m x 2-3 m	Very prickly, large, open shrub. Flowers red and cream.
Grevillea vestita	2-3 m x 2-3.5 m	Large shrub with pointed, greyish leaves. Flowers white.
Hakea purpurea	1-2 m x 1-1.5 m	Has prickly foliage and bright red flowers.
Hakea sericea	2-4 m x 1-3 m	Popular nesting plant. Has prickly foliage and white to pink flowers.
Hakea suaveolens	3-6 m x 3-5 m	Foliage is prickly. Flowers white to cream.
Lambertia formosa	2-3 m x 2-3 m	Has dark green, pointed leaves. Tubular flowers orange to red.
Leptospermum laevigatum	3-6 m x 3-6 m	Trunk has papery bark. Flowers white.
Melaleuca leucadendron	15-25 m x 8-15 m	Trunk has papery bark. Flower-spikes are cream.
Melaleuca linariifolia	5-10 m x 3-6 m	Trunk has papery bark. Has showy clusters of white feathery flowers.

14—Coping with Drought Conditions in the Garden

Australia is an extremely dry continent over much of the total land area.

In the major cities we are sometimes not fully aware of how dry our land really is. We can turn on the tap and obtain a seemingly endless supply of water with which to water our gardens, fill swimming pools, wash cars, and even hose down paths and driveways. In very dry seasons, however, when restrictions govern the degree to which mains water can be used, we are forced to consider whether we have taken for granted this luxury of an unlimited water supply.

In rural areas where residents must rely on tank, dam or bore water, there is greater awareness regarding this precious and limited resource. This is reflected in gardening practices.

Because our continent is so arid, a large percentage of the native plants has evolved to cope successfully with very dry situations. This is a tremendous advantage when we are planning low maintenance gardens if only we can learn to use these plants to their full potential.

In several overseas countries with serious water shortage problems and areas of high population, drought-resistant Australian plants are becoming extremely popular, as little or no hand watering is required for their survival.

It must again be pointed out here that *not all* Australian plants occur naturally in arid regions. Therefore *all are not* drought-tolerant. Some species occur in swamplands and waterways throughout the country, or in fern gullies and other moist, shaded regions.

Plants native to many coastal areas of Queensland have adapted to both high rainfall and high humidity. They grow best if given similar conditions in cultivation and some are best suited to indoor or glasshouse cultivation in cool temperate zones.

All *Eremophila* species are tolerant of dry conditions, and the name *Eremophila* means 'desert-loving'. Seen here is *E. clarkei.*

THE IMPORTANCE OF GOOD PLANNING

Low maintenance Australian gardens can be established by grouping together plants which require a high level of moisture intake throughout the year. The rest of the garden will, with adequate planning, be able to cope with minimal or no hand watering, even during extremely dry periods.

PLANTING TIME

The time of the year when planting is carried out is also of considerable importance. This is particularly true in areas where no hand watering at all will be possible during the first year when the plant is becoming established.

Small plants, if they are planted in autumn with an initial light application of slow-release fertiliser at the time of planting, will usually be able to cope from that time onwards, when suitable species have been chosen.

All plants do need to be watered thoroughly when first planted.

MULCHING

Mulching around garden plants is a valuable help to moisture conservation. One test reported in the CSIRO publication *When Should I Water* indicated that a layer of straw 4 cm thick can reduce evaporation from the soil by 73 per cent.

There are various types of mulching materials from which you can choose. Each has advantages and some also have disadvantages. Information regarding mulching materials will be found in Chapter 6.

WATERING AND FERTILISING

The maintenance methods used within the garden have a considerable bearing on whether plants will survive during drought conditions.

New growth occurs on plants only when there is adequate water available. In their natural environment plants from dry areas generally grow quite slowly, at a rate well below that which we often seek to achieve in our gardens.

If we apply liberal amounts of fertiliser and water to garden plants, the result is likely to be seen in new foliage growth or profuse flowering. Such growth must then be sustained by continued watering, or the fresh young tips will wilt and perhaps die back beyond recovery.

Fertilising and watering only to the level where healthy and sturdy plants can be maintained is therefore recommended, as this will ensure their ongoing good development. In many cases there is no need to fertilise at all if the soil is of good quality.

Further information regarding garden watering and watering systems will be found in Chapter 5. Fertilising is covered in detail in Chapter 7.

The following charts provide details of Australian plants which will tolerate extended periods of dryness. These species can be useful both for low maintenance gardens in urban areas and for farms and other broad-acre planting.

Chart 10 — Plants which will tolerate extended periods of dryness

(a) Groundcovers and plants to around 1 m high: A selection of 20 species

Plant Name	**Height x width**	**Brief comment — for further description see Section 2**
Acacia cometes	0.2-0.3 m x 0.5-0.8 m	Low, spreading wattle with globular yellow flower-heads.
Acacia depressa	0.1 m x 1 m	Cushion-like dwarf shrub with yellow flower-heads.
Acacia pravissima 'Golden Carpet'	0.3 m x 3-5 m	Has a profuse display of bright yellow flower-heads.
Acacia pulviniformis	0.3-1 m x 0.5-2.5 m	Dwarf, spreading shrub with profuse cream to yellow flowers.
Cheiranthera alternifolia	0.5-1 m x 0.5-1 m	Flowers are deep blue with yellow anthers.
Clianthus formosus	Prostrate x 1-4 m	Sturt's Desert Pea. Has showy red with black pea-flowers.
Crinum flaccidum	0.5-1 m	Member of the Lily family. Flowers white or yellow.
Dampiera rosmarinifolia	0.4 m x 1-3 m	Has dense spikes of light blue or mauve flowers.
Dampiera teres	0.3-0-5 m x 0.5-1 m	Dwarf shrub with blue-mauve or pink flowers.
Enchylaena tomentosa	0.3-1 m x 0.5-1.5 m	Foliage is bluish-green. Has colourful fruits.
Frankenia pauciflora	Prostrate x 1 m	Has small, greyish leaves. Flowers are commonly deep pink.
Glishrocaryon behrii	0.3-0.5 m x 0.5-1 m	A clump-forming plant with bright yellow flowers.
Grevillea ilicifolia	Prostrate to 1 m x 1.5-3 m	Has deeply lobed leaves and cream with red flowers.
Grevillea juniperina, prostrate forms	Prostrate x 1-5 m	Variable. Foliage prickly. Flowers buff, yellow or red.
Grevillea repens	Prostrate x 2-4 m	Has holly-like leaves and deep red flower-heads.
Kunzea pomifera	0.5 m x 1-3 m	Dense spreading plant with white to cream flowers.
Myoporum parvifolium	0.2-0.4 x 1-3 m	Has bright green or purplish leaves. Flowers white or pale pink.
Phyla nodiflora	Prostrate	Spreading plant useful as a non-mow lawn. Flowers pink.
Rhagodia spinescens	Prostrate to 1 m x 1.5-3 m	Dense groundcover with greyish foliage.
Spyridium parvifolium 'Austraflora Nimbus'	Prostrate x 0.5-1 m	Has decorative foliage and white to cream flowers.

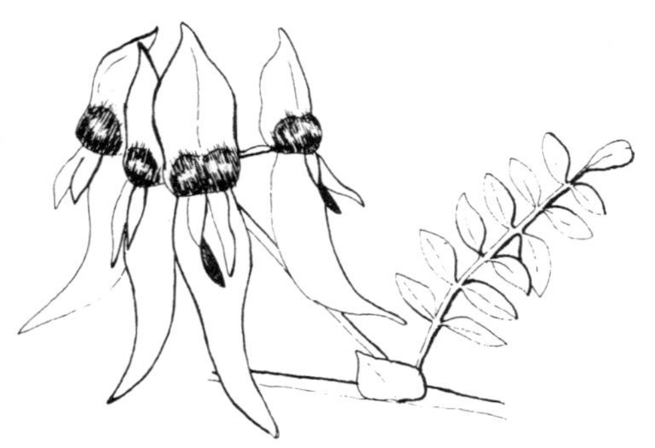

Clianthus formosus, Sturt's Desert Pea.

Chart 10 — Plants which will tolerate extended periods of dryness

(b) Medium shrubs around 1-4 m high: A selection of 20 species

Plant Name	Height x width	Brief comment — for further description see Section 2
Acacia redolens	1-4 m x 3-8 m	Has grey-green foliage and yellow flower-heads.
Allocasuarina muelleriana	1-4 m x 0.5-1.5 m	Tall, shrubby she-oak with grey-green foliage.
Atriplex rhagodioides	0.5-2 m x 1-2 m	A very hardy shrub with silver foliage.
Banksia baueri	2-5 m x 2-4 m	Bushy shrub with large mauve-grey or orange-brown flower-heads.
Beaufortia orbifolia	2-3 m x 2-3 m	Flower-heads are lime-green with red tips.
Calocephalus brownii	0.2-2 m x 0.5-3 m	Has silvery foliage and yellow and white flower-heads.
Calothamnus gilesii	2-4 m x 2-4 m	Has clusters of red flowers tipped with gold.
Cassia artemisioides	1-2 m x 1 m	Has silvery, ferny foliage and yellow bell flowers.
Chamelaucium uncinatum	2-5 m x 2-6 m	Open-petalled flowers are white to reddish-purple.
Eremaea beaufortioides	1-2 m x 1-2 m	Has showy, orange flower-heads.
Eremophila denticulata	1-2.5 m x 1-3.5 m	Tubular flowers are yellow then age to red.
Eremophila maculata	0.5-3 m x 1-3 m	Variable species with tubular flowers in several colours.
Eucalyptus kruseana	3-4 m x 3-4 m	Has oval, blue-grey leaves. Clusters of yellow flowers.
Eucalyptus preissiana	2-5 m x 3-10 m	Spreading plant with smooth bark and yellow flowers.
Grevillea lavandulacea	0.5-2.5 m x 0.5-3 m	Variable species. Has greyish foliage and pink to red flowers.
Grevillea pinaster	1.5-2.5 m x 2-4 m	Has narrow green leaves and bright red flowers.
Hakea cinerea	1-2 m x 1-2 m	Foliage is blue-green. Flowers yellowish-green.
Melaleuca wilsonii	1-2.5 m x 1-3 m	Has clusters of lilac to reddish-pink flowers.
Petrophile serruriae	2-3 m x 2-3 m	Has finely divided, prickly leaves and pink to yellow flowers.
Regelia velutina	2.5-4 m x 1-2 m	Has decorative, greyish foliage and bright red flower-spikes.

Chart 10 — Plants which will tolerate extended periods of dryness

(c) Tall shrubs or trees over 4 m high: A selection of 20 species

Plant Name	Height x width	Brief comment — for further description see Section 2
Acacia jibberdingensis	3-5 m x 3-4 m	Has long, narrow phyllodes and deep yellow flowers.
Acacia lasiocalyx	3-5 m x 4-6 m	Stems and branches silvery. Has bright yellow flower-heads.
Acacia rossei	2-5 m x 1-3 m	Has deep yellow, globular flower-heads.
Acacia salicina	4-10 m x 3-5 m	Branches pendulous. Has pale yellow, globular flower-heads.
Acacia victoriae	3-12 m x 4-6 m	This wattle often has spines on the branches. Flowers pale yellow.
Brachychiton discolor	10-30 m x 5-15 m	Has pink to red, bell-shaped flowers.
Brachychiton rupestre	10-20 m x 5-15 m	Has bottle-shaped trunk, decorative foliage and yellowish flowers.
Callitris rhomboidea	3-6 m x 2-3 m	A conifer-like tree with green or glaucous foliage.
Casuarina cristata	8-25 m x 5-10 m	Has fine, green to greyish foliage.
Eucalyptus eremophila	3-5 m x 3-6 m	Has reddish buds and cream to yellow or red flowers.
Eucalyptus gardneri	2.5-9 m x 3-6 m	Leaves green or bluish-purple. Flowers cream to yellow.
Eucalyptus lansdowneana	3-6 m x 3-6 m	Slender tree with smooth bark. Flowers crimson.
Eucalyptus macrandra	5-10 m x 3-6 m	Has smooth trunk and large clusters of yellow-green flowers.
Eucalyptus sideroxylon	10-20 m x 5-10 m	Bark is black and deeply furrowed. Flowers pink.
Eucalyptus stricklandii	6-12 m x 5-10 m	Has smooth trunk and bright yellow flowers.
Eucalyptus websteriana	3-6 m x 3-6 m	Has decorative trunk and profuse cream to yellow flowers.
Geijera parviflora	4-9 m x 5-9 m	Foliage is pendulous. Has small, white flowers.
Grevillea robusta	10-25 m x 6-15 m	Has attractive foliage and bright orange flowers.
Melia azedarach var. *australasica*	6-8 m x 4-6 m	Deciduous tree with purple and white flowers and yellow-orange berries.
Pittosporum phylliraeoides	3-6 m x 1.5-3 m	Has pendulous branches with yellow flowers and fruits.

Brachychiton rupestre leaf.

15—Growing Plants in Wet Areas

Frequently in a garden we need plants which are moisture tolerant. There may be a natural depression in the slope of the land where moisture tends to gather or an area of natural drainage can result in certain portions of the garden being constantly moist.

The planting of moisture-loving species is a very effective method of draining excess moisture from wet areas. Chart 3, Chapter 3, provides a list of such species.

Sometimes we seek to create areas of water as features of our gardens. Ponds give a very pleasant dimension to an area. Reflections of trees and sky can be attractive and add an illusion of greater space. Ponds can also provide the important feature of permanent water necessary for native birds and insects within the garden.

Not infrequently water gardens are constructed primarily for the purpose of enabling some of the attractive moisture-loving Australian plants to be grown.

Chart 11, which follows in this chapter, lists a selection of ornamental, moisture-loving plants, suitable for a wide range of situations.

PLANTS WHICH WILL TOLERATE BOTH WET AND DRY SEASONS

'It never rains but it pours' is a well known saying and applicable to many areas of Australia.

In some places both wet and dry conditions can occur at different seasons of the year. Fortunately there are many Australian plants which have adapted to cope with both extremes.

A list of some of these species can be found in Chart 2, Chapter 3.

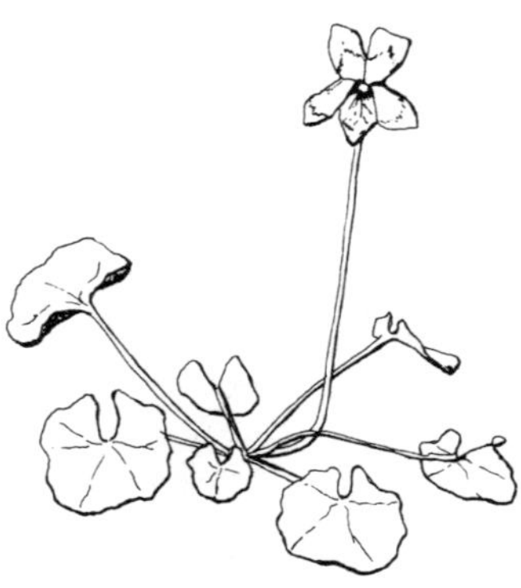

Viola hederacea.

Chart 11 — Moisture-loving plants

A selection of 20 species

Plant Name	Height x width	Brief comment — for further description see Section 2
Baeckea virgata	0.2-6 m x 2-3 m	Variable species. Has showy display of small, white flowers.
Banksia paludosa	0.5-1.5 m x 0.5-1.5 m	A low, spreading shrub with yellow to brownish flower-heads.
Bauera rubioides	0.2-3 m x 1-3 m	Has white to pink flowers for most of the year.
Callistemon citrinus	2-8 m x 2-6 m	Has bright red bottlebrush flower-spikes.
Callistemon sieberi	1-5 m x 1-5 m	Flower-spikes are cream to yellow.
Dianella tasmanica	0.6-1.7 m x 0.5-2 m	A clumping plant with strap-like leaves and blue flowers.
Diplarrena moroea	0.5-1 m x 0.5-1 m	Has strap-like leaves and white, 3-petalled flowers.
Epacris microphylla	0.5-1 m x 0.5-1 m	Dwarf shrub. Pink buds open to mainly white flowers.
Eucalyptus spathulata	6-12 m x 4-8 m	Trunk is smooth. Has clusters of small, cream flowers.
Gleichenia dicarpa	2-4 m tall	A wiry fern which can spread to form a thicket.
Leptospermum squarrosum	1-3 m x 1-3 m	Bushy shrub with prickly foliage. Has white to deep pink flowers.
Melaleuca decussata	2-4 m x 2-4 m	Has small, grey-green leaves and mauve flower-brushes.
Melaleuca thymifolia	0.5-1.5 m x 1-1.5 m	Compact shrub with mauve to purple flowers.
Patersonia occidentalis	0.5-0.8 m x 0.5 m	Has rush-like leaves and purple, 3-petalled flowers.
Restio tetraphyllus	1.5-2 m x 1-2 m	A decorative rush with brown or reddish flowers.
Sowerbaea juncea	0.3-0.5 m x 0.3-0.5 m	Has grass-like leaves and globular clusters of mauve flowers.
Sprengelia incarnata	1-2 m x 0.5-0.7 m	An erect plant with clusters of starry, pale pink flowers.
Stypandra caespitosa	0.3-0.5 m x 0.5 m	A tufting plant with usually blue flowers.
Todea barbara	2-3 m x 2-4 m	Large fern with a short broad trunk.
Viola hederacea	0.1 m x 1-2 m	Native violet. Has small, purple-blue and white flowers.

16—Plants for Wind Protection

Plants can be used for wind protection in the suburbs as well as in rural situations.

Windbreak plants can have a marked effect on temperatures within houses or other buildings. In winter, warmth can be increased by preventing the direct flow of cold air onto walls and window areas. Summer temperatures can be effectively reduced through moisture evaporation from the foliage of plants.

For windbreak planting to be fully effective species of different heights should be planted simultaneously. This will provide a dense foliage cover from ground level to the height desired and allow the wind to be gradually directed up and above the height of the tallest plant.

In areas where strong winds come from more than one direction, as is the case with many farm windbreaks, at least five plant height groupings will prove the most successful.

The establishment of plants in exposed and windy conditions is neither quick nor simple.

It is recommended that sturdy, young plants be used in preference to more mature specimens which would then need to be staked for support.

Do not over fertilise or force growth, or the new, soft foliage is likely to be burnt by strong winds. Allow the plants to develop at their own pace.

In the case of young plants it may be desirable to erect some form of screen to shelter them through their initial growth stages. If this has been necessary, ensure that the screen is removed gradually so that plants can cope with the change.

A partial screen, which provides some protection but also allows the plants to receive some degree of wind, is often the best solution. This will encourage the development of stronger plants than if total protection is given. See also Chapter 8.

TREATMENT OF WIND-DAMAGED PLANTS

In strong winds branches can sometimes be broken or split and it is wise to repair such damage as soon as possible.

Prune away any jagged or broken areas and paint cuts with a wound sealant. Information regarding correct methods of pruning will be found in Chapter 9.

If a plant is beginning to split from a major fork, it may be wise to remove one section completely. An alternative is to brace the branches affected by the split by using bolts or wooden or wire supports to assist the healing process. In the case of large trees, you should seek the advice of an experienced tree surgeon if you wish to save the tree.

Plants may also suffer wind damage in the form of burnt foliage. This can be caused by very cold winds, hot drying winds, or salt-laden winds in coastal areas. As mentioned earlier in this chapter, it is usually the fairly soft new growth which is affected in this way. Minimum use of fertilisers will avoid an excess of new foliage growth likely to be damaged. Generally no treatment is necessary and the plants will recover naturally after such a setback.

One of the best ways of avoiding wind damage to plants is to select species which are known to be tolerant of the conditions likely to be experienced in your area.

The plants in the following chart have all been found to tolerate strong winds. They are also generally regarded as being hardy to a range of different soil and climatic conditions.

The height and width dimensions given refer to their normal average size under favourable garden conditions. In very exposed situations it can be anticipated that the plants will not grow to these dimensions. It is therefore suggested that you select species with stated dimensions slightly greater than you need in order to achieve plants of the size desired.

An effective screen and windbreak planting, using species of different sizes.

Chart 12 — Plants suitable for use in a windbreak

(a) Plants up to around 4 m high: A selection of 20 species

Plant Name	Height x width	Brief comment — for further description see Section 2
Acacia boormanii	3-5 m x 2-5 m	An adaptable wattle. Can sucker lightly. Bright yellow flowers.
Atriplex nummularia	1-3 m x 2-4 m	A hardy shrub with bluish-grey foliage.
Brachysema lanceolatum	0.5-2 m x 1-3 m	Leaves are silvery underneath. Has red pea-flowers.
Callistemon phoeniceus	2-4 m x 3-5 m	Has large, red or pink bottlebrush flower-spikes.
Correa alba	0.5-2 m x 1-2 m	Dense shrub with starry, white flowers.
Grevillea rosmarinifolia	2-3 m x 2-4 m	Has narrow, pointed leaves and pink to red with cream flowers.
Grevillea tripartita	2-3 m x 2-3 m	Has prickly leaves and clusters of red and cream flowers.
Hakea nitida	1-2.5 m x 2-2.5 m	Has prickly green leaves and profuse cream flowers.
Kunzea ambigua	1-3 m x 1-2 m	Leaves are small and crowded. Has profuse, white flowers.
Leptospermum flavescens	3-4 m x 3-4 m	Large shrub with white to cream, tea-tree flowers.
Leptospermum 'Horizontalis'	0.5-1 m x 2-4 m	Dense, spreading shrub with white tea-tree flowers.
Leptospermum scoparium	1.5-2.5 m x 2-3 m	Has white to pale pink or purplish flowers.
Melaleuca diosmifolia	2-4 m x 2-4 m	A dense shrub with crowded leaves and lime-green flowers.
Melaleuca elliptica	3-5 m x 2-5 m	Has oval, grey-green leaves and red flower-brushes.
Melaleuca lateritia	2-4 m x 1.5-3 m	Has narrow leaves and bright orange-red flower-spikes.
Melaleuca violacea	1-2 m x 1-2 m	Has greyish-green leaves and purple to violet flowers.
Melaleuca wilsonii	1-2.5 m x 1-3 m	Has clusters of lilac to reddish-pink flowers.
Regelia ciliata	1.5-2.5 m x 2-3 m	Has small leaves and globular, mauve-purple flower-heads.
Rhagodia spinescens	Prostrate to 1 m x 1.5-3 m	A dense groundcover with greyish, hairy foliage.
Westringia fruticosa	2-3 m x 2-3 m	A hardy shrub. The white flowers have purple markings.

Chart 12 — Plants suitable for use in a windbreak

(b) Tall shrubs or trees over 4 m high: A selection of 20 species

Plant Name	Height x width	Brief comment — for further description see Section 2
Acacia floribunda	4-8 m x 4-6 m	Likes moist position. Has pale yellow flower-heads.
Acacia howittii	4-8 m x 3-6 m	Branches are pendulous. Flower-heads are pale yellow.
Acacia pravissima	4-8 m x 4-8 m	Has dense foliage with triangular phyllodes. Flowers bright yellow.
Acacia prominens	5-20 m x 4-15 m	Dense tall shrub to medium tree. Flowers lemon-yellow.
Acacia saligna	3-10 m x 3-6 m	An adaptable wattle with golden-yellow flower-heads.
Allocasuarina verticillata	4-11 m x 3-6 m	Attractive she-oak with dark, furrowed bark and pendulous foliage.
Angophora floribunda	10-25 m x 6-15 m	Has a profuse display of white to cream flowers.
Angophora hispida	3-10 m x 3-6 m	Spreading tree with reddish branchlets and cream flowers.
Callistemon salignus	5-15 m x 3-5 m	New leaf growth pink to red. Flower-spikes white to pink.
Casuarina glauca	8-30 m x 4-12 m	An adaptable she-oak which can sucker to form a copse.
Eucalyptus cladocalyx nana	6-8 m x 6-8 m	Has a mottled, smooth trunk and creamy-yellow flowers.
Eucalyptus cornuta	6-20 m x 5-10 m	An adaptable species with large heads of light yellow flowers.
Eucalyptus doratoxylon	3-7 m x 4-7 m	Spreading tree with smooth bark and whitish flowers.
Eucalyptus kitsoniana	3-10 m x 3-8 m	A mallee with clusters of cream flowers.
Eucalyptus platypus	4-10 m x 5-10 m	Has a decorative, smooth trunk and profuse yellowish flowers.
Hakea suaveolens	3-6 m x 3-5 m	Has prickly foliage and white to cream flower-heads.
Lophostemon confertus	10-35 m x 6-12 m	Has shiny, dark green leaves and feathery, white flowers.
Melaleuca armillaris	4-8 m x 3-6 m	Adaptable and quick growing. Has narrow, green leaves and cream flowers.
Pittosporum undulatum	4-14 m x 2-6 m	Has shiny, dark green leaves, fragrant cream flowers and orange fruits.
Tristaniopsis laurina	Usually 3-15 m x 2-15 m	Has glossy, green leaves and yellow flowers.

Melaleuca armillaris.

17—Useful Screening Plants

A common need, particularly in suburban gardens, is for quick-growing plants which will provide a screen. The purpose of the screen may be to block out the view of some unattractive structure or frequently to protect one's privacy.

Sometimes a new house is built next door and suddenly our privacy has disappeared. Or we may have put in a new swimming pool and need screen plants around it.

A dense screen can also be used to reduce noise levels and dust from a major roadway. It may be necessary for species selected for this purpose to be tolerant of air pollution from car exhaust fumes. Further details on this particular aspect will be found in Chapter 12, page 89.

In nearly all cases where screen plants are considered desirable, our need for them is *now*! We want to be able to plant the plants today and have the screen by tomorrow if possible.

ESTABLISHING A QUICK-GROWING GARDEN SCREEN

There are native trees which can grow 3 to 4 m in one year. They often, however, continue growing to a total of 50 to 60 m or even higher. At that stage the bushy foliage is on the upper section, leaving only a trunk with little screening effect below. In addition we will have a large tree which may cause problems, due to its size or its extensive root system, and can be difficult and costly to remove.

Careful selection of species is necessary to ensure that an effective and lasting screen is provided.

If you want to achieve a dense screen, it is wise to plant a combination of shrubs of different sizes to ensure good foliage growth to ground level. Once larger shrubs have become well established, it is much more difficult to grow smaller plants underneath.

As with any area of the garden, the successful development of the young plants will depend to a great extent on the preparation of the soil before planting, as well as good garden maintenance afterwards.

Pruning can also be of major importance in regard to establishing an effective screen. Tip pruning of plants from an early stage helps to promote a dense framework of growth.

The plants listed in Chart 13, which follows, are all relatively quick-growing and generally regarded as hardy species. They can be allowed to develop to their full size or pruned to develop bushier growth if desired.

Chart 13 — Quick-growing shrubs and small trees for use as screen plants

A selection of 20 species

Plant Name	Height x width	Brief comment — for further description see Section 2
Acacia adunca	4-8 m x 3-5 m	An adaptable wattle with dark green foliage and yellow-orange flowers.
Acacia boormanii	3-5 m x 2-5 m	Has grey-green foliage and bright yellow flowers. Can sucker.
Acacia fimbriata	5-8 m x 4-6 m	A graceful species with deep cream to yellow flower-heads.
Acacia longifolia	4-8 m x 4-8 m	Very quick growing. Has yellow, rod-like flower-heads.
Acacia podalyriifolia	3-5 m x 3-4 m	Has oval, silvery-grey phyllodes. Flower-heads are golden-yellow.
Acacia pravissima	4-8 m x 4-8 m	Has dense foliage with triangular phyllodes. Flowers bright yellow.
Albizia lophantha	2-8 m x 1-3 m	Quick growing. Has ferny leaves and yellowish-green soft bottlebrushes.
Alyogyne huegelii	1-2.5 m x 1-3 m	Has dark green, lobed leaves and mauve, hibiscus-like flowers.
Eucalyptus burdettiana	4-10 m x 3-6 m	Trunk is smooth. Has clusters of yellow-green flowers.
Eucalyptus conferruminata	5-10 m x 4-8 m	Dense small tree with clusters of yellow-green flowers.
Eucalyptus crenulata	6-15 m x 5-10 m	Has grey-green foliage and clusters of white to cream flowers.
Goodia lotifolia	2-4 m x 2-3 m	Quick growing. Has clusters of yellow pea-flowers.
Grevillea longifolia	2-4 m x 3-5 m	Large, spreading shrub with serrated leaves and pink-red flower-heads.
Grevillea shiressii	3-8 m x 2-5 m	Quick growing bushy shrub with bluish-green flowers.
Hakea salicifolia	3-7 m x 2-5 m	Quick-growing bushy plant with clusters of white to cream flowers.
Melaleuca armillaris	4-8 m x 3-6 m	Hardy and quick growing. Has narrow leaves and cream flower-spikes.
Melaleuca linariifolia	5-10 m x 3-6 m	Has papery bark and clusters of white, feathery flowers.
Melaleuca styphelioides	4-15 m x 3-8 m	Has papery bark and creamy white flower-spikes.
Prostanthera lasianthos	2-6 m x 2-3 m	Has aromatic dark green leaves and white with purple flowers.
Westringia glabra	1-2 m x 1-2 m	A hardy and bushy shrub with mauve-purple flowers.

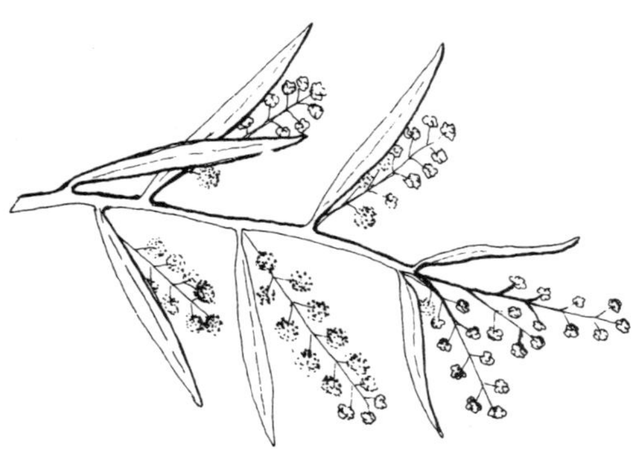

Acacia fimbriata.

ESTABLISHING A NARROW GARDEN SCREEN

Often the areas in which we desire to grow screening plants are very narrow and there is insufficient space to grow the bushy shrubs listed in Chart 13.

By judicious pruning we can restrict the spread of shrubs or it is even possible to develop certain species in an espalier fashion if we so desire. Climbing plants provide a further very useful alternative in such situations. If plants are given an adequate framework on which to climb, a dense yet narrow screen can be successfully established. Always ensure that the framework is strong enough to support the climbers being grown, and that it is of long lasting materials. Timber should be durable, such as red gum, jarrah or treated pine, particularly if it is in contact with the soil, and the use of galvanised nails and copper wire where necessary will avoid problems with rusting.

Australia is rich in native climbing plants, ranging from light twining species through to more vigorous or even rampant climbers. A selection is given in the following chart.

In addition to being valuable for providing a foliage screen, climbers do of course have many other useful functions. They can be used to provide colour on fences or walls, to cover logs or stumps, or as groundcover plants.

As with all other plants, adequate attention should be paid to the selection of suitable species and soil preparation prior to planting if best results are to be achieved with climbing plants. Regular light pruning, or tip pruning, will help to encourage bushy growth.

Hibbertia scandens has large, golden yellow flowers for most of the year.

38 *Above:* Sawfly larvae often cluster around a eucalypt stem during daylight hours, then move away to feed at night.

39 *Top right: Banksia ericifolia* has large, showy flower-heads which are highly attractive to native honey-eating birds.

40 *Right: Grevillea juniperina* is a bushy shrub with sharply pointed leaves. It is an excellent bird-attracting species.

41 *Left: Grevillea* 'Pink Pearl' has clusters of bright pink flowers throughout most of the year. It can grow to 4 m high by a similar width and has prickly leaves, making it an excellent screen plant.

42 *Bottom left:* The NSW Christmas Bells, *Blandfordia grandiflora*, seen here with a background of native ferns.

43 *Below: Grevillea alpina* is an extremely variable species. This form from Tooborac, Victoria, has greyish foliage and showy clusters of reddish flowers.

44 *Right: Epacris longiflora* is an outstanding small plant, with spectacular red and white tubular flowers which can be produced throughout most of the year.

45 *Below: Grevillea tripartita* is a large shrub with prickly foliage, making it useful as a screen plant to restrict access to a particular area. It bears a showy display of red and cream flowers.

46 *Bottom right: Brachychiton discolor*, seen here as a street tree in Melbourne, has lobed leaves and decorative pink flowers.

48 *Above: Calocephalus brownii* is grown primarily for its unusual and decorative, silvery foliage. It is also ideal for coastal situations.

47 *Left: Melaleuca wilsonii* grows to around 2.5 m high, and provides a colourful display during spring.

49 *Below:* The Bushy Sugar Gum, *Eucalyptus cladocalyx nana*, is widely grown in rural areas. It can be used, with other species, in the establishing of an effective windbreak.

Chart 14 — Climbing plants suitable for a narrow screen

A selection of 20 species

Plant Name	**Habit**	**Brief comment — for further description see Section 2**
Billardiera cymosa	Light climber	Has white, to green, pink or blue tubular flowers and oblong fruits.
Billardiera longiflora	Light climber	Tubular flowers are greenish-yellow. Fruits deep bluish-purple.
Billardiera ringens	Light climber	Flowers are initially orange then deepen to red.
Chorizema diversifolium	Light twining shrub	Pea-flowers are orange, yellow and pink to purple.
Clematis aristata	Vigorous climber	Creamy white, starry flowers are followed by feathery seed-heads.
Clematis microphylla	Dense climber	Greenish-cream starry flowers are followed by feathery seed-heads.
Hardenbergia comptoniana	Dense climber	Has racemes of small bluish-purple pea-flowers.
Hardenbergia violacea	Climber or trailer	Has racemes of usually mauve-purple pea-flowers.
Hardenbergia violacea 'Happy Wanderer'	Vigorous climber	Has long racemes of mauve-purple pea flowers.
Hibbertia scandens	Vigorous climber	Has shiny green leaves and bright yellow open-petalled flowers.
Jasminum suavissimum	Slender climber	Clusters of highly fragrant white flowers.
Kennedia beckxiana	Fairly vigorous	Twiner, climber or groundcover with red pea-flowers.
Kennedia macrophylla	Strong climber	Also twiner or groundcover. Pea-flowers red with yellow.
Kennedia nigricans	Vigorous climber	Has deep purple-black with greenish-yellow pea-flowers.
Kennedia retrorsa	Vigorous climber	Has racemes of purple pea-flowers.
Kennedia rubicunda	Vigorous climber	Pea-flowers are dusky pink to dark red.
Pandorea jasminoides	Strong climber	Has shiny, dark green leaves and white to pink trumpet-flowers.
Pandorea pandorana	Strong climber	Has profuse tubular flowers often cream with reddish markings.
Passiflora cinnabarina	Vigorous climber	Flowers bright coppery-red. Has oval, green fruits.
Sollya heterophylla	Hardy climber	Dense, bushy species with blue, pink or white flowers.

18—Plants Suitable for Embankment Planting and Soil Erosion Control

A natural asset, which unfortunately we frequently accept without question, is topsoil. It is not until we have attempted to garden without a rich layer of topsoil that we appreciate its true value.

Many of the residential areas around our major cities are established on sloping land. All too frequently topsoil has been washed away into the gutter, because adequate steps to protect and retain it have not been taken.

It is essential that we should be aware of the value of the upper layer of the soil. It is this layer which contains the most important nutrients for plant growth. Once lost, it is very difficult to replace.

We should also make sure we use to the greatest advantage any topsoil removed in the course of house or garden construction.

On steep embankments we may need some means of landscape construction like terracing to help retain the soil. Plants also play a major role here, as their root systems penetrate the soil and the fine feeder roots secure the loose particles.

The plants included in the following chart have proved their usefulness in erosion control. They are suitable for home garden use, as well as for roadside embankments and other large projects. They will withstand exposure to long hours of sunlight and extended periods of dryness, once they have become well established. Some will also tolerate relatively high levels of pollution, e.g. from car exhaust systems, and this is indicated where relevant.

Callistemons are useful plants for soil erosion control.

A new garden area prepared for planting. Plants will help prevent soil erosion which would otherwise occur, even on a relatively gentle slope such as this.

Terracing of garden beds is an effective method of coping with a sloping garden area.

Chart 15 — Plants suitable for embankment planting and soil erosion control

A selection of 20 species

Plant Name	Height x width	Brief comment — for further description see Section 2
Acacia boormanii	3-5 m x 2-5 m	An adaptable wattle which can sucker. Has bright yellow flowers.
Acacia pravissima 'Golden Carpet'	0.3 m x 3-5 m	Has a profuse display of bright yellow flower-heads.
Brachysema sericeum	Prostrate to 1 m x 1-4 m	Dense groundcover with yellow-green, cream or blackish pea-flowers.
Callistemon viminalis	1-12 m x 1.5-6 m	Variable species with red bottlebrush flower-spikes.
Dampiera linearis	0.3-0.5 m x 1-2 m	A variable species with several suckering forms. Flowers usually deep blue.
Darwinia grandiflora	0.1-0.5 m x 1.5-2.5 m	Low, spreading shrub. Flowers are white then age to red.
Eremophila serpens	Prostrate x 1.5-3 m	Has purple and lime-green flowers most of year.
Eucalyptus viridis	2-10 m x 2-7 m	Mallee species with glossy green leaves and white flowers.
Goodenia lanata	Prostrate x 1 m	Trailing plant which roots at nodes. Flowers bright yellow.
Grevillea longifolia	2-4 m x 3-5 m	Large shrub with serrated leaves and pink-red flower-heads.
Hardenbergia violacea	Climber or trailer	Has racemes of usually mauve-purple pea-flowers.
Kennedia beckxiana	Strong groundcover	Also climber or twiner. Has red with green pea-flowers.
Kennedia macrophylla	Strong groundcover	Also climber or twiner. Pea-flowers red with yellow.
Kennedia rubicunda	Vigorous climber	Also useful as groundcover. Pea-flowers pink to dark red.
Leptospermum 'Horizontalis'	0.5-1 m x 2-4 m	Dense spreading shrub with white, tea-tree flowers.
Melaleuca wilsonii	1-2.5 m x 1-3 m	Has short narrow leaves and clusters of reddish flowers.
Myoporum parvifolium	0.2-0.4 m x 1-3 m	Hardy groundcover which spreads by layering. Flowers white or pale pink.
Myoporum viscosum	1-2 m x 1-2 m	Has shiny, dark green foliage and mainly white flowers.
Nephrolepis cordifolia	0.5-1 m x 0.5-2 m	Hardy fern with fish-bone fronds. Spreads to form a clump.
Scaevola striata	0.2-0.5 m x 1-2 m	Groundcover which suckers lightly. Has showy mauve to bluish-purple flowers.

19—Planting in Coastal Areas

Agonis flexuosa.

Many keen Australian gardeners choose to live by the sea. Others may have land or holiday houses on the coast. There is consequently a keen interest in, and demand for, plant species which will grow well in coastal areas.

In these areas there is often a need for trees and shrubs to act as windbreaks and screening plants. The winds are frequently salt-laden and plants which are not accustomed to these conditions are often unable to cope.

Fortunately in Australia we do have many hardy and attractive plants which occur naturally in exposed coastal situations. It is these species which can form the basis of a successful coastal garden. Once a protective screen has been established, other less tolerant plants can then be grown.

Even with species which are native to exposed coastal regions, strong salt-laden winds are still likely to burn new growth. This can have an effect similar to tip-pruning and plants grown under such conditions are consequently often very bushy. Take this into account when selecting suitable species for planting, as plants may not reach their full height. Growth may also be slower than normal.

In very exposed locations, young plants will often give better results than those which have been grown to a larger size in containers before planting out. A temporary screen of sticks and leaves, light tea-tree stakes, or hessian-type fabric can give initial protection, while still allowing some penetration by wind or salt spray. Light staking can be used if necessary. See Chapter 8.

While many coastal areas have sandy soils, this is not always the case. Similarly, not all coastal areas are well-drained and this aspect should also influence your choice of suitable plants.

The code reference of C1 (see Section 2) has been used throughout this book to indicate plants which are suited to protected coastal situations. The reference C2 has been used for plants which will tolerate exposed coastal conditions. Chart 16 lists a selection of Australian plants that have proved to be excellent for cultivation in coastal areas and from which an initial garden framework can be established.

Other charts which may be of assistance include Chart 1, Plants Suitable for Cultivation in Sandy Soils, and Chart 4, Plants Suitable for Use in Saline Soils, both in Chapter 3.

Kennedia rubicunda, seen here growing on a brick wall adjacent to an exposed ocean beach.

Chart 16 — Plants suitable for coastal situations

A selection of 20 species

Plant Name	**Height x width**	**Brief comment — for further description see Section 2**
Acacia sophorae	2-8 m x 4-10 m	Bushy wattle with rod-like yellow flower-heads.
Agonis flexuosa	8-15 m x 5-15 m	Has long, narrow leaves and clusters of small, white flowers.
Allocasuarina verticillata	4-11 m x 3-6 m	Attractive she-oak with dark, furrowed trunk and narrow pendulous foliage.
Astartea fascicularis	1-2.5 m x 2-3 m	Long flowering. Pink buds open to usually white flowers.
Atriplex nummularia	1-3 m x 2-4 m	Saltbush, with dense, bluish-grey foliage.
Banksia integrifolia	10-20 m x 5-10 m	Leaves have silver undersurface. Flower-heads pale yellow.
Banksia serrata	10-20 m x 5-12 m	Leaves are toothed. Has large, greenish-yellow flower-heads.
Banksia speciosa	3-6 m x 3-8 m	Has showy, greyish to yellow flower-heads.
Callistemon pallidus	2-5 m x 2-5 m	Dense shrub with cream to yellow bottlebrush flower-spikes.
Calocephalus brownii	0.2.-2 m x 0.5-3 m	Has silvery branches and leaves with white to yellow flower-heads.
Casuarina equisetifolia	5-20 m x 5-10 m	A graceful she-oak with drooping branches.
Correa alba	0.5-2 m x 1-2 m	Dense shrub with starry, white flowers.
Eucalyptus conferruminata	5-10 m x 4-8 m	Dense small tree with large clusters of yellow-green flowers.
Hibbertia scandens	Climber or trailer	Has shiny green leaves and bright yellow, open-petalled flowers.
Kunzea ambigua	1-3 m x 1-2 m	Has small leaves and profuse small, white flowers.
Kunzea baxteri	2-4 m x 2-4 m	Bushy shrub with red bottlebrush flower-spikes tipped with gold.
Lagunaria patersonii	8-13 m x 3-6 m	Single-trunked tree with pink, open-petalled flowers.
Leptospermum laevigatum	3-6 m x 3-6 m	A bushy shrub with papery bark and white flowers.
Melaleuca nesophila	3-6 m x 2-5 m	Dense shrub with globular, mauve-pink flower-heads.
Myoporum insulare	3-5 m x 4-8 m	Hardy and bushy shrub with white, starry flowers.

20—Transplanting Established Plants

Generally, Australian plants respond most favourably to cultivation from an early age in the position in which they will be grown permanently and it is not a common practice to transplant them from one garden location to another.

In some cases, however, building extensions, relocation of drains, or major earthworks necessitate the removal of a plant from its position in the garden. If it is a species which cannot be easily replaced, or if the plant is slow-growing, attempts should be made to transplant it to another site.

The initial preparations should begin, if possible, at least three months before the final removal of the plant.

Step 1 (3 months before transplanting)

Using a sharp spade, cut down vertically in a circle around the base of the plant. The distance from the main trunk should vary according to the size of the plant and, in the case of large plants, the equipment available to assist in the removal. The area within the circle will contain the portion of the root system to be lifted at the time of transplanting, the roots outside the circle having been cut.

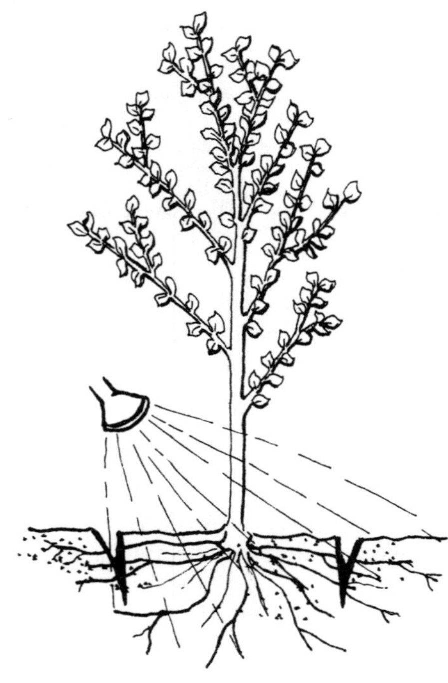

Step 2
To compensate for the loss of root area through roots being cut, the foliage of the plant should be reduced by light to medium pruning.
Step 3
Water the plant thoroughly, using a root stimulant to encourage new feeder root growth on the now reduced root system.
Step 4 (1 week before transplanting)
Dig again around the perimeter of the area to be lifted and water the plant once more with a root stimulant.
Step 5 (transplanting)
When lifting the plant, slide a sheet of hessian or similar material under the root system, in order to retain as much as possible of the soil attached to the roots.

Step 6
Relocate the plant in a prepared hole, then water thoroughly. Be careful to avoid the creation of a waterlogged area (see page 23), as this may prevent the roots from getting enough air and some roots may die.
Step 7
Further pruning of the foliage at this time will reduce the stress on the root system and increase the chance of the plant surviving.

Plants should, if possible, be moved during cool weather. If transplanting must be undertaken during hot summer months, a temporary screen erected immediately after transplanting to protect the plant from wind and direct sunshine will be of assistance.

Temporary staking (see Chapter 8) may also help to stabilise a transplanted plant until the root system has a chance to become re-established.

Several landscaping firms specialise in the moving of large shrubs and trees using equipment specifically designed for this purpose. Professional assistance in this regard can simplify what would otherwise be a difficult task for the home gardener.

For the transplanting of tree ferns, see Chapter 23.

21—Replanting amongst Existing Trees and Shrubs

From time to time almost every garden needs some replanting. This can be one of the more difficult tasks of garden maintenance.

Plants may die or suffer so much damage that they must be removed, or it may be discovered that a plant is unsuitable for the position in which it is growing. Having grown well initially it may then have lost all vigour or, on the other hand, it may have developed to a much larger size than that required, or envisaged. If you have moved into a new house, you may wish to introduce some Australian plants into a European-type garden without removing all the existing plants.

There are several difficulties in the introduction of young plants to an already mature garden area. Situations which were previously open and sunny, allowing young plants to grow vigorously, have often become densely shaded by the established trees and shrubs. The soil also becomes matted with roots, which absorb all available moisture.

Special care is therefore needed in selecting plant species which will cope with these conditions. Some extra assistance should also be given to the young plants to help them become established, despite the existing competition from other plants.

It is very probable that the new plants will grow at a slow rate, because of the factors mentioned above, and their mature size may be smaller than it would otherwise be. It is reasonable therefore to allow for this in choosing species of a desired size.

The following steps will assist the development of new plants in well established garden areas.

Step 1
If the area has dense overhead shade, thin out some branches to allow sunshine and rain to penetrate.

Step 2
Dig the soil to a spade's depth. Break it up thoroughly.

Step 3
Water well until penetration is down to the full depth of digging.

Step 4
Leave fallow for several days, then repeat watering.

Step 5
Add to the soil some peat moss, ligna-peat, vermiculite or decomposed organic material such as compost or leaf mould until the soil is friable.

Step 6
Water the soil until moist, but not wet. The use of a soaker hose is often beneficial because run-off of water is not likely to occur, as it can do with heavier sprinklers.
Step 7
Plant the plants selected, following the planting methods outlined in Chapter 4. Incorporate a small amount of slow-release fertiliser in the base of each planting hole.
Step 8
Ensure that the plants are regularly watered during the next few months. They should be soaked thoroughly during watering to encourage the roots to extend deeper in search of moisture.

The following chart lists a selection of Australian native plants which have been found to tolerate dry, semi-shaded conditions, such as often exist beneath established trees and shrubs.

Melaleuca hypericifolia. In this photograph branched stamens which distinguish a *Melaleuca* from a *Callistemon* (see page 20) can be clearly seen. (Photograph by courtesy *Your Garden* magazine.)

Chart 17 — Plants suitable for dry, semi-shaded conditions

A selection of 20 species

Plant Name	Height x width	Brief comment — for further description see Section 2
Acacia acinacea	0.5-2.5 m x 2-4 m	Has deep golden, globular flower-heads.
Banksia marginata	1-10 m x 0.5-5 m	Variable species with yellow flower-spikes.
Brachysema lanceolatum	0.5-2 m x 1-3 m	Leaves grey-green above and silver below. Pea-flowers red.
Correa backhousiana	1-2 m x 2-3 m	Dense shrub with oval leaves and cream to green tubular flowers.
Correa reflexa	0.3-3 m high	Variable in size and also in flower colour. Flowers are bell-shaped.
Dianella revoluta	0.3-1 m x 0.5-2.5 m	A clumping plant with pale blue flowers.
Dodonaea sinuolata ssp. *acrodentata*	2-3 m x 2-3 m	Shrubby plant with attractive reddish hops.
Eriostemon myoporoides	1-2 m x 1.5-3 m	Has aromatic, dark green leaves and white, starry flowers.
Grevillea arenaria	1.5-2.5 m x 1.5-2.5 m	Has grey-green foliage and reddish or yellow-green flowers.
Grevillea dimorpha	1-2 m x 1-3 m	A variable species with clusters of bright red flowers.
Grevillea glabrata	2-3 m x 2-4 m	Has grey-green, lobed leaves and white to cream flowers.
Grevillea pilulifera	1 m x 1 m	Has cream flowers with yellow, orange or red styles.
Grevillea shiressii	3-8 m x 2-5 m	A quick-growing bushy plant with bluish-green flowers.
Isopogon anethifolius	1.5-3 m x 1-2 m	Has finely divided leaves and yellow flower-heads.
Kunzea pomifera	0.5 m x 1-3 m	Dense, spreading plant with white to cream flowers.
Melaleuca hypericifolia	3-6 m x 2-5 m	Has pendulous branchlets and orange-red flower-spikes.
Pandorea pandorana	Strong climber	Tubular flowers are commonly cream with reddish markings.
Prostanthera monticola	1 m x 2 m	Tubular flowers are green streaked with purple.
Regelia ciliata	1.5-2.5 m x 2-3 m	Has small leaves and mauve to purple, globular flower-heads.
Sollya heterophylla	Climber	A bushy species with blue, pink or white, bell-shaped flowers.

22—Growing Australian Annuals

An *annual* is the term used to describe a plant with a life cycle which is completed within any one year.

The seed may germinate fairly rapidly after planting or it may lie in the soil until rain occurs and soil temperatures are right for germination to take place. In arid regions of Australia some seeds lie in the ground for several years, until there are suitable conditions to promote the growth of young seedlings. The plants grow rapidly to maturity, flower, set seed, then finally die.

A large range of annual flowering plants from overseas is commonly grown in Australian gardens and can be purchased either as seed or in small trays of seedlings.

There are quite a number of Australian native annuals. However to date only a few have been widely grown in cultivation as the seed of the many other species has been difficult to obtain. Due to an increased demand for these annuals, both in Australia and overseas, a wider range is now being grown commercially for seed production and further developments in this area are likely to take place in the near future.

Annual plants are excellent for providing a showy display of colour in a garden, although it is usually for a limited period only.

In many gardens, particularly where a sand mulch is used, it is common for annual species to re-seed naturally. They will therefore re-appear in subsequent seasons, without further planting.

Otherwise it is recommended that seed be sown initially into seedling containers (see Chapter 26). The young seedlings can be pricked out and further developed in small individual pots or, if their growth in the seedling tray has been good, they can be transferred directly into the garden.

Not all species commonly referred to as annuals are strictly within that category. Some plants may continue for two years (these are called biennials) or some even longer. Pruning almost to ground level when flowering has finished will in some species give new vigour to the plants and prolong their life for a further season. All these plants should, however, be considered as having a limited life span and extension of their life cycle beyond one year should not be relied upon.

WATERING

As mentioned earlier, annuals are usually very quick-growing plants and therefore their need for moisture is relatively high.

Plants should be kept moist throughout their period of growth, without being waterlogged. Good drainage is important for all Australian annuals, particularly those which come from fairly dry, sandy regions.

If annuals are allowed to dry out, flower production will usually be poor or the plants may die prematurely.

FERTILISING

Combined with a high need for moisture in annual species is a high need for readily available nutrients.

A complete garden fertiliser should be used at the time of planting out young seedlings, then there should be regular light applications of soluble fertilisers to maintain good, vigorous growth.

PRUNING

It has already been mentioned that pruning after flowering will prolong the life of some annual plants.

Pruning from the early seedling stage is also highly recommended with most species. This will encourage bushy growth and in most cases an increased number of flowers.

If plants are being grown for cut flower production, any pruning carried out is likely to reduce the length of the flower-stems being produced and this should be borne in mind.

PESTS

The lush growth of some annual species often makes them particularly attractive to garden pests such as slugs and snails. The use of snail bait or other precautions may be desirable to protect the plants from these creatures.

A SELECTION OF AUSTRALIAN ANNUALS

The following chart lists a selection of the many Australian annual flowering plants. Some are widely grown, whilst others are not yet so well known. Seed of most of the species listed is available commercially at the present time, although perhaps without wide distribution in some cases.

Actinotus helianthi, Flannel Flower.

Chart 18 — A selection of Australian annuals

A selection of 20 species

Plant Name	Height x width	Brief comment — for further description see Section 2
Actinotus helianthi	0.3-1.5 m x 0.5-1 m	Herbaceous plant with soft grey foliage and whitish 'flannel flowers'.
Actinotus leucocephalus	0.3-1 m x 0.2-2.5 m	Has smaller flowers than *A. helianthi* (above).
Actinotus superbus	0.3-1 m x 0.2-2.5 m	Similar to other flannel flowers but with more hairy bracts.
Angianthus tomentosus	0.1-0.4 m x 0.2-0.5 m	Has pale yellow, cylindrical flower-heads.
Brachyscome iberidifolia	0.3-0.5 m x 0.3-1 m	Has white, blue or purple daisies with yellow centres.
Cephalipterum drummondii	0.2-0.5 m x 0.2-0.75 m	Has globular, white or yellowish flower-heads.
Clianthus formosus	Prostrate x 1-4 m	Sturt's Desert Pea. Has soft, greyish foliage and red with black pea-flowers.
Helichrysum bracteatum	0.5-1.5 m x 0.3-1 m	Has papery, everlasting daisies of white, yellow, gold or pink.
Helichrysum cassinianum	0.3-0.5 m x 0.1-0.3 m	Has clusters of small, pink everlasting flowers.
Helipterum albicans	0.2-0.3 m x 0.2-0.3 m	Has yellow or white papery flower-heads.
Helipterum floribundum	0.2-0.4 m x 0.1-0.3 m	Has many white, papery flower-heads.
Helipterum humboldtianum	0.3-0.6 m x 0.2-0.3 m	Has clusters of yellow, everlasting flowers.
Helipterum manglesii	0.3-0.5 m x 0.3 m	A widely grown annual with pink, papery flower-heads.
Helipterum roseum	0.5-1 m x 0.5 m	Has pink or white everlasting flowers.
Myriocephalus stuartii	0.5 m x 0.1-0.2 m	Has white everlasting daisies with large yellow centres.
Swainsonia maccullochiana	1.5-2 m x 1-2 m	Has ferny leaves and rose-pink pea-flowers.
Trachymene caerulea	0.5-1 m x 0.3-0.5 m	Has soft heads of delicate blue flowers.
Waitzia acuminata	0.3-0.6 m x 0.3-0.6 m	Everlasting flowers are usually golden-yellow. Can be white or pink.
Waitzia aurea	0.4 m x 0.1-0.3 m	Has golden everlasting flower-heads.
Waitzia suaveolens	0.3-0.6 m x 0.1-0.3 m	Everlasting flower-heads are white, often with pink tonings.

23—Growing Australian Ferns

Most gardeners will be familiar with at least some species of ferns, perhaps even some Australian ferns. There are around 10 000 different fern species throughout the world, with over 400 of them being native to Australia.

Botanically, ferns are very different from the flowering plants in our gardens, as they produce neither flowers nor seeds.

Ferns reproduce by means of spores, which are produced in spore cases on the fronds, though not all fronds are fertile. It is relatively common for gardeners to think that their plant is diseased when they see the brown spore cases dotted on the undersurface of a frond. The spore cases are sometimes in regular patterns of dots or stripes, or they can be irregular. On large fronds such as those of the Elkhorns and Staghorns (*Platycerium* spp.) the spore cases can cover large areas on the undersurface, forming a felt-like mass.

PROPAGATING FERNS FROM SPORES

Many fern species will propagate readily in nature or in the garden under favourable conditions. The spore falls to the ground when ripe and develops into a minute, heart-shaped plant of about 5 mm diameter, called a prothallus. Each prothallus produces male and female sections. Sperm from the male section travels through moisture accumulated beneath the prothallus to unite with the female part and achieve fertilisation. The new fern then begins to grow and feeds initially on the nutrients contained in the prothallus.

Spore can be collected from a fern by removing the fertile frond and placing it in a dry paper bag. The spore will be released within a few days, provided the frond was mature and the spore had not already been shed at the time of collection.

To propagate the spore you will need some peat moss, sphagnum moss, or other propagating mix with a high degree of moisture-retaining ability. It is wise to cover this with boiling water just before use to minimise the growth of algae and fungi, etc., which could have a detrimental effect on the developing ferns. After allowing the medium to cool, place it in a sterilised plant pot, leaving about 6 to 8 cm between the top of the mix and the top of the pot. Scatter the fern spore lightly over the surface.

Place the pot into a tray of water, as shown for the 'Bog Method of Seed Germination' in Chapter 26. Cover the top of the pot with a piece of glass or polythene. Position the unit in a warm, well lit situation, but not in direct sunlight.

In about 4 to 8 weeks a green scum-like substance will be seen on the surface as the prothalli develop. It will be several more months before the true fronds begin to appear. When the plants reach this stage the cover should be removed from the pot. They should be left in the pot for one further week, then they will be ready for potting into individual containers.

As with other methods of plant propagation, there are many different propagating mediums and practices employed by amateur and professional fern growers. Fern propagation, although not quick, is fascinating, and those who wish to gain further information on this topic are referred to the specialised publications listed in the Bibliography.

VEGETATIVE PROPAGATION OF FERNS

Some ferns, including the commonly grown *Asplenium bulbiferum* and *Polystichum proliferum*, provide a very effective short-cut to propagation by producing small ferns or bulbils at or near the tips of some of the mature fronds.

In nature, the fronds gradually lower to ground level as they age and under favourable conditions the developing bulbils will then take root and grow as independent plants.

Well developed bulbils can be removed from the parent plant and transferred to individual pots to become established in preparation for planting into the garden. Alternatively they can be pegged down into a pot while still attached to the parent plant and separated after the roots have developed in the new pot. (See 'Layering', Chapter 28.)

Another commonly used method of fern propagation is that of division.

Many ferns spread by means of a creeping rhizome or stem. Sections of the plant can be cut from the parent and potted into individual containers. (See 'Root Division', Chapter 28.)

On ferns such as the Elkhorns, young plant sections commonly known as offsets are produced. These can be carefully removed with a knife and developed as separate plants either by potting into sphagnum moss or by mounting onto a pad of sphagnum moss on a wooden slab. See page 133.

Fern divisions are best carried out during the warm months of the year, when growth is active rather than dormant.

Tissue culture, as discussed in Chapter 28, is also used for fern propagation, although generally it seems that those species which propagate most readily from the methods mentioned above are those which also provide best results from tissue culture.

CULTIVATION OF FERNS

In general most ferns grow best in shady, moist locations. There are some, however, that are tolerant of full sunshine and also relatively dry conditions. The specific needs of each particular fern are therefore included in the chart later in this chapter.

Because ferns grow well in constant shade, they are extremely valuable for planting along the south side of the house or in other spots in the garden which are shaded for most of the time. In such positions the cultivation of flowering garden plants can be difficult. Before planting in these situations, as for all areas of the garden, it is wise to check first that the species chosen are suited to the conditions. There are some ferns which will require at least filtered sunlight to grow well.

WATER

As mentioned in Chapter 5, it is recommended that, if possible, moisture-loving plants should be grouped together in the garden to minimise maintenance through hand watering and also assist in water conservation. This applies particularly to the cultivation of ferns.

Most ferns prefer a moist, cool root area, but few are tolerant of stagnant, waterlogged conditions. Garden areas for ferns therefore need to be adequately drained. By placing ferns in shade or semi-shade the soil is less likely to dry out and need regular watering than if plants are in direct sunshine. Those species which are tolerant of full sunshine usually still require a moist, cool root area. This can be achieved by planting the fern on the protected side of a rock or log, so that the roots can extend into the cool area below it.

Ferns take in moisture from the atmosphere through their fronds. Humidity will therefore help to supplement moisture intake from the soil and prevent the plants drying out. The placing of ferns near garden pools or other areas of water in the garden will add to the humidity in the atmosphere, particularly on a warm day when evaporation is high.

When it is necessary to water plants by hand, the general procedures and advice contained in Chapter 5 are also applicable in regard to ferns.

SOILS

Best results are usually achieved in soils which have a relatively high organic content. Mountain soils and clay-loams are usually excellent, as they are rich in plant nutrients and are also able to retain more water than sandy soils.

In a garden where these conditions do not exist naturally, the soil can be improved by adding materials such as compost, peat moss, or leaf mould.

For further information, see Chapter 3, 'Soil Preparation'.

MAINTENANCE REQUIREMENTS

1 Air and Air Movement

Adequate air circulation is important to the good growth of most plant species. Ferns also need protection from strong winds, whether they be hot or cold.

2 Fertilising

Most species appreciate an application of slow-release fertiliser at the time of planting (see Chapter 7). In some areas ferns will need little or no further fertilising to maintain good growth. If the fronds appear green and healthy the application of a fertiliser is usually unnecessary.

Light applications of slow-release fertilisers can be made or liquid fertilisers can be used if desired. The recommended time for fertilising is during the warmer months of the year, when the ferns are usually making new growth.

3 Mulching

Mulching will help to maintain a cool root area and thus aid the growth of ferns. Chapter 6 includes a list of various mulching materials suitable for use with ferns and other plants. The use of an organic mulch such as bush litter or compost is of particular value when establishing ferns in a garden.

4 Pests and Diseases

Ferns are subject to pests and diseases as discussed in Chapter 12, although the hardy species are generally able to cope with most attacks.

The uncurling new fronds can present a particularly tasty meal for many creatures including slugs, snails, caterpillars and parrots. If there are possums in your garden they may also seek out this succulent new growth.

A number of sucking insects will be found on the fronds from time to time, including aphids, leaf hoppers, mealy bugs, scale insects, thrips and white flies. Most of these can be controlled by using a contact spray of low toxicity. Weak applications of white oil and a pyrethrum based spray will usually achieve the desired results.

Ferns can suffer from rust and other fungal diseases. This occurs mainly on weak plants or it can be an indication of overwatering or excessive humidity. Affected fronds should be removed and burnt and if the problems mentioned are rectified further control methods will usually not be needed.

Wind burn and heavy frosts can also damage ferns, particularly young fronds. Plants will usually recover naturally, unless the damage has been particularly severe, and protection against these elements will help to avoid subsequent burning.

CULTIVATION OF FERNS IN CONTAINERS

Many ferns make extremely attractive container plants and their cultivation in this way is very popular.

A potting mixture with a high organic content is recommended for best results. A basic mixture is 4 parts peat moss or leaf mould with 1 part of good quality topsoil and 1 part coarse river sand. Any mix should be able to support the plant roots, provide aeration and be able to retain moisture and nutrients for use by the plant. Commercially prepared mixes are readily available for the potting of ferns. Other ingredients used by fern growers in their potting mixes include bark (crushed or shredded), compost, cow manure (well rotted), perlite, vermiculite, wood chips and wood shavings (aged).

Further information on the potting and maintenance of plants in containers will be found in Chapter 25.

CULTIVATION OF EPIPHYTIC FERNS

Epiphytic ferns, which grow naturally on trees or rocks, can be cultivated in containers or on slabs. If they are being grown in pots the drainage of the containers should be excellent, and the potting mixture should be coarse and well drained. If this is not the case the plants will soon rot and die. *Asplenium australasicum* (the Bird's Nest Fern) is an epiphytic species which, because of its large size and upright habit is best grown in a container, rather than on a slab. It can also be grown in the garden if the right conditions are available.

Those epiphytes with pendulous habit are particularly suited to cultivation in hanging baskets.

Platycerium species such as *P. bifurcatum* (Elkhorn) and *P. superbum* (Staghorn) are commonly grown on slabs of tree-fern, cork or weathered hardwood. A pad of sphagnum moss is placed between the fern and the slab, then the plant is tied securely with a length of fishing line or plastic coated wire. For best results these ferns should be hung in situations that receive protection from strong winds and full sunshine. Young plants should be given frequent watering until they become established. Elkhorn and Staghorn ferns will usually benefit from liquid fertilisers applied two or three times per year, or from compost placed between the fern and the slab.

Both these *Platycerium* species are popular in cultivation and *P. bifurcatum* is sometimes also referred to (incorrectly) as a Staghorn. *P. bifurcatum* produces new plantlets which can be separated from the parent plant, but *P. superbum* does not.

FERN HOUSES

Structures known as bush houses, fern houses, greenhouses, lathe houses, or shade houses are commonly used for the cultivation of ferns. In gardens where there is no site available with ideal conditions for good fern growth, the construction of a special fern area will enable these plants to be grown with success.

Fern houses generally provide some degree of shade plus protection from strong winds. Conditions should still be both light and airy. In recent times the material most commonly used in their construction is the product known as 'shadecloth'. It is a synthetic fabric of open weave, designed especially for garden use. It is durable and very simple to erect. Shadecloth is available in several different shade ratings to provide from light to dense shade. Around 50 per cent shade is suitable for the cultivation of ferns in all but very hot regions.

Ferns can also be grown successfully in glasshouses, although the degree of warmth and humidity provided is not essential for the majority of Australian species.

PROTECTION OF NATIVE FERNS

Australian ferns are protected by law and it is illegal for them to be removed from the bush without a permit. Whilst many species are propagated under nursery conditions, a large percentage of the plants offered for sale have been collected under licence from areas such as those being logged for timber. To avoid illegal exploitation of our native flora, it is wise to check on the origin of ferns, particularly tree-ferns and epiphytic species, before purchase.

TRANSPLANTING TREE FERNS

The commonly cultivated Soft Tree-fern (*Dicksonia antarctica*) can be successfully transferred from one site to another and trunks are frequently available for purchase in nurseries. The trunk is sawn through near the base and the fronds are cut off in preparation for transplanting. The trunk should then be kept moist by wrapping it in damp hessian or through frequent light waterings, until re-located in the desired position.

If the trunk is tall, staking may be necessary to provide support until the root system becomes re-established.

The transplanted fern should be kept moist, but not wet, during the months following planting, to enable new feeder roots to develop. The plant should be watered from the top of the trunk. A very slow trickle from a hose, for 1 to 2 hours, 2 or 3 times per week in warm weather will be needed if a fern has recently been moved. The most favourable season for transplanting ferns is in autumn or early winter.

It should be noted that the Rough Tree-fern (*Cyathea australis*) which can be found growing with or near *Dicksonia antarctica* is not as easy to transplant. It should be dug from the soil and moved with as much of the root system as possible. Nevertheless trunks of this species are sometimes seen offered for sale, with the differences being accounted for, falsely, as those of male and female tree-ferns. The plants are very similar in general appearance; however, the frond bases on *Cyathea australis* (the Rough Tree-fern) have a rasp-like, rough texture.

AUSTRALIAN FERN SPECIES FOR GARDENS OR CONTAINERS

The following chart lists a selection of Australian native ferns, all of which are widely grown either as garden or container plants. These plants are also suitable for cultivation indoors, although some will grow too large for many domestic situations. See also 'Cultivation of Plants Indoors', page 147.

A fern garden showing some of the variety in the shapes of fern fronds. (Photograph by courtesy *Your Garden* magazine.)

Chart 19 — A selection of Australian ferns

A selection of 20 species

Plant Name	Height x width	Brief comment — for further description see Section 2
Adiantum aethiopicum	0.3 m x 1 m	Common Maidenhair Fern. Fronds have small, rounded segments.
Asplenium australasicum	1-2 m x 1-2 m	Bird's Nest Fern. Has large, undivided fronds.
Asplenium bulbiferum	1-2 m x 1.5 m	Has large fronds to 1.2 m long.
Asplenium simplicifrons	0.6 m x 0.5-1 m	Has long, narrow, strap-like fronds.
Blechnum fluviatile	0.5 m x 1 m	A prostrate fern with spreading fronds.
Blechnum minus	0.5-1 m x 0.5-1 m	Soft Water-fern. Has large, erect or arching fronds.
Blechnum nudum	1-2 m x 0.5-1 m	Fishbone fronds are around 1 m long. Can develop a trunk.
Blechnum penna-marina	0.2 m x 1 m	A low, spreading fern with small, divided fronds.
Blechnum wattsii	0.5-1 m x 0.5-1 m	Has dark green, deeply divided fronds.
Cyathea australis	To 12 m x 4-6 m	Rough Tree-fern. Fronds are to 4.5 m long.
Cyathea cooperi	3-12 m x 3-6 m	Scaly Tree-fern. Fronds are to 6 m long.
Dicksonia antarctica	To 15 m x 2-9 m	Soft Tree-fern. Will usually transplant successfully.
Dicksonia youngiae	2-5 m x 2-5 m	Bristly Tree-fern. Has a slender trunk and finely divided fronds.
Doodia aspera	0.3-0.6 m x 0.5-1 m	Has fishbone-shaped fronds and pink to reddish new growth.
Doodia media	0.3-0.6 m x 0.5-1 m	Has fishbone-shaped fronds and purplish-red new growth.
Nephrolepis cordifolia	0.5-1 m x 0.5-2 m	A hardy fern with fishbone-shaped fronds.
Pellaea falcata	0.3-0.6 m x 0.5-1 m	Has fishbone-shaped fronds with narrow segments.
Platycerium bifurcatum	Clump-forming epiphyte	Elkhorn. Has large, irregular fronds.
Polystichum proliferum	0.5-1.5 m x 1-2 m	Has arching, dark, dull green fronds.
Todea barbara	2-3 m x 2-4 m	Has bright green fronds to 2 m long. Develops a short, broad trunk.

Adiantum aethiopicum, Common Maidenhair Fern.

24—Growing Australian Orchids

There are over 600 species of Australian native orchids. They can be divided into two major categories. Terrestrial orchids are those which grow in the ground, while epiphytic species are usually found growing on trees. Lithophytic orchids which grow on rocks are very similar to epiphytic species and have similar requirements.

All Australian orchids are protected by law. They should not be collected from any property, private or public, without written permission. The picking of flowers or collecting of plants is certainly not recommended, unless the area is to be cleared in the very near future. Alternative methods of propagation should be sought if possible. Orchid societies provide opportunities for plants or tubers to be purchased or exchanged.

EPIPHYTIC ORCHIDS

Approximately 40 per cent of Australia's native orchids come into the category of epiphytic. They grow naturally on the trunks and branches of trees, or on rocks in the case of lithophytic species. The host is used primarily for support, as these plants are not parasitic and take no nutrient from host plants.

Epiphytic orchids are widely grown by enthusiasts, and there is also a large number of hybrids in cultivation. Some have extremely showy flowers, perhaps the best known being the Cooktown Orchid (*Dendrobium bigibbum*), which is the floral emblem of Queensland. The white to pink-purple flowers are often around 7 cm in diameter. Some species are highly fragrant, such as the white-flowered Beech Orchid (*Dendrobium falcorostrum*) which has a sweet perfume.

Epiphytic orchids are commonly cultivated on tree trunks within gardens, or are grown on slabs of wood, cork, bark, weathered tree-fern fibre or other similar material.

To mount an epiphytic orchid you should trim roots where necessary so that the plant will sit firmly onto the selected backing. A pad of sphagnum moss behind the orchid will help the roots become established and retain moisture for use by the plant. Tie the orchid securely, using a durable material such as plastic string or nylon fishing line. Water well.

Epiphytic orchids can also be potted as container plants. Excellent drainage is essential for good results, and any potting mix must be selected with this in mind. A mixture of 2 parts aged bark or woodchips plus 1 part charcoal is suitable for a large number of species. Particles should be around 1 cm diameter and any fine dust should be removed by washing or sieving.

Orchids which are naturally epiphytic usually develop thick roots which are very efficient at absorbing moisture and nutrients. They can survive on relatively small amounts of nutrients, derived from decaying leaves and any other matter which becomes lodged in crevices of the orchid, or host bark. In cultivation they will usually respond well to applications of half strength liquid fertiliser, applied at around fortnightly intervals during the main growing season between November and April.

During this growing period plants also require regular watering. They will usually need at least one watering daily, although they should also be allowed to dry out between waterings.

Recommended time for division and potting or re-potting of epiphytic orchids is during September-October, just prior to the growing period when plants will become re-established.

A large number of Australian epiphytic orchids come from the tropical areas of the Cape York Peninsula in Queensland. Many of these species require the protection of a glasshouse if they are to be grown successfully in cool temperate climates. Some will do well in an unheated glasshouse, while others require heating during winter to survive.

It is recommended that orchid enthusiasts start by growing some of the generally hardy and readily obtainable species, then refer to specialised publications which are available before attempting to grow any rarer or more difficult plants.

TERRESTRIAL ORCHIDS

Terrestrial orchids are those species which grow naturally in the ground. There are around 400 Australian species in this category.

Terrestrial orchids are not as common in cultivation as the epiphytic species. Some can be grown with success, however, and a selection is included in the list which follows.

Most enthusiasts prefer to grow terrestrial orchids in containers, rather than in the garden. A potting mix can be more adequately adjusted to the needs of the orchids, as can moisture requirements at different times of the year.

A basic potting mix contains 2 parts coarse river sand, plus 1 part good quality topsoil, 1 part hardwood or softwood chips, and 1 part leaf mould. (Treated pine, cedar or chipboard wood chips are not suitable.) To improve the drainage of this mixture, additional coarse river sand can be used. Approximately one dessertspoon of blood and bone per bucket (9 litre) of mix can be added just prior to potting.

Terrestrial orchids are generally re-potted around December, when the foliage of most species has died down and the plants are dormant.

Any pot being re-used should be thoroughly washed to avoid transfer of disease. A circle of shadecloth can be placed in the base of the pot to prevent slaters and earwigs from entering through the drainage holes. The pot should be filled with the selected potting mix to around 5 cm from the top. The tubers are then arranged on this, with the growing eyes on top, and another layer of 2 to 3 cm of potting mix added. Avoid overcrowding of the tubers. A pot of 10 to 15 cm diameter will comfortably hold around 10 to 20 tubers. A light mulch of coarse river sand on the top of the pot will help avoid fungal disease of the leaves.

Adequate labelling of pots is extremely important to avoid containers being tipped out and tubers unintentionally thrown away whilst dormant.

Terrestrial orchids generally require moist soil during their growing period between April and November, followed by drier conditions during the dormant period. A light watering once a week will be sufficient at this time to avoid dessication of the dormant tubers. Tubers can rot if the potting mix remains warm and moist for extended periods.

One of the main problems with growing terrestrial orchids is that of slugs and snails. By growing the plants in containers it is easier to protect them from these creatures than if the orchids were in the garden.

Plants can also be affected by fungal diseases, but these can be minimised through using a well drained mixture plus a quick drying surface mulch and avoiding excess watering. Any diseased plants should be removed as soon as noticed, to avoid spread of the fungus.

Terrestrial orchids generally respond favourably to cultivation in a shadehouse rather than a glasshouse. A solid roof will enable watering to be seasonally adjusted to suit the needs of the plants, whilst at least one wall of shadecloth will ensure adequate air movement around the plants.

GETTING STARTED IN ORCHID CULTIVATION

Although some Australian orchids can be grown fairly readily with good success, a detailed study of their needs must be carried out if the best results are to be achieved.

To provide a fully comprehensive guide to their cultivation would require a complete book and there are already many excellent publications on this subject. Some of these are included in the Bibliography. There are also different groups and societies where orchid growers can meet together to discuss various aspects of their cultivation.

The following chart lists a selection of Australian native orchids which are all commonly grown by collectors and enthusiasts. The list includes both epiphytic and terrestrial species. It is, of course, a selection only from the much wider range being grown. However, these species should provide a starting point for those who may wish to enter into the fascinating world of orchid growing.

Chart 20 — A selection of Australian orchids

A selection of 20 species

Plant Name	Habit	Brief comment — for further description see Section 2
Chiloglottis trapeziformis	0.05-0.12 m tall	Broad-lip Bird Orchid. A small terrestrial species.
Corybas diemenicus	Small plant	Slaty Helmet-orchid. Ground-hugging terrestrial orchid.
Corybas dilatatus	Small plant	Ground-hugging terrestrial orchid.
Cymbidium madidum	0.3-1 m x 0.2-0.5 m	An epiphytic species with fragrant, yellow-green and brown flowers.
Cymbidium suave	Clump forming	Olive-green flowers are highly fragrant.
Dendrobium aemulum	Clump forming	An epiphytic species with fragrant white, cream or pinkish flowers.
Dendrobium bigibbum	Forms slender clump	Cooktown Orchid. Very showy epiphytic species. Various flower colours.
Dendrobium x *delicatum*	0.3-0.5 m x 0.5-1 m	Has arching racemes of white flowers, often with pink or mauve.
Dendrobium falcorostrum	0.2-0.4 m x 0.3-0.5 m	Has racemes of fragrant white to cream flowers.
Dendrobium x *gracillimum*	0.3-0.75 m x 0.5-1 m	Has racemes of fragrant, white and yellow flowers.
Dendrobium kingianum	0.2-0.5 m x 0.5-1 m	A popular species with usually pink flowers.
Dendrobium speciosum	0.3-1 m x 0.5-1.5 m	Has large, terminal racemes of white, cream or yellow flowers.
Dendrobium tetragonum	0.2-0.3 m x 0.2-0.5 m	Has fragrant, dpider-like green to yellowish flowers.
Diuris longifolia	To 0.5 m tall	Terrestrial orchid with mainly yellow flowers.
Diuris maculata	To 0.5 m tall	Leopard Orchid. The yellow flowers have many brown spots.
Lipparis reflexa	0.2-0.5 m x 0.2-0.5 m	A lithophytic orchid with greenish-white to yellow-green flowers.
Pterostylis concinna	To 0.3 m high	Trim Greenhood. Flowers are green with white and brown markings.
Pterostylis curta	To 0.3 m high	Blunt Greenhood. Flowers are green with red and brown markings.
Pterostylis nutans	To 0.3 m high	Has nodding, translucent, green flowers.
Pterostylis pedunculata	To 0.3 m high	Flowers are green and white with reddish-brown hood-tip.

25—Growing Australian Plants in Containers

The cultivation of Australian plants in containers has become very popular in recent years, possibly because we now realise that there are many species suitable for growing in this way.

There are three main reasons containers may be chosen in preference to garden cultivation.

1. We may have only limited garden space, as is the case in inner suburban areas, flats or retirement villages, etc. Container-cultivation enables us to utilise additional areas such as verandahs, patios and paved areas for the growing of plants.
2. The growing of plants in containers allows us to provide the optimum conditions for successful cultivation. Potting mixtures can be adjusted to suit the exact requirements of each plant being grown, as can watering, and the containers can be positioned to suit the climatic requirements of the plant at different times of the year.
3. We can display the plants to our own advantage by being able to move them both around the garden and also indoors, as desired.

Other reasons for cultivating plants in containers include the ability to grow plants where it might otherwise not be possible, such as above drainage pipes or other underground structures. Container cultivation is also useful for those whose occupation or way of life involves moving from house to house frequently.

Whatever your reason for wishing to grow plants in containers, you will find there is a large range of Australian species from which to choose, in addition to the many introduced plants that have been grown in this way for a number of years.

CHOOSING A CONTAINER

Sometimes we have or purchase a particular container, then choose plants to grow in it, whilst on other occasions we may have a particular plant and wish to select a suitable container. Whichever is the case, the container and the plant should complement each other and also be suited to the area where the pot will be located.

There are three important aspects in regard to container selection. These are Design, Drainage and Durability.

1. DESIGN

The size and shape of the container must be suitable for the plant being grown.

Some mat plants or low tufting species can be grown quite successfully in containers which are relatively shallow. However, species which require a deeper root area need more depth in the container design.

It is also desirable that the container should be widest at the top. Many ceramic containers are attractively shaped but, if the neck is narrower than the middle of the pot, re-potting of plants becomes extremely difficult and the plant may be severely damaged during removal. Slow-growing species which require re-potting rarely can usually be grown successfully in a container of this type, or plants which will withstand root damage can be used. For hanging baskets, see page 146.

2. DRAINAGE

Any container must be able to retain moisture for sufficient time to allow absorption by the plant, but also any excess must be able to drain away. It is not possible to over-estimate the importance of having adequate drainage holes in plant containers.

In addition to having good drainage within the pot, any container should be placed on a surface which will allow excess water to drain away from its base. If a container is placed on an area of soggy clay the drainage holes will become clogged up and the advantage of a well designed pot and suitable potting mix will be wasted. Pots can be raised from the soil on a bed of gravel or a layer of bricks to overcome this problem.

3. DURABILITY

Containers should be constructed of a material which is durable and able to withstand regular watering without breaking down.

Ceramic containers, glazed and unglazed, have been used for many years for potted plants and are highly successful for this purpose. It should be borne in mind that unglazed pots are porous and therefore will dry out more quickly than those which are glazed. The main disadvantages of ceramic containers are that they are relatively heavy to move around, particularly when filled with a potting mix, and they can be broken.

Plastic pots are possibly now the type most commonly used for the growing of plants, both in homes and nurseries. They are light to handle and generally fairly durable. Many designs are available and most of these allow for the good development of plants. It is also easy for the plastic pots to be thoroughly washed for re-potting or the growing of new plants.

Timber is widely used for the construction of planter boxes, into which plants which are perhaps being grown in plastic pots can be placed. When plants are being potted directly into wooden containers, such as barrels, it should be remembered that the timber may decay over a period of time. This is less likely to happen if it is of a durable species such as Jarrah or River Red Gum.

Logs, stumps and containers formed from tree-fern fibre are also used successfully for the cultivation of plants.

Metal containers such as those of copper and brass are used to a limited extent. Containers of these materials should not be placed in direct sunlight, as they can become very hot and damage to plant roots can result.

POTTING MIXES

There are many different potting mixtures used with success for the cultivation of Australian plants in containers. Prepared potting mixes can be purchased from garden stores and, for plants with specific needs, products such as fern and orchid mixes are also obtainable.

A basic potting mixture suitable for a large range of Australian plants is about 5 parts coarse river sand, with 4 parts of peat moss or other organic material and 3 parts of friable soil. This mixture can be varied to suit the needs of the plant being grown. Prepared potting mixtures can also be varied, if necessary, by the addition of extra sand or organic material. Coarse sand serves the purpose of providing good drainage within the mixture while peat moss or other organic material will increase the retention of moisture in the container.

In addition to the ingredients mentioned above, a wide range of other materials is commonly used in potting mixtures. These include mushroom compost, perlite, pine bark chips, rice hulls, scoria, sawdust, straw and vermiculite.

It is recommended that any potting mixture used should be sterilised. This will reduce the possibility of root diseases and also minimise any initial weed seed germination in the mixture. Commercially prepared potting mixtures are generally pre-sterilised. For advice on home sterilisation, see page 154.

SELECTION OF SUITABLE PLANTS

Plants for container cultivation should be selected in the same way as those chosen for the garden. Nearly all small to medium Australian plants can be grown successfully in containers, provided the containers are of adequate size.

If the container is not likely to be moved from time to time, consideration must be given to the position in which it is located. If it is in an open, sunny situation, any plant chosen must be suited to these conditions. The same plant may not grow successfully if the container is in a very shaded spot.

Having thought through aspects such as container position and the species you would like to grow, your native plant nursery will be able to offer advice regarding any particular needs of the plant and the type of container necessary for adequate root development of that species. Code references included in the plant descriptions in Section 2 will assist you to find out the needs of each species, and additional information can be found in *Australian Plants for Small Gardens and Containers*, see Bibliography.

POTTING OF PLANTS

Small plants can be successfully potted directly into large containers if desired. Some growers prefer to re-pot plants progressively from small to medium then larger containers over a period of time; this is generally a matter of personal preference.

Step 1

Partly fill the container with potting mixture. The level to which you fill it will depend on the size of the plant being potted and especially its root development.

Step 2
A small amount of slow-release fertiliser can be added at this stage if desired. Approximately half the recommended rate is likely to be adequate as excessive growth is usually unwanted, rather than being desirable, in container-grown plants. Mix the fertiliser through the soil in the container. Do not leave it in one small area.

Step 3
Remove the plant from its original container and carefully inspect the root system. If the roots are matted they should be gently teased out so that the small feeder roots will be able to penetrate into the new potting mix. Straighten any coiled roots; if too long for the new container they should be cut with secateurs. Don't be alarmed if the soil breaks away more than you intended at this stage. If the plant is handled with care both during and after potting, it is likely to cope adequately even if the roots are disturbed.

Step 4
Place the plant on the potting mix in the new container and add further mixture to achieve a soil level just slightly higher than that of the original pot. Some settling of the potting mix will take place later. If plants are planted too deeply, collar rot can result. If they are not deep enough the roots can dry out very quickly.

Step 5
Firm down the potting mixture, then water the plant thoroughly.

Step 6
If desired, a mulch of coarse sand or other material can be placed on top of the potting mix to help retain moisture and to maintain a more even temperature around the root system. For further information on mulches, see Chapter 6.

TWO OR MORE PLANTS IN ONE CONTAINER

It is a relatively common practice for more than one plant to be potted into a medium to large container. Some tubs will adequately accommodate 3 to 4 plants, while containers such as planter boxes hold many.

Any species used in combination plantings must have very similar cultivation requirements if good results are to be achieved.

The plants may flower at similar times, or the flowering periods can be staggered so that there is a colourful display in the container over a longer period.

The eventual size and habit of the plants should also receive careful consideration. Two small plants which will intertwine can be planted together, or you may combine one plant of upright habit with a small mat plant to cover the potting mix and act as a living mulch.

MAINTENANCE OF CONTAINER-GROWN PLANTS

The ongoing maintenance of container-grown plants differs only slightly from general garden practices as described in earlier chapters.

Watering is perhaps the area which causes the most concern in regard to pot plants or tub plants.

As the plant is unable to draw water from the garden soil through its root system it will be reliant on rainfall or hand watering for survival. Many plants suffer from over-watering. Pots should never be allowed to stand in containers of water for extended periods, unless the plants are naturally aquatic or semi-aquatic species.

To check whether a plant is in need of water you can poke your finger into the potting mix. If it is dry and powdery as you scrape down a little, it is likely that the plant needs watering. Other methods of recognising when a plant requires moisture are mentioned in Chapter 5.

Always aim to water container-grown plants with a soft, broad flow of water. A strong spurt can dislodge the topsoil and uncover or damage the roots.

One of the most successful methods of watering plants grown in containers is through trickle irrigation. Trickle irrigation systems are also discussed in Chapter 5.

Generally, container-grown plants should not be forced by artificial feeding, unless you are striving for maximum growth and then intend to replace the plants after a relatively short time.

Light top-dressings of slow-release fertiliser can be applied at six-monthly intervals if desired. Liquid seaweed fertilisers can also be used to maintain good, healthy and attractive growth.

Excessive use of fertilisers can result in container-grown plants becoming root-bound and increase the need for re-potting or replacing them.

Other aspects of garden maintenance, such as pruning, weed control and pests and diseases, are covered in earlier chapters. The information contained therein can be applied also to container-grown plants.

RE-POTTING CONTAINER-GROWN PLANTS

Some Australian plants can be left, undisturbed, in tubs for several years. Other species which are perhaps more quick-growing will benefit from re-potting after 2 to 3 years.

Re-potting can also be desirable if the potting mixture becomes infested with weeds such as couch, oxalis or sorrel, which are difficult to eradicte by any other means.

Step 1

Remove the plant from the container. You may have to tap the outside of the container lightly with a rubber hammer or mallet in the case of large tubs. A knife inserted around the edge of the pot will not harm the root system. Immersing the pot in water can also help. With large tubs the help of a second person will make the task much easier.

Step 2

Reduce the size of the root system by about 25 to 30 per cent. Fibrous roots can be removed with the fingers, but sharp secateurs should be used for the removal of any large roots. Cut away any dead or damaged roots, and tease out the outer roots in readiness for replanting. Carefully remove any weed roots that may be intertwined through the root system. In cases of bad infestation it may even be necessary to wash all soil from the plant roots in an endeavour to remove the weeds completely.

Step 3
The container into which the plant is to be re-potted should be washed thoroughly then rinsed well.
Step 4
Re-pot the plant, using the potting method described earlier in this chapter. Take care to maintain the original soil level of the plant. Water well.
Step 5
If the root system has been reduced in size the plant will benefit from light pruning of the foliage also.

HANGING BASKETS

Hanging baskets provide a very popular form of container-cultivation.

When choosing and planting a hanging basket it should be borne in mind that in most situations the container is likely to dry out more quickly than a standing pot. Additional peat moss or other organic material can be added to the mixture to help rectify this problem.

The choice of the material from which the basket is constructed will also affect its moisture-retaining ability. Wire framed baskets lined with moss or the fibre liners available commercially for this purpose can dry out very quickly, especially if baskets are hung in an exposed position. Glazed ceramic containers will retain moisture more effectively than those which are unglazed, and plastic containers are also non-porous. Plastic hanging baskets have the added advantage of being comparatively light in weight.

All hanging baskets can become quite heavy once filled with potting mixture and the hooks as well as the chain or rope hangers must be able to cope with the weight. The structure from which the basket will hang must also be more than adequate to support its weight.

Hangers which extend around and under the basket are recommended in preference to those which are attached only through loops at the top. This is particularly applicable in regard to plastic containers, which can become brittle after long periods of exposure so that the hanging loops snap.

Trailing plants are ideally suited to hanging baskets, particularly if the plant is to be above eye level, with foliage hanging down. Plants such as *Dampiera diversifolia*, *D. linearis* and *Pultenaea pedunculata* can all be grown with success in this way.

MAINTENANCE OF PLANTS IN HANGING BASKETS

General maintenance procedures, as described for container-grown plants and also in earlier chapters of this book are recommended for hanging baskets.

Particular attention in regard to watering is important and watering methods will depend largely on the location of the baskets. Gentle watering from a hose will be the most suitable method in many situations, or if plants are located on verandahs or patios and can be easily removed from their hangers it may be preferable to take them down and stand them in a tray of water when watering is needed. Some gardeners will find that a combination of both methods will provide the best results.

50 An attractive garden screen featuring a wide selection of Australian plants. The smooth white trunk of the Lemon-scented Gum, *Eucalyptus citriodora*, is seen near a dwarf form of *Banksia spinulosa* with yellow flower-heads. *Melaleuca armillaris* with its cream flower-spikes is also in flower.

51 *Persoonia pinifolia* has showy yellow flowers, produced over a long period, and it is also an excellent screening plant. It is seen here growing with *Grevillea* x *gaudichaudii* as a groundcover, and the sculptured trunks of *Allocasuarina littoralis*.

52 *Acacia adunca* bears masses of bright golden flower-heads over a long period, mainly during winter-spring.

54 *Above:* Feathery seed-heads follow the creamy-white, starry flowers on female plants of the climber, *Clematis aristata.*

55 *Top right: Goodia lotifolia* is a quick-growing shrub of 2 to 4 m high, with clusters of yellow pea-flowers in spring.

58 *Right: Scaevola striata* is a low-growing, suckering plant with a colourful display of bluish-purple flowers during October-February.

Opposite:
53 *Top left:* The Qld Silver Wattle, *Acacia podalyriifolia,* has decorative foliage and buds, as well as showy golden-yellow flower-heads, seen during winter-spring.

56 *Extreme left:* The purple-flowered *Hardenbergia violacea* has here been allowed to climb informally through the lower branches of a smooth-barked *Eucalyptus leucoxylon.*

57 *Left: Billardiera longiflora* is a light climbing plant. It has the common name of Purple Apple-berry because of the deep bluish-purple fruits which follow the tubular greenish flowers seen here.

59 *Left: Helipterum manglesii* is a popular Australian annual species with papery, everlasting daisies of white through to deep pink.

60 *Bottom left: Isopogon anethifolius* has attractive yellow flower-heads of around 4 cm diameter. Plants can grow to 3 m high, but respond well to regular light pruning from an early age.

61 *Below:* The Flannel Flower, *Actinotus helianthi* is well known for its showy, long-lasting, creamy-white flowers. It can be grown as an annual, or plants may continue to grow for several years in the garden.

THE CULTIVATION OF FERNS AND ORCHIDS IN CONTAINERS

Ferns are very popular as container plants, both for outdoor and indoor use. Readers are referred to Chapter 23 for information regarding this particular group of plants.

The majority of Australian terrestrial orchids are cultivated in containers. Epiphytic species are also commonly grown in pots, or attached to slabs of bark or other material. Details regarding the growing of orchids is contained in Chapter 24.

CULTIVATION OF PLANTS INDOORS

In many homes potted plants are featured as part of the indoor decor. While in a garden or glasshouse we aim primarily to provide conditions to suit the plants, this is not the situation indoors. Usually we have no wish to change the conditions within a house to suit the needs of our plants, and we therefore must seek plants that can tolerate the conditions we have chosen for our way of life.

The potting and general maintenance of indoor plants is very similar to that already described for other container-grown plants. There are, however, some additional specific needs of which we should be aware in regard to plants grown indoors.

All plants have a basic need for light, which must be supplied from natural or artificial sources. However, they should not be placed where hot sun will shine through a window or the foliage will be scorched. Plants have also adapted to taking in some moisture through their leaves. Most houses have a dry atmosphere so a bowl of water placed near indoor plants can be of assistance.

To enable good growth plants require carbon dioxide, taken in from the air. Foliage can become very dusty indoors, restricting the plant's ability to breathe through the leaves. Leaves should therefore be wiped over regularly with a damp cloth or sponge.

Generally plants will benefit from a few hours outside every few weeks, if possible during light rain. Try to select a time when the difference in temperature from indoors to outdoors is not great.

Those plants which grow best in indoor locations are usually those which occur naturally in tropical or temperate rainforests.

Ferns are grown frequently as indoor plants and many species respond very favourably to indoor situations. These include *Adiantum aethiopicum* (Common Maidenhair Fern), *Asplenium australasicum* (the Bird's Nest Fern), *Asplenium bulbiferum* (Mother Spleenwort) and *Nephrolepis cordifolia* (the Fish-bone Fern) all of which are included in Chart 19.

Other suitable plants listed in earlier charts include *Acmena smithii* (8c), *Brachychiton populneus* (2c), *Brachychiton rupestre* (10c), *Castanospermum australe* (8c), *Cordyline stricta* (23), *Grevillea robusta* (10c), *Nothofagus cunninghamii* (1c), *Pittosporum undulatum* (12b), *Stenocarpus sinuatus* (1c) and *Syzygium coolminianum* (1c). Full descriptions of these plants can be found in Section 2. Plants of these species can be grown for several years in containers, but as all will eventually grow to tree size, they have a limited life span as indoor plants. Generally they are grown only as foliage plants indoors, as most would be unlikely to flower unless planted in an outdoor garden.

A combination of indoor and outdoor gardening provides one of the best solutions for those who do not necessarily want the same plant indoors for an indefinite period. Most plants will tolerate short periods indoors, ranging from a few days to several weeks. By this means container-grown plants can be grown primarily in an outdoor situation, then brought inside when in bloom or another attractive stage of growth. From even a small selection of containers it is possible to have plants which will provide flowers throughout most of the year.

SPECIALISED CONTAINER CULTIVATION

There are some forms of specialised container-plant cultivation, including bonsai and hydroponics, which are not covered here. However, there are Australian plant species which have been found to be suited to these areas. Experimental work is being undertaken by enthusiasts and undoubtedly the range of Australian plants being grown by these methods will increase considerably in the future.

26—Propagating Plants from Seed

Much pleasure can be gained from propagating your own garden plants. There is usually also the added bonus that you end up with more plants than you need for your own garden. They can make useful gifts for friends or neighbours, or no doubt will be very welcome at the next local school or charity fete.

Propagating your own plants can also be valuable if the species you seek is not readily obtainable through nurseries. You may want an unusual plant, or one with a low commercial value and therefore not widely grown. Provided you can locate propagation material, you will not be dependent upon nurseries.

Propagation of plants from seed is the method most commonly used. Very little equipment is necessary to achieve good results and what is required is usually available in the average household.

COLLECTION OF SEED

Australian plants have a wide range of different seed and fruit types. Many are dry and woody fruits (e.g. *Eucalyptus* capsules), some are soft, fleshy fruits (e.g. *Billardiera* berries), seeds of the pea plants and *Acacia* species are produced in pods, whilst plants such as daisies have seeds which are carried on the wind by light, feathery wings.

Because of this wide variation, several different methods are required for collecting the seeds.

1. SEED CAPSULES

Among the Australian plants which produce dry, woody seed capsules are species of *Callistemon, Eucalyptus, Leptospermum* and other plants in the family Myrtaceae. The seeds of lilies such as *Blandfordia* and *Patersonia* are also contained in capsules, although these are dry and papery when mature, rather than dry and woody.

Many species bearing woody capsules retain the seed in the capsules for a number of years. It is released relatively soon after the capsule is removed from the plant, or in the event of the plant dying. The collection of seed from these plants is relatively simple.

Choose the mature capsules from a plant. Seed from the latest flowering period usually takes several months to become completely ripe.

Place the capsules in a bag of paper or cloth, or in an open container. Never use a plastic bag or closed container as even a small amount of moisture can cause the seed to become mouldy. Label with the plant name and date of collection.

Some of the many different *Eucalyptus* seed capsules.

Store the container of seed in a warm, dry place for 1 to 2 weeks. The capsules will open and the seed will be released.

If no seed is released, this indicates that either the plant had shed the seed prior to collection, or the capsules gathered were immature.

Some plants, such as certain species of *Eucalyptus*, do shed their seeds as the capsules mature. In such cases a careful watch must be maintained in order to collect some of the seed before it is dispersed.

In addition to containing seed, some capsules also carry a quantity of packing material. This is most noticeable in *Eucalyptus* species. The seed is usually black or dark brown, whilst the packing material is a light brown or reddish brown. It is not necessary to separate the two before planting, but it helps to know the difference between the seed and other material if you wish to estimate the number of potentially viable seeds being planted.

2. FLESHY FRUITS

The percentage of Australian plants with fleshy fruits is relatively small, but amongst those common in cultivation are species of *Astroloma*, *Billardiera*, *Coprosma* and *Sollya*.

The fruits should be collected when ripe, then cut or broken apart to expose the seed. Good results can often be obtained by sowing the seeds immediately after collection. Alternatively the flesh and seed can be allowed to dry out so that the seed can be separated, then stored for later planting.

Whilst some plants in this group, e.g. *Sollya* species, will be found to germinate readily, others including *Astroloma* and *Persoonia* have proved fairly difficult to grow from seed.

3. SEED PODS

All native pea-flowered plants produce their seed in pods. So too do the wattles and there are over 1000 species in this genus of *Acacia.*

In these plants seed collection is a relatively easy matter, although many pods split when dry and the seeds either fall or are catapulted to the ground. Seeds usually ripen in summer and frequently large numbers are produced.

The majority of these seeds have a very hard coating. Moisture cannot penetrate readily through to the seed and this allows it to remain viable for many years.

To hasten germination, treatment of the seed just prior to planting is necessary. The most commonly used method is to place the seeds in a mug or similar container. Cover them with very hot water and leave them to soak for about 8 to 12 hours before planting. The hard exterior layer will be softened and the seeds will become noticeably swollen following the intake of moisture.

An alternative method is to rub the seeds between two sheets of sandpaper, breaking down the hard outer coating but avoiding damage to the soft interior.

4. SEED FOLLICLES

Follicles are dried, papery or woody fruits, like the seed capsules. Whilst a capsule opens with several splits, a follicle has only one big split.

Well known Australian plants with seeds produced in follicles are members of the Proteaceae family, including *Banksia, Grevillea, Hakea* and *Telopea* (Waratahs). A follicle may contain one, two or several seeds.

In *Banksia* species, seed-cones are produced and each usually contains a number of follicles. In the majority of species the cones will remain, unopened, on the plants for many years. In the event of a bushfire the heat causes the follicles to

A selection of follicles from plants in the Proteaceae family.

open. They continue to open further as the fire passes and they cool once more. The seed is then released to allow regeneration to occur. Seed is released in a similar manner following the death of a plant, or if a branch bearing cones becomes broken and dies, or in some cases if a borer grub eats into the base of the cone.

A small number of banksias release their seeds as they mature, whilst others do so in times of drought or if the plant is under similar conditions of stress.

The maturity of *Banksia* follicles can be tested by scraping the surface with a fingernail. If it is dry and woody the seed is ready for collection. If it is green or a light tan, the seed may still be immature.

To extract *Banksia* seed successfully, the cones can be placed in a warm to moderately hot oven for 30 minutes, or until the follicles open. Alternatively they can be lightly burnt on a barbecue or open fire until the follicles open. Each follicle contains one or two winged seeds, separated and protected by a piece of woody packing material. The seeds are placed well in the interior of the cone, giving them protection against damage by fire.

Whilst some banksias release their seed readily, others have proved to be much more difficult. In very difficult cases soaking in water for days or even weeks, then again treating with heat has achieved success. If cones are immature when collected they may not open to release the seeds.

Grevillea follicles have a somewhat leathery texture and they are not produced in cones, as are the banksias. In most cases they split to release the seeds as soon as they mature and the timing of seed collection is therefore critical. One commonly used method is to place a nylon stocking over the ripening seeds. The stocking should be fine enough to allow both light and air to reach the fruits. As the seeds mature and are shed they will be held within the stocking for collection.

Hakea seeds are retained within their woody follicles on the plants, at least in most species. A few shed their seeds when ripe, but this is usually over a period of time, enabling collection of at least some of the seed.

Most hakea follicles will open soon after collection, if stored in a warm, dry place (see instructions for seed capsules). If the follicles fail to open, place them on a tray in a warm to moderately hot oven for around 30 minutes. Should they still fail to open, it is probable that they have been collected whilst immature.

The follicles of *Telopea* or Waratah plants contain several seeds and it is many months after flowering until the seed is ripe. As the follicles mature they will turn brown and slowly begin to split open. They should then be collected, placed in an open container and left in a warm, dry situation to open fully.

Other follicle-bearing plants can be treated using one of the methods described for the above genera.

5. GRAINS AND OTHER DRY SEEDS

The collection of these seeds generally presents very little difficulty. The main requirement is to be in the right place at the right time.

The seeds must of course be mature when gathered and thoroughly dry before being stored.

SOME PROBLEMS WITH SEED COLLECTION

When seed is collected from garden plants there is often the possibility that cross-pollination between two separate species may have occurred, thus resulting in a plant hybrid.

In the natural environment also plant hybrids do sometimes occur, but the possibility of cross-pollination is increased when closely related species, often from different areas, are brought together in the garden.

In some plant families or individual genera hybridisation is relatively common, whilst others are regarded as generally being stable and few if any hybrids exist.

Just by looking through books or catalogues of Australian plants it is easy to see those plants which hybridise readily. Grevilleas are outstanding in this regard. A hybrid is usually indicated by listing the plant's generic name (underlined or in italics) followed by the given name quoted in parenthesis, e.g. *Grevillea* 'Poorinda Firebird'.

Variation within a species can also occur with plants propagated from seed. *Acacia pravissima* (the Ovens Wattle) is a good example of this. A prostrate form, *Acacia pravissima* 'Golden Carpet' is the result of a chance seedling which developed as a groundcover rather than having the normal bushy habit of the parent plant, which has a height of around 4 to 8 m. Here the name of the plant includes both the generic and species names, *Acacia pravissima*, followed by the given name of 'Golden Carpet'. This indicates that it is a form of the species stated and not a hybrid between two separate species.

Callistemons are also noted for the variety of forms which can occur within individual species, e.g. *Callistemon citrinus* and *C. viminalis*. Another well known example is the Red-flowering Gum (*Eucalyptus ficifolia*) of which there are forms with many different flower colours.

Should you wish to establish plants which will have exactly the same characteristics as the parent plant, this can be achieved through vegetative methods, such as propagation from cuttings or grafting.

SEED STORAGE

All seed should be labelled at the time of collection with the plant name, the date, and location of collection. You may also wish to include further details such as the flower colour, size of plant, etc. for future reference.

Seed should be thoroughly dry before storage. Paper envelopes can be used to store the seed or, if there is likely to be a problem with pests such as mice, airtight jars are recommended. Seed should not be stored in direct sunlight. A cool, dark place is ideal.

Generally it is suggested that seed be sown within one year from the time it is collected. As earlier mentioned, however, in some species such as *Acacia* the seed can remain viable for several decades.

PURCHASING SEED

There are now several commercial sources of Australian plant seed. These are listed in *Australian Plants*, which is the quarterly journal of the Society for Growing Australian Plants, as well as in other major Australian gardening magazines. The seed can be bought from selected nurseries and stores or by mail order.

Groups such as the Society for Growing Australian Plants frequently operate 'seed banks', where members can obtain seeds of a wide range of species.

WHEN TO SOW SEED

In areas with warm climates, seed can be planted throughout most of the year with success. This is also possible in cooler regions if heated glasshouses or propagation beds are being used.

The recommended sowing time, particularly in temperate zones, is during late winter to spring. Seed can be germinated at this time of the year without the use of artificial heating and early development of the young seedlings will be stimulated by the spring warmth. Growth can continue during the summer months and in many cases the young plants will be ready for planting out in the following autumn.

CONTAINERS FOR SEED PROPAGATION

Any clean, small container can be used, provided it has adequate holes in the base to allow good drainage. Plastic margarine, yoghurt or ice-cream containers are commonly used. Seedling punnets and plant pots can be re-used, but should be washed thoroughly, preferably in a solution of bleach or germicide to ensure they are free from disease. They should then be left to air for 2 to 3 days.

PROPAGATION MIXTURES

Mixtures used for seed sowing should drain well, yet be able to retain sufficient moisture to sustain the young seedlings.

The basic ingredient used in most mixtures is coarse river sand and a commonly adopted mix is —

3 parts coarse river sand, plus
1 part peat moss.

The sand provides excellent aeration and drainage, and the peat moss has a high water-holding capacity, yet at the same time allows good aeration of the mixture.

A number of other materials have been used in propagation mixes, some with greater success than others. The aim of this chapter is to describe a simple and successful method of plant propagation, so readers are advised to refer to specialised publications on propagation as listed in the Bibliography if they wish to experiment with alternative materials.

It is strongly recommended that any propagation mixture should be pasteurised or sterilised before use. Pasteurisation assists in the control of soil-borne diseases and will also prevent the germination of most weed seeds.

Packs of sterile sand, peat moss or prepared propagation mixes can be purchased from garden suppliers. These may seem somewhat expensive, but many plants can be propagated in relatively small quantities of propagation mix and the use of properly treated material can be thoroughly justified.

If you are unable to purchase a sterilised mix, you can treat small quantities yourself by placing the mixture in a shallow tray and heating it in an oven for 45 minutes at 60 °C.

One of the major plant diseases affecting Australian gardens is the Cinnamon Fungus (*Phytophthora cinnamomi*), see Chapter 12. Control and eradication of this fungal disease is usually very difficult, therefore prevention of its introduction wherever possible is strongly recommended.

PLANTING THE SEED

Step 1

Fill the container with potting mix and press down firmly. There should be sufficient space at the top for the seed to be spread and then covered, leaving another 1 to 2 cm empty to allow for watering.

Step 2

Place the seeds on top of the mix.

The number of seeds which can be planted in one container will depend both on the size of the container and the size of the seeds. *Banksia* seed, for example, can be quite large and is suitable for planting with just one or two seeds per container. Other seeds such as those of *Callistemon* species are very fine, but they should not be planted too thickly or overcrowding will occur. Overcrowding creates ideal conditions for the young seedlings to be attacked by fungal disease.

Fine seed can be sprinkled from a pepper shaker to assist in an even and light distribution, or the seed can be mixed with a small amount of fine sand before sowing.

As mentioned on page 150, some seeds are accompanied by a quantity of packing material, so that the number of seeds being planted may look to be greater than is actually the case.

Step 3

Cover the seeds with about their own depth of very fine potting mix. The mixture can be sieved to remove any large lumps. Large seeds can be covered with a deeper layer than the very small ones.

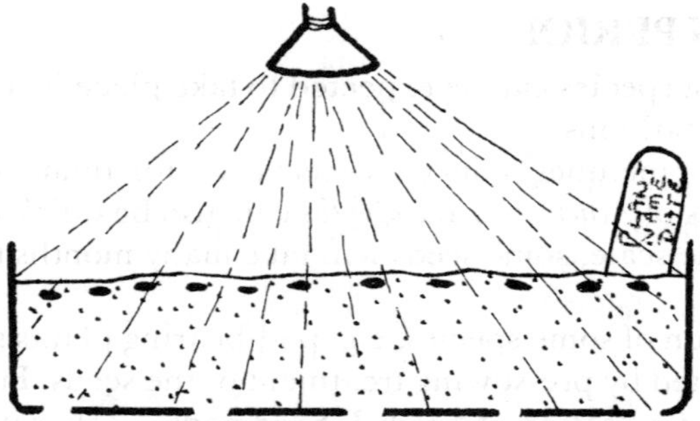

Step 4
Water gently, but thoroughly. See also 'Bog Method of Seed Germination', below.
Step 5
Label with plant species and date of planting.
Step 6
Place the container in a warm place protected from strong winds and direct sunlight. It should be kept moist, but not wet.

BOG METHOD OF SEED GERMINATION

This method is used very successfully with plants in the Myrtaceae family, including *Callistemon*, *Calothmanus*, *Eucalyptus*, *Leptospermum* and *Melaleuca* seeds. Several other species, particularly those tolerating moist conditions, can also be germinated in this way.

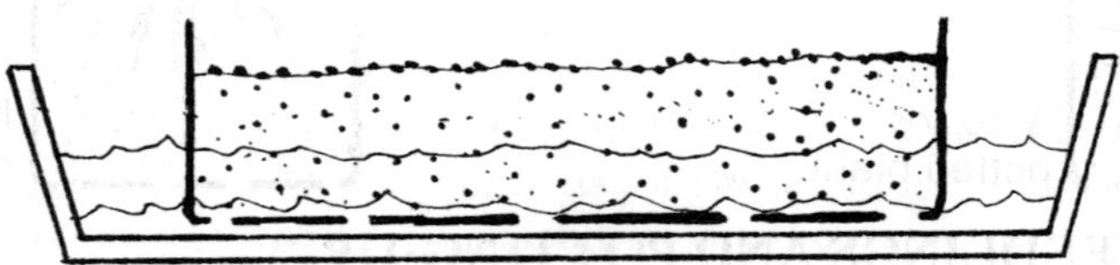

After completing planting Steps 1 and 2, the seedling container is placed in a dish or tray which does not have drainage holes. Water is then added to the dish until the level is approximately halfway up the level of propagating mix in the seedling container. The water is absorbed into the propagating mix, and the level should be maintained by adding additional water as necessary until germination occurs.

It is not necessary to cover the seeds with potting mix; however a very fine cover layer can be used if desired.

Place the container in a warm situation protected from strong winds and direct sunlight.

One of the main advantages with this method is that there is no danger of the fine seed being dislodged as may happen with normal overhead watering methods. A further advantage is that it is easy to ensure that the container of seed does not dry out during the germination period. This is particularly useful if you are going away for a few days or even if you have to spend many hours a day away at work.

Following germination of the seeds, the container should be removed from the water tray and the plants watered in the normal manner.

GERMINATION PERIOD

Germination of most species can be expected to take place in around 8 to 12 weeks under favourable conditions.

This period is sometimes reduced, especially with annual or other short-lived plants. Some species of *Acacia* and *Eucalyptus* can also be quick to germinate. At the other end of the time scale, some seeds will take many months to begin to show signs of growth.

The germination of some species, e.g. pod-bearing plants such as pea-plants and wattles, is affected by pre-sowing treatment of the seeds. Further information can be found under 'Collection of Seed: 3. Seed pods', earlier in this chapter.

As a general rule it is wise to avoid throwing out any pots of mixture containing seed for at least one year after planting. Seeds of several genera, including *Billardiera*, *Patersonia* and *Sollya*, can remain in the container for several months, then suddenly spring to life during autumn rains.

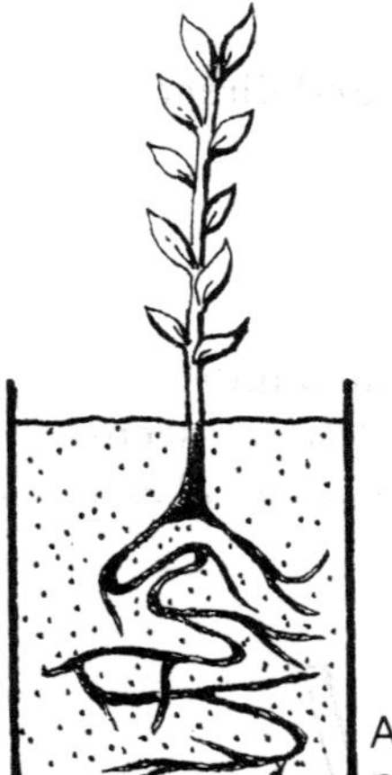

A poorly potted plant.

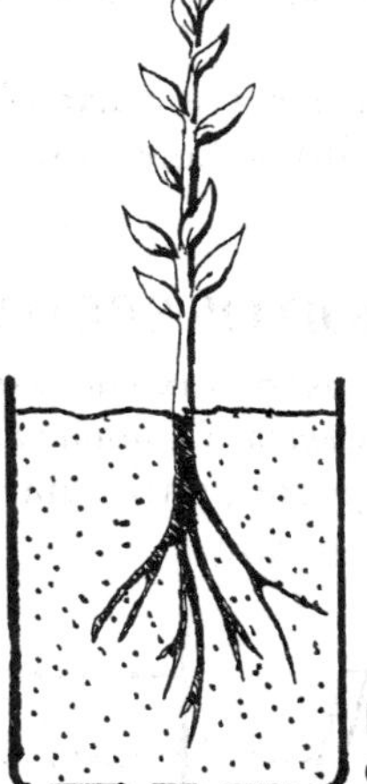

Plant correctly potted.

CARE OF SEEDLINGS AND POTTING-UP

Following germination, over-watering of seedlings should be avoided. The most likely problem at this stage of their developme t is known as 'damping off'. This is a fungal disease, and it can occur if the seedlin s are overcrowded or over-watered.

Transplanting the small seedlings into inuividual pots as soon as they are large enough to be handled will help to avoid 'damping off'.

If long roots have developed in the seedling container, these should be broken or cut at the time of transplanting so that the roots can be spread out in the plant pot rather than bunched, twisted or coiled. This is extremely important. If the root system is not correctly handled at this stage of the plant's development, it may *never* develop properly. It is not uncommon to see mature shrubs or trees, which have been blown down by strong winds, reveal a root system which had developed in a tight knot or coil due to incorrect potting at a very early stage in their growth.

Most seedlings will benefit from a light application of slow-release fertiliser at the potting-up stage. The fertiliser should be mixed through the soil in the pot and *not* left in one area next to the plant roots.

After potting, plants should be watered thoroughly. The addition of a root stimulant and fungicide to the water is beneficial. Your garden supplier will be able to advise you regarding suitable products available for this purpose.

POTTING MIXTURES

A recommended basic mixture for the potting of seedlings, or cutting-grown plants, is —

5 parts coarse river sand,
4 parts peat moss or organic material, plus
3 parts good quality topsoil.

As with propagation mixtures, any potting mix should be well-drained and aerated, yet able to maintain sufficient moisture to meet the needs of the plant. It must be able to support the young seedling and hold adequate nutrients for plant development.

Because the above ingredients can be both costly and in some areas difficult to obtain, experiments have been carried out with a wide range of alternatives. These include brown coal, compost, leaf litter, peanut shells, pine bark, polystyrene balls, rice hulls and sawdust. Some nurseries now use potting mixes consisting of one or more of these ingredients. The advantages and problems associated with each material are not detailed here, but books containing this information are listed in the Bibliography for those who may wish to experiment with these, or other materials. For the beginner, at least, the use of a standard potting mixture is recommended.

ESTABLISHING HEALTHY PLANTS

Following the potting of seedlings or rooted cuttings into individual containers, the plants should be held in a sheltered situation for 1 to 2 weeks.

After this period they are usually sufficiently developed to allow them to survive and grow in a more open location. Moving them to a fairly open situation is recommended in order that sturdy plants may result. These will then be capable of being successfully planted into garden conditions.

If the climatic conditions at the time of potting are particularly unfavourable, as in a spell of very hot weather during summer, it may be desirable to keep them in a sheltered location for a longer period. Similarly, if some particular species being grown are known to be very susceptible to the normal climatic conditions of the region, special precautions will be necessary to ensure their survival.

Young plants should, if possible, be allowed to grow without staking. If seedlings or cuttings have been potted on at an early stage after propagation, staking will usually be unnecessary.

Plants should not be over-fertilised or 'forced' during their development. If this is done, an imbalance of root growth as compared to foliage growth may occur, and plants can become top heavy. Fertilisers should be used simply to provide sufficient nutrients for the maintenance of plant vigour and healthy, sturdy growth.

27—Propagating Plants from Cuttings

Cuttings are sections of plant material removed from the parent plant for the purpose of propagation. They are kept under favourable conditions to enable the formation of roots, following which the cuttings will develop and grow as separate plants.

This method of propagation is widely used for Australian shrubs and groundcover plants. Large shrubs or trees with a height of over 4 m are best grown from seed, as this helps in the development of the root system natural to the species which is preferable for tall plants.

The majority of plants propagated from cuttings are in the classification of dicotyledons. Although a small number of monocotyledons can be propagated by this method, most are generally reproduced from seed or by root division.

There are several advantages in regard to the propagation of plants from cuttings.

(a) Plants can be propagated in cases where seed is not readily available.

(b) The characteristics of the parent plant will be reproduced without the variations which can occur in plants grown from seed. Plant hybrids or cultivars *must* be propagated by vegetative means, such as cuttings, to ensure true reproduction.

(c) It is widely accepted that cutting-grown plants will flower and fruit at a much earlier age than those grown from seed.

Stem cuttings are the most commonly used for the propagation of Australian plants and it is this procedure that will be covered here. Individual leaves can be used for the successful propagation of some plants, the best-known example being the introduced African violets. Bud cuttings and root cuttings are also used in particular situations.

PROPAGATION STRUCTURES

In order to enable the formation of roots on cuttings, they must be kept in an atmosphere which is moist and slightly warm. They need to be able to receive both air and light, but must be protected from direct sunlight and hot or cold winds.

There are various structures which will help to provide these conditions, ranging from a simple upturned glass jar to a fully equipped glasshouse.

Small propagation units should not be placed in direct sunlight; they will heat very quickly so the plants may be burnt. Cold frames and larger structures are commonly covered with shadecloth for protection when necessary, or painted with

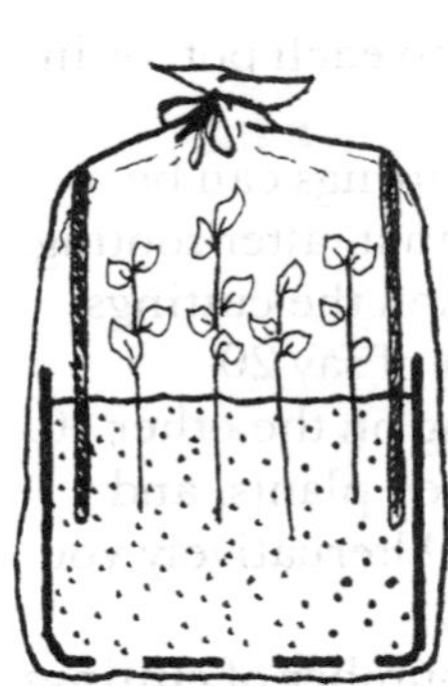

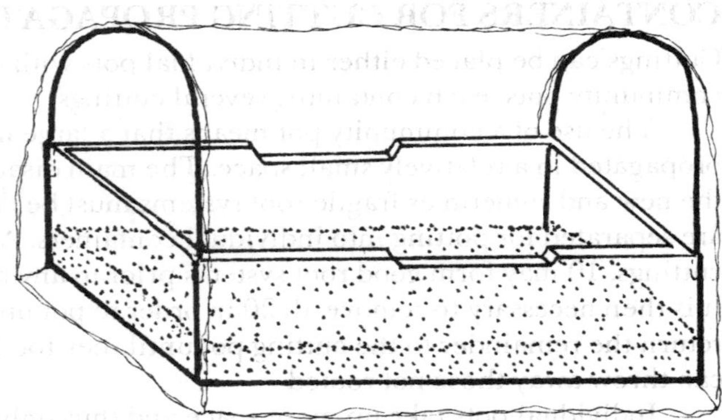

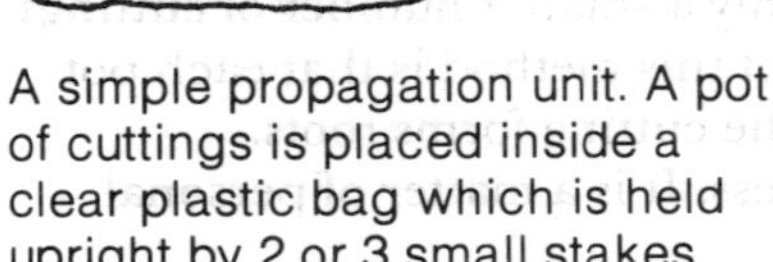

A simple propagation unit. A pot of cuttings is placed inside a clear plastic bag which is held upright by 2 or 3 small stakes.

A propagation unit using a polystyrene fruit box. Two wire hoops support a clear plastic sheet cover. Pots of cuttings are placed on a layer of coarse sand in the base of the box.

glasshouse paint, which can be applied during the hot summer months then partially or completely washed off during winter.

It is not necessary to spend large sums on setting up sophisticated equipment unless you really wish to do so. If cuttings are put down during the warmer months of the year, artificial heating will not be necessary to obtain good results.

A polythene propagating house with sprinkler system, suitable for large numbers of plants.

CONTAINERS FOR CUTTING PROPAGATION

Cuttings can be placed either in individual pots with one cutting to each pot, or in community pots, each containing several cuttings.

The use of a community pot means that a large number of cuttings can be propagated in a relatively small space. The main disadvantage is that, after rooting, the new and sometimes fragile root systems must be disturbed when the cuttings are separated for potting into individual containers. Also, in a pot of say 20 cuttings, 10 may form good root systems prior to any roots forming on the other 10. It is then necessary to remove all 20 in order to pot up the 10 rooted plants, and return the remainder to the cutting pot until they too form roots. Alternatively you can throw away those not rooted.

Individual pots take up more space and thus only a smaller number of cuttings can be propagated at the one time. The advantage of this method is that each pot can be removed from the propagation structure as the cutting forms roots.

Both these methods are used widely with success. It is a matter of personal preference as to which is selected.

Any containers used should have adequate drainage holes in the base and should be clean and free from disease. See also 'Containers for Seed Propagation', page 154.

PROPAGATION MIXTURES

A similar mixture to that recommended for the germination of seed can be used for the rooting of cuttings.

3 parts coarse river sand, plus
1 part peat moss.

Cuttings can be rooted successfully in a medium composed entirely of coarse river sand; however this has very little moisture-retaining ability and therefore care must be taken to ensure the cuttings do not dry out. The addition of peat moss helps to provide a moisture retaining ability within the propagating mix.

A range of other mixtures, many of which are regarded as being very successful, are commonly used for the rooting of cuttings.

The selection of the most suitable mixture for your own use will depend to a large extent on the conditions under which you will be propagating, i.e. in a cold frame or heated glasshouse, whether watering is by hand or by constant mist, etc. Another relevant factor is whether you are using individual small pots or community pots. If community pots are used, the potting mix must allow the rooted cuttings to be easily separated without excessive damage to the young roots.

The mixture listed here is recommended as a starting point, and in many cases there will be no need to consider variations. Through experience you will be able to determine whether the mixture is retaining too much moisture, drying out readily, or causing other problems. Variations can then be considered, having regard to the availability of various ingredients in your particular area.

TYPES OF CUTTINGS

As earlier mentioned, the type of cutting most commonly used for the propagation of Australian plants is the stem cutting. Stem cuttings are further divided into the

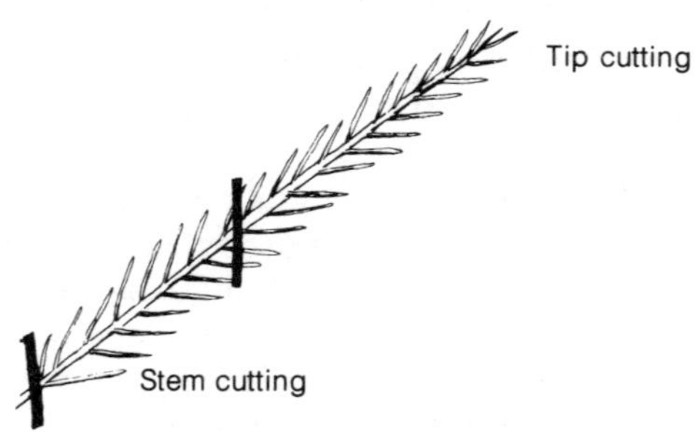

three main types of tip, stem and heel cuttings. Cuttings taken are usually from 5 to 15 cm long.

In some plant species the leaves are fairly close together, whilst in others they are widely spaced. The point at which a leaf joins the stem is known as the leaf node and it is necessary in most plant species to plant at least one of the cutting's leaf nodes, from which roots can develop, below the soil. It is also necessary to have one upper node, or more if possible, from which new shoots and leaves can grow.

Heel cuttings.

COLLECTION AND CARE OF CUTTINGS

Cuttings should be collected early in the morning if possible. At this time of day the material will usually be in good condition. Secateurs and other cutting instruments should be clean and sharp.

Material chosen should include fresh young growth which has developed to the stage of being able to spring back fairly quickly if bent over.

If you have a heated propagation unit with automatic misting, softer cutting material can be used and here, as in most aspects, experience will probably provide the most reliable guide as to the best material for your own particular conditions.

If there is a delay between the collection of cuttings and their preparation for planting, they should be kept moist in a cool location. They can be placed in a large plastic bag or wrapped in moist newspaper. An insulated cooler can provide a suitable storage unit in warm weather. If cutting material is exposed to heat or direct sunlight, through the windows of a car, for example, the chances of successful propagation will be very considerably reduced.

Cutting prepared for planting.

PREPARATION OF CUTTINGS

Carefully remove the leaf or leaves from the lower half of the cutting. They can be cut with secateurs or they may come away easily with a short, sharp pull.

Generally the bark should not be ripped or damaged during this process, although sometimes the stripping of the bark from the lowest node to the base of the cutting is thought to hasten rooting. This is known as 'wounding', and is used commonly on *Grevillea* species such as *G. x gaudichaudii* and other plants where the leaves are widely spaced on the stems.

Many propagators choose to use a root-promoting hormone mixture when propagating from cuttings. Such mixtures are readily obtainable in powder or liquid form and a small container is sufficient for a large number of cuttings. The use of a rooting hormone is certainly not essential for success, but it usually assists in the quicker formation of stronger roots.

Before planting, simply dip the cutting in the powder then shake off any excess. If you use a liquid preparation it is only necessary to place the base of the cutting in the liquid for a very short period, as directed on the bottle.

Cutting of *Grevillea* x *gaudichaudii* showing base leaf pulled down to achieve 'wounding' of the stem.

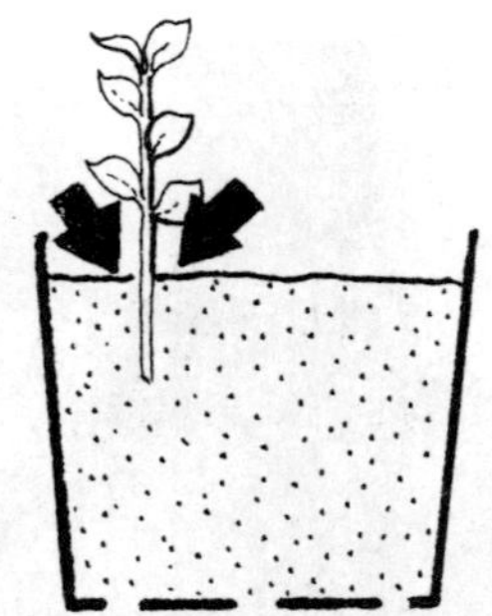

Firm mixture around base of cuttings where indicated by arrows.

PLANTING THE CUTTINGS

Having organised the propagating structure, filled the pots with propagating mix and collected and prepared the cuttings, the actual planting becomes a very simple task.

Gently water the propagating mixture in the selected container and allow the water to drain through.

Make a hole in the mixture with a clean stick or similar object, insert a cutting and firm the mixture around the base of the stem. Repeat as many times as necessary if several cuttings are being placed in a community pot. Do not overcrowd the cuttings, as there must be air movement to avoid the development of fungi.

Water gently after the desired number of cuttings have been placed in the pot.

Again water the pot gently, without allowing the mixture to become waterlogged.

Label with plant name and the date on which the cuttings are put down, then place the pot in the propagating unit.

ROOTING OF CUTTINGS

Formation of roots can take place within a few weeks; however, with some difficult species it can take up to a year or more. If artificial heating is not used, the period involved is usually between 2 and 6 months.

During this period cuttings should be kept moist, but not wet. In hot weather it is best not to let the foliage dry out too often. Regular light spraying will help to prevent this.

As the cuttings form roots, the roots will be seen appearing through the drainage holes of the pot. New leaf growth will also develop as the roots provide greater moisture intake.

A gentle pull on the cutting may indicate whether or not roots have formed, although this can sometimes be deceptive. Alternatively, small pots can be tipped out to see if there are roots forming around the edges of the mixture. The success of this method will depend to some extent on the mixture used and whether it can be tipped out without falling apart.

Regardless of the method used to check rooting, this is a very exciting stage and it is always a thrill to see roots formed at the base of the cuttings and new plants begin to develop.

POTTING ROOTED CUTTINGS

A recommended basic mixture for the potting of rooted cuttings is —

5 parts coarse river sand,
4 parts peat moss or organic material, plus
3 parts good quality topsoil.

It will be noted that potting mixtures have a greater percentage of organic material than propagation mixtures, which are primarily composed of coarse sand. The additional organic material helps to retain nutrients necessary for the healthy growth of the young plant.

If desired, slow release fertiliser can be added at the time of potting. This should be mixed through the soil in the pot, rather than being placed in one position.

Cuttings being transferred from community pots should be handled with care to avoid excessive damage to the new root systems. Any very long roots should be cut, rather than squashed into the new pot. See also 'Care of Seedlings and Potting Up' in Chapter 26.

If a cutting rooted in an individual pot has developed a very strong root system, the roots should be gently teased out before potting on to avoid any coiling of the root system as the plant grows.

Plants should be watered thoroughly after potting. For further information regarding the subsequent care of young plants, see 'Establishing Healthy Plants' in Chapter 26.

If cuttings have been rooted in individual pots and have developed good healthy root systems, they can be planted directly into the garden without further potting. This is best done in cool weather and they should be watered regularly until they have become established in their new location. It is wise to mark small plants in some way, to prevent them being accidentally broken or 'lost' amongst other larger plants.

Chart 21 — Plants which can be propagated readily from cuttings

A selection of 20 species

Plant Name	Height x width	Brief comment — for further description see Section 2
Bauera rubioides	0.2-3 m x 1-3 m	White to pink flowers for most of year.
Bauera sessiliflora	2-3 m x 2-3 m	Rosy-purple flowers. Excellent for shaded places.
Brachyscome multifida	0.5 m x 1-1.5 m	Small daisy flowers for most of year.
Dampiera diversifolia	Prostrate x 1-2 m	Profuse, small, deep blue flowers.
Grevillea baueri	1-2 m x 1.5-2.5 m	An adaptable shrub with clusters of red flowers.
Grevillea rosmarinifolia	2-3 m x 2-4 m	Large shrub with clusters of pink to red with cream flowers.
Helichrysum baxteri	0.5 m x 1 m	Has white with yellow everlasting daisies.
Helichrysum bracteatum 'Dargan Hill Monarch'	0.5-1 m x 1 m	Has large, golden everlasting daisies most of year.
Kunzea pomifera	0.5 m x 1-3 m	Has clusters of cream to white flowers in spring.
Lechenaultia biloba	0.5-1 m x 0.5-1 m	Has very showy blue flowers.
Lechenaultia formosa	0.1-0.6 m x 0.5-1 m	Flowers can be yellow, orange, pinks or reds.
Leptospermum 'Horizontalis'	0.5-1 m x 2-4 m	Dense, spreading shrub with white, tea-tree flowers.
Leptospermum scoparium var. *rotundifolium*	1.5-2.5 m x 2-3 m	Tea-tree flowers are white to pink and purple or bluish-mauve.
Myoporum parvifolium	0.2-0.4 m x 1-3 m	Hardy groundcover with small white or pale pink flowers.
Prostanthera cuneata	0.3-1.5 m x 0.5-1.5 m	Has white flowers and aromatic foliage.
Prostanthera rotundifolia	1.5-2.5 m x 1-3 m	Has mauve-purple flowers and aromatic foliage.
Scaevola 'Mauve Clusters'	Prostrate x 1-2 m	Goundcover with profuse small mauve flowers.
Thryptomene saxicola	0.5-1.5 m x 1-2 m	Long-flowering, with small pale to deep pink flowers.
Westringia fruticosa	2-3 m x 2-3 m	Hardy shrub with white flowers.
Westringia glabra	1-2 m x 1-2 m	Hardy shrub with mauve-purple flowers.

28—Other Propagation Methods

ROOT DIVISION

This is a very simple and usually successful method of establishing new plants from species which form bulbs, tubers or rhizomes as part of their root systems.

Most of these plants cannot be propagated from cuttings, as described in Chapter 27.

Popular Australian plants propagated by root division include *Anigozanthos* or Kangaroo Paws, *Blandfordia*, *Conostylis* and *Patersonia* species.

Clumps are dug from the ground or tipped from a container. They can then be divided either by firmly pulling them apart with the hands or by careful cutting with a sharp knife or secateurs. Be sure that each division has a healthy root area, including active, fine feeder roots. The divisions should also have sufficient growth points for the development of new leaves.

The divided plants should be potted into clean containers; a potting mix as suggested for seedlings or rooted cuttings will be satisfactory. If the divisions are left in clumps of a good size they can be planted directly into the garden.

It is best to undertake root divisions during autumn or spring. If the work is being done in spring, you may notice new leaves and flower-stems developing. Be careful to avoid damaging this new growth. However, you can remove some of the flower-stems if desired, to promote better initial plant growth.

LAYERING

Plant layering occurs in some species when stems come in contact with the ground and roots grow down from the nodes.

It is a relatively simple matter to separate new plants from the parent plant. Simply cut the stem joining the rooted sections with a sharp knife or secateurs. Potting mixtures and procedures are the same as those described for seedlings in Chapter 26.

After the potting of layers, they should be placed in a warm, sheltered area, until the plants have become established.

Chart 22, which follows in this chapter, lists plants that spread naturally by layering.

Layering can also be initiated by pegging a stem into the soil beside the plant or into a pot containing propagating mixture. Wounding of the stem (removing a piece of the bark) before pegging will assist in the formation of roots and some root-producing hormone can be brushed on the wound if desired. This method of propagation can be used for any species normally propagated from cuttings and with branches at or near ground level.

AERIAL LAYERING

Aerial layering is similar in theory to simple layering as described above; however, it is used on the upper stems of a plant which do not extend down to ground level.

Propagation takes place while the stem is still part of the parent plant. The selected stem is wounded (a small section of the bark is removed), wrapped in damp sphagnum moss, then secured with a wrapping of polythene film. When roots have developed, the layered section of stem can be removed from the parent plant and potted up in the manner recommended for rooted cuttings.

More detailed information regarding this method of propagation can be obtained from textbooks dealing specifically with propagation techniques, see Bibliography.

SUCKERING

Suckering takes place when new shoots develop from underground buds along the root system.

The young suckers can be dug up and cut free from the parent plant, then potted into separate containers, using the methods described for the potting of seedlings.

If a sucker has little or no root growth, it should be treated in the same way as a cutting. This is common in some species of *Dampiera* and such cuttings usually form roots more readily than stem cuttings from older material.

A selection of plants which spread naturally by suckering is listed in Chart 23.

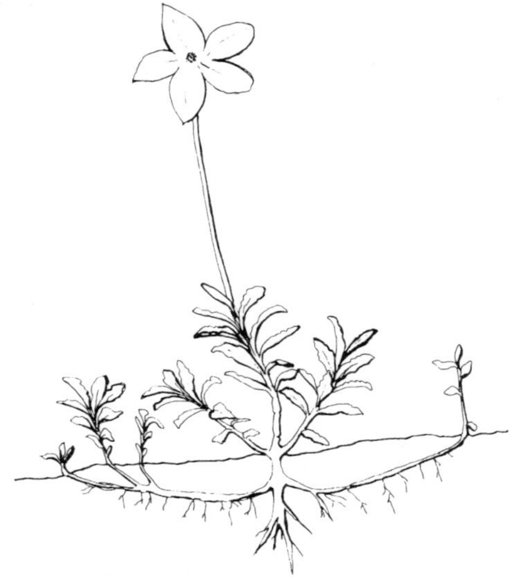

The suckering growth habit of *Wahlenbergia gloriosa*.

TISSUE CULTURE

Tissue culture is a means of establishing large numbers of plants from very small sections of tissue, or even single cells. Specialised equipment and sterile laboratory conditions are necessary for good results.

Whilst propagation of this nature is not likely to be attempted by the majority of home gardeners, it is nevertheless of considerable relevance to all plant growers. It is likely that our gardens will, in the future, include one or maybe many plants that have been propagated in this way.

Tissue culture can be used for the propagation of species which present difficulties in regard to other methods of propagation, because the plants may not bear sufficient quantities of good seed or propagation from seed may not be desired, as is the case with hybrids and cultivars. Some plants do not produce large quantities of good cutting material, or propagation by this method may not be possible, e.g. with Kangaroo Paws.

In view of the minimum amount of propagation material required, tissue culture is particularly useful in regard to rare and endangered plants.

Propagation by tissue culture also enables the production of disease free plants, which is of major importance if living plants are being transported from one area or country to another.

Australian plant species which have to date been propagated by tissue culture include ferns, orchids, *Anigozanthos* species (Kangaroo Paws), *Dampiera* species, some of the hybrid grevilleas, and the spectacular and well-known Waratah. The list is being constantly increased.

For further information readers are referred to *Tissue Culture for Plant Propagators* (see Bibliography).

Anigozanthos flavidus x *pulcherrimus*, a showy yellow Kangaroo Paw.

Chart 22 — Plants which spread naturally by layering

A selection of 20 species

Plant Name	Height x width	Brief comment — for further description see Section 2
Baeckea ramosissima ssp. *prostrata*	0.1-0.5 m x 1-1.5 m	Has white to deep pink flowers.
Brachysema species	Prostrate x 1-2.5 m	Has dark green leaves and mainly red pea-flowers.
Claytonia australasica	Prostrate x 1-2 m	Has fragrant, white flowers.
Conostylis seorsiflora	Prostrate x 0.3-0.5 m	Has tubular yellow flowers.
Darwinia glaucophylla	Prostrate x 1-2.5 m	Has purplish foliage and greenish-cream to pink flowers.
Darwinia grandiflora	0.1-0.5 m x 1.5-2.5 m	Flowers are white then age to dark red.
Dichondra repens	Prostrate x 1-2 m	Useful as a non-mow lawn.
Frankenia pauciflora	Prostrate x 1 m	Has greyish leaves and white to pink flowers.
Goodenia hederacea	Prostrate x 1-2 m	Has yellow to orange flowers.
Goodenia lanata	Prostrate x 1 m	Trailing plant with dark green leaves and bright yellow flowers.
Hibbertia pedunculata	Prostrate x 0.5-1 m	Has profuse bright yellow flowers.
Isotoma fluviatilis	Spreading mat plant	Flat, layering plant with small, blue starry flowers.
Mentha diemenica	0.2 m x 0.5-1 m	Highly aromatic native mint.
Myoporum parvifolium	0.2-0.4 m x 1-3 m	Hardy groundcover with small white or pale pink flowers.
Phyla nodiflora	Spreading mat plant	Can be used as a non-mow lawn. Pink flowers.
Pratia pedunculata	Prostrate x 0.5-2 m	Mat plant with small blue or white, starry flowers.
Pultenaea pedunculata	0.5 m x 1-2 m	Has profuse orange or yellow with red pea-flowers.
Pultenaea pedunculata 'Pyalong Gold'	0.5 m x 1-2 m	Profuse golden pea-flowers.
Pultenaea pedunculata 'Pyalong Pink'	0.5 m x 1-2 m	Profuse pink pea-flowers.
Viola hederacea	0.1 m x 1-2 m	Native violet with purple-blue and white flowers.

Chart 23 — Plants which spread naturally by suckering

A selection of 20 species

Plant Name	Height x width	Brief comment — for further description see Section 2
Acacia boormanii	3-5 m x 2-5 m	An adaptable wattle with showy yellow flowers.
Brachyscome sp. aff. *melanocarpa*	0.05-0.4 m x 0.2-1 m	Daisy flowers are mauve-pink with yellow centres.
Casuarina glauca	8-30 m x 4-12 m	A hardy she-oak.
Commersonia pulchella	0.6-1.5 m x 0.5-1 m	Compact shrub with pink to red buds and white flowers.
Cordyline stricta	2-5 m tall	Erect plant with sprays of purplish flowers.
Dampiera diversifolia	Prostrate x 1-2 m	Profuse, small, deep blue flowers.
Dampiera linearis	0.3-0.5 m x 1-2 m	Variable species. Has deep blue flowers.
Dampiera rosmarinifolia	0.4 m x 1-3 m	Low shrub with spikes of blue or mauve flowers.
Dampiera teres	0.3-0.5 m x 0.5-1 m	Has spikes of blue-mauve or pink flowers.
Dianella revoluta	0.3-1 m x 0.5-2.5 m	Clumping plant with strap-like leaves. Pale blue flowers.
Dianella tasmanica	0.6-1.7 m x 0.5-2 m	Clumping plant with leaves to 1 m long. Flowers blue.
Glishrocaryon behrii	0.3-0.5 m x 0.5-1 m	Has bright yellow flowers.
Goodenia geniculata	Prostrate x 0.5-1 m	Has dark green leaves and bright yellow flowers.
Goodenia hederacea	Prostrate x 1-2 m	Flowers are yellow to orange.
Halgania cyanea	0.5 m x 0.5-1 m	Has clusters of deep blue flowers.
Lechenaultia biloba	0.5-1 m x 0.5-1 m	Has very showy blue flowers.
Lechenaultia formosa	0.1-0.6 m x 0.5-1 m	Flowers can be yellow, orange, pinks or reds.
Mazus pumilio	Prostrate x 1-2 m	Mat plant with tubular, mauve or white flowers.
Pimelea humilis	0.1-0.3 m x 0.3-1 m	Has heads of white to cream flowers.
Whalenbergia gloriosa	Prostrate x 0.5-1 m	Has deep blue-purple flowers on slender stems.

29—Learning more about Australian Plants

SOCIETY FOR GROWING AUSTRALIAN PLANTS

For those interested in growing a wider range of Australian plants, it is helpful to join and participate in the activities of the Society for Growing Australian Plants. There are branches of the Society in all Australian States, as well as in the Australian Capital Territory. In addition to groups in the capital cities, many states also have regional groups in suburban and country areas. Your local native plant nursery will almost certainly be able to give you the address of your nearest group.

Within the Society for Growing Australian Plants there are numerous plant study groups, catering for those members with specific interests. Some deal with particular plants, such as the Grevillea Study Group, whilst others cover a range of genera, such as the groups studying Rainforest Plants, Everlastings, and Plants Useful as Food.

OTHER GROUPS

In addition to the Society for Growing Australian Plants, there are other groups which may be of interest to particular readers. The Australian Native Orchid Society has branches in several states and there are also Fern Society groups throughout Australia.

For those particularly interested in attracting birds to the garden, further information can be obtained from The Bird Observers Club, the Australian headquarters of which are at 183 Springvale Road, Nunawading, Victoria 3131.

FURTHER READING

In this book we have looked in detail at approximately 500 Australian native plants, out of several thousand currently in cultivation and a total number of over 20 000 separate plant species. Australia does indeed have a very rich native flora.

It must be obvious that there is much more information and knowledge available regarding our indigenous plants than can be contained within the pages of any one book.

There is now a very wide range of books available on Australian plants and their cultivation. Many books cover one particular group of plants, one particular region of Australia, or selected aspects relating to propagation or cultivation.

Most books in the Bibliography are obtainable through major booksellers. Any which are no longer in print can usually be borrowed from public libraries.

Section 2

Plant Descriptions

KEY TO THE CULTIVATION CODE

There is a logical sequence to the code in the plant descriptions which will assist the reader to recognise immediately the conditions under which a plant may be expected to grow successfully.

H	— Hot	Tolerates sun for most of the day.
O	— Open	An open position is suitable, but not necessarily exposed to hot sun for extended periods.
S	— Shade	Will grow well in full shade.
SS	— Semi-shade	Will grow well in situations that are shaded for some part of the day; or in positions that receive dappled sunlight through an overhead foliage canopy.
D	— Drainage	Needs or prefers well-drained soil.
M	— Moist	Will grow well in soil that is moist for most of the year.
W	— Wet	Will withstand extended wet periods.
L	— Loam	Suitable for loam, or clay-loam.
SA	— Sand	Suitable for sandy soils or sandy loam.
G	— Gravels	Suitable for coarse, open gravels.
CA	— Calcareous	Suitable for alkaline soils.
C1	— Coastal	Suited to protected coastal situations.
C2	— Coastal	Suited to exposed coastal situations.
F1	— Frost	Moderately frost-resistant.
F2	— Frost	Frost-resistant at all stages of growth.
B	— Birds	Attractive to birds.

PLANT DESCRIPTIONS

The numbers printed in the margins refer to illustrations in the colour section.

Acacia acinacea, Gold Dust Wattle
0.5-2.5 m x 2-4 m NSW, Vic, SA
Has oblong or oval phyllodes to around 2.5 cm long. Deep golden, globular flower-heads are produced during Aug.-Dec. This species is adaptable to a wide range of situations and will grow in dry or moist conditions if drainage is good.
H O SS D M L SA CA C1 F2
Chart 17, Chapter 21

Acacia aculeatissima, Thin-leaf Wattle
Prostrate to 0.5 m x 1-2 m NSW, Vic
Has an open habit with slightly prickly foliage. Pale to bright yellow flower-heads are produced in June-Nov. An adaptable low wattle. Likes well-drained soils and partial or filtered sun. Drought-tolerant.
O SS D L SA G C1 F2
Charts 1a, Chapter 3; 7a Chapter 10

Acacia acuminata, Raspberry Jam Wood
6-10 m x 3-5 m WA
A quick-growing small tree with narrow foliage and bright yellow, rod-like flower-heads produced during July-Oct. Likes well-drained soils and a sunny situation. Freshly cut wood has the aroma of raspberry jam.
H O SS D L SA G CA C1 F2
Chart 2c, Chapter 3

52 **Acacia adunca**, Wallangarra Wattle
4-8 m x 3-5 m Qld, NSW
Has long, narrow, dark green phyllodes. Masses of fluffy, yellow-orange flower-heads are produced during April-Nov. An extremely showy small tree. Plants are adaptable to a fairly wide range of well-drained situations.
H O SS D L SA G C1 F2
Chart 13, Chapter 17

Acacia baileyana, Cootamundra Wattle
5-8 m x 5-8 m NSW
A hardy and very widely grown wattle, with bluish, ferny leaves which can have silvery, yellow, red or purplish new growth. Masses of bright yellow flower-heads are produced, mainly during June-Aug. The seeds are often eaten by native parrots and bronze-wing pigeons.
H O SS D L SA G C1 F2
Chart 7c, Chapter 10

Acacia boormanii, Snowy River Wattle
3-5 m x 2-5 m NSW, Vic
An adaptable wattle, with grey-green foliage and a showy display of bright yellow flower-heads, produced during July-Oct. It likes well-drained soils but also tolerates wet periods. A good windbreak and screen plant. Can spread by suckering.
H O SS D M L SA G C1 F2
Charts 12a, Chapter 16; 13, Chapter 17; 15, Chapter 18; 23, Chapter 28

Acacia brownii, see **A. ulicifolia** var. **brownei**

Acacia buxifolia, Box-leaf Wattle
2-4 m x 2-4 m Qld, NSW, Vic
A hardy wattle with grey-green, leathery phyllodes of around 1.5 cm x 1 cm. There is a profuse display of yellow flower-heads during July-Dec. This species has many ornamental and landscape uses. Prune lightly after flowering.
H O SS D L SA G C1 F2
Chart 1b, Chapter 3

Acacia calamifolia, Wallowa
2-5 m x 2-4 m NSW, Vic, SA
A medium to tall shrub, with long, narrow phyllodes. It has profuse, golden, globular flower-heads during July-Nov. Requires a warm, well-drained situation and is drought-tolerant. Ornamental and useful also as a screen plant.
H O SS D L SA G CA C1 F2
Chart 5, Chapter 3

Acacia cometes
0.2-0.3 m x 0.5-0.8 m WA
A low, spreading shrub, with globular, yellow flower-heads, produced in dense spikes mainly during Oct.-Nov. It likes partial or full sun, and is a good groundcover for use on embankments.
H O SS D L SA C1 F1
Chart 10a, Chapter 14

Acacia cultriformis 'Austraflora Cascade'
0.3 m x 2-4 m
A selected form of *A. cultriformis* (which usually grows to 4 m high). Bright yellow flower-spikes are produced mainly during Aug.-Oct. Is adaptable to most well-drained situations. All forms are frost-tolerant.
H O SS D L SA G C1 F2
Chart 7a, Chapter 10

Acacia decora, Western Silver Wattle
2-5 m x 3-5 m Qld, NSW, Vic
Although this species can reach 5 m in height, plants respond well to regular light pruning. Phyllodes are 2-5 cm long, leathery and grey-green. Terminal racemes of golden flower-heads are produced in Aug.-Oct. Adaptable to a very wide range of well-drained situations.
H O SS D L SA CA C1 F2
Chart 2b, Chapter 3

Acacia depressa
0.1 m x 1 m WA
A cushion-like dwarf shrub, with small, divided leaves. Small, yellow, globular flower-heads are produced mainly during Dec.-Jan. This species is not well-known in cultivation, but is suitable for well-drained to dry situations.
H O SS D L SA G C1 F1
Chart 10a, Chapter 14

62 *Right:* The Rock Orchid, *Dendrobium speciosum*, produces large racemes with numerous white, cream or yellow flowers.

63 *Below:* The Prickly Rasp-fern, *Doodia aspera*, is suited to a wide range of situations in gardens or containers. It is noted for its colourful pink to reddish new growth.

64 *Bottom right: Cyathea cooperi* in a glazed ceramic container.

65 *Top left:* The use of containers enables successful cultivation of plants such as *Hibbertia stellaris* which can prove difficult to grow in garden situations.

66 *Above: Thryptomene saxicola* is an arching shrub of around 1 m high. The small, open-petalled flowers are borne in profusion during winter and spring. This particular form is known as *T. saxicola* 'Mingenew'.

67 *Left:* The Round-leaf Mint-bush, *Prostanthera rotundifolia*, has several colour forms, including this pink-mauve form commonly available as *P. rotundifolia* 'Rosea'. The foliage is highly aromatic.

68 *Lechenaultia formosa* is a variable species, but all forms make excellent container plants.

69 The Round-leaf Tea-tree, *Leptospermum scoparium* var. *rotundifolium* has large open-petalled flowers in various shades from white to pink or bluish-purple.

70 An attractive garden in the grounds of Monash University, Clayton, Victoria. The blue-flowered *Dampiera rosmarinifolia* is seen in front of the red *Grevillea thelemanniana* and the pink and white flowers of *Hypocalymma angustifolium*. *Acacia drummondii* is in the background.

71 *Top left: Conostylis seorsiflora* is a clump-forming species which can spread by layering. Yellow flowers are produced during spring to early summer.

72 *Above: Isotoma fluviatilis* is a matting plant which is ideal for use in rockeries and also for cultivation in small or large containers. It grows well in moist situations.

73 *Left:* The clusters of deep blue flowers produced by *Halgania cyanea* are seen during September-February.

Acacia elata, Cedar Wattle
10-20 m x 5-10 m NSW
A large tree with dark green, bipinnate leaves to 40 cm long. Pale yellow, globular flower-heads of almost 1 cm diam. are produced in Dec.-March. Normally a hardy and long-lived wattle, but can be attacked by borers. Can also be frost-tender whilst young.
H O SS D L SA C1
Chart 1c, Chapter 3

Acacia fimbriata, Fringed Wattle
5-8 m x 4-6 m Qld, NSW
An upright to spreading, graceful wattle. Racemes of deep cream to yellow, globular flower-heads are produced near the ends of the branches in Aug.-Oct. Adaptable to a fairly wide range of soil and climatic conditions.
O SS D W L SA G CA C1 F1
Charts 2c, Chapter 3; 13, Chapter 17

Acacia flexifolia, Bent-leaf Wattle
1-2 m x 1-2 m Qld, NSW, Vic
The foliage of this shrub is usually grey-green. Many globular, pale yellow flower-heads are produced during May-Nov. Likes a sunny, well-drained situation. Responds well to pruning, and is useful for screen or wind-break purposes.
H O SS D L SA G CA C1 F2
Chart 7b, Chapter 10

Acacia floribunda, White Sallow Wattle
4-8 m x 4-6 m Qld, NSW, Vic
An ornamental species with phyllodes to 12 cm x 1 cm. There is a profuse display of pale yellow, rod-like flower-heads mainly during July-Oct. Plants will grow in partial or full sun, and have a preference for a moist situation.
H O SS M W L SA CA C1 F2
Charts 7c, Chapter 10; 12b, Chapter 16

Acacia gracilifolia
2.5-5 m x 2-5 m SA
A large shrub of fairly open habit. It has long, narrow, dark green phyllodes. Golden yellow flower-heads are produced in clusters during Aug.-Oct. Is suited to well-drained soils with partial or full sun, and is drought-tolerant.
H O D L SA G CA C1 F2
Chart 1b, Chapter 3

Acacia howittii, Sticky Wattle
4-8 m x 3-6 m Vic
A graceful tree with pendulous branches. Fragrant pale yellow flower-heads are produced near the ends of the branches in Sept.-Nov. An adaptable species which will grow in full or partial sun. Likes a moist yet well-drained situation.
H O SS M W L SA G C1 F2
Charts 7c, Chapter 10; 12b, Chapter 16

Acacia inophloia, Fibre-barked Wattle
3-4 m x 3-4 m WA
An upright shrub, with brown, string-like bark on the trunk. Yellow flower-heads are produced during Sept.-Nov. Grows best in a warm, well-drained situation. The fibrous bark provides good nesting material for birds.
H O SS D L SA C1 F1
Chart 9, Chapter 13

7 **Acacia iteaphylla**, Flinders Range Wattle; Gawler Range Wattle
3-5 m x 3-6 m SA
Has blue-green foliage with pink new growth. Some forms are pendulous. Globular pale yellow flower-heads are produced over a long period during March-Sept. A hardy species suited to a range of well-drained situations. Is drought-tolerant.
H O SS D L SA G CA C1 F2
Chart 5, Chapter 3

Acacia jibberdingensis
3-5 m x 3-4 m WA
A medium to tall shrub with long, narrow phyllodes of 10-25 cm x 0.2 cm. Deep yellow, rod-shaped flower-heads to 3 cm long are produced mainly during May-Dec. A showy species, with a preference for very well-drained soils. It is popular in cultivation as it flowers over a long period.
H O SS D L SA G CA C1 F1
Chart 10c, Chapter 14

Acacia lasiocalyx
3-5 m x 4-6 m WA
The stems and branches of this medium-sized wattle have a silvery appearance. The phyllodes are long and narrow. Bright yellow, rod-shaped flower-heads are produced mainly during Aug.-Nov. Although this species prefers a well-drained situation it will tolerate short periods of waterlogging.
H O SS D L SA G CA C1 F1
Chart 10c, Chapter 14

Acacia ligulata, Umbrella Bush
2-5 m x 4-7 m NSW, Vic, SA, WA, NT
A hardy and decorative wattle, bushy to ground level unless pruned. It has globular bright yellow to orange flower-heads mainly during Aug.-Oct., but with odd blooms throughout the year. It prefers full sun and is drought-resistant.
H O SS D L SA G CA C2 F2
Chart 4, Chapter 3

Acacia longifolia, Sallow Wattle; Sydney Golden Wattle
4-8 m x 4-8 m NSW, Vic, Tas, SA
This species has green phyllodes to 20 cm long. Bright yellow, rod-like flower-heads are produced near the ends of the branches during July-Oct. It is a very quick-growing tree which can sometimes be short-lived but provides an excellent initial screen.
H O SS W L SA G C1 F1
Chart 13, Chapter 17

Acacia longifolia var. **sophorae**, see **A. sophorae**

Acacia myrtifolia, Myrtle Wattle
1-3 m x 2-3 m All states
A small shrub, often with reddish stems. Has a profuse display of globular, cream or yellow flower-heads, mainly during July-Oct. It is an adaptable species although not always long-lived. It produces a good quantity of seed which is enjoyed by parrots and pigeons.
H O SS D M L SA CA C1 F2 B
Chart 8b, Chapter 13

53 **Acacia podalyriifolia**, Mount Morgan Wattle; Qld Silver Wattle
3-5 m x 3-4 m Qld, NSW
The decorative, silvery-grey phyllodes of this wattle are oval and up to 4 cm long. Racemes of golden-yellow flower-heads are produced usually during July-Oct. Plants will grow in a wide range of well-drained situations. Pruning after flowering is recommended to encourage bushy growth.
H O SS D L SA G C1 F1
Chart 13, Chapter 17

Acacia pravissima, Ovens Wattle
4-8 m x 4-8 m NSW, Vic
This wattle has dense foliage and often pendulous branches. The phyllodes are triangular to about 2 cm long. There is a profuse display of bright yellow flower-heads mainly during Aug.-Oct. It is a widely cultivated and highly ornamental wattle.
H O SS M W L SA G C1 F2
Charts 12b, Chapter 16; 13, Chapter 17

Acacia pravissima 'Golden Carpet'
0.3 m x 3-5 m
This prostrate form of *A. pravissima* (above) also has a profuse display of bright yellow flower-heads mainly during Aug.-Oct. It is a hardy plant that will tolerate dry conditions and also moist situations. Prostrate plants are propagated from cuttings of the prostrate form to retain this growth habit.
H O SS M W L SA G C1 F2
Charts 10a, Chapter 14; 15, Chapter 18

Acacia prominens, Golden Rain Wattle
5-20 m x 4-15 m NSW
A dense tall shrub to medium tree. Racemes of globular, lemon-yellow flower-heads are produced mainly during Aug.-Oct. This species is useful as a shade, screen or windbreak plant.
H O SS D L SA C1 F2
Charts 7c, Chapter 10; 12b, Chapter 16

Acacia pulchella, Western Prickly Moses
0.5-1.5 m x 1-2 m WA
A variable small wattle, with ferny leaves and small spines at the nodes. Flower-heads in July-Nov. are golden-yellow and profuse. Suited to a range of well-drained situations. Responds well to pruning after flowering.
H O SS D L SA C1 F1
Chart 2b, Chapter 3

Acacia pulviniformis
0.3-1 m x 0.5-2.5 m WA
A dwarf, spreading shrub, with small phyllodes. Profuse cream to yellow flower-heads are seen mainly during Aug.-Nov. This species will grow in partial or full sun and is drought-tolerant. It is not well-known in cultivation at present.
H O SS D L SA C1 F1
Chart 10a, Chapter 14

Acacia pycnantha, Golden Wattle
3-10 m x 2-6 m NSW, Vic, SA
This wattle has large, globular, golden-yellow flower-heads mainly during July-Oct. It is an adaptable species with a preference for well-drained soils. Birds and insects are attracted to nectar from glands on the phyllodes, and parrots and pigeons eat the seeds. It is the species often used to depict Wattle as the floral emblem of Australia.
H O SS D L SA CA C1 F1 B
Chart 8c, Chapter 13

Acacia redolens
1-4 m x 3-8 m WA
This species has grey-green foliage, with phyllodes to 7 cm long. Yellow flower-heads are produced during Aug.-Oct. It is an excellent screen plant which can be pruned if desired. A low, spreading form is also available.
H O SS W L SA G CA C1 F2
Chart 10b, Chapter 14

Acacia retinodes, Wirilda
3-5 m x 3-6 m Vic, Tas, SA
A variable wattle. Phyllodes can be broad or narrow, and foliage is weeping on some forms. Lemon-yellow flower-heads are produced mainly during Nov.-May, but can be seen throughout the year. It is a quick-growing small tree.
H O SS D W L SA G CA F1 F2
Charts 2c, Chapter 3; 8c, Chapter 13

Acacia rossei
2-5 m x 1-3 m WA
An open-branched shrub with short, narrow phyllodes. Deep yellow, globular flower-heads are produced during July-Dec. This decorative plant is best suited to warm, well-drained situations. It is not widely available at present, but seed can be purchased.
H O SS D L SA G CA C1 F2
Chart 10c, Chapter 14

Acacia salicina, Coobah; Native Willow
4-10 m x 3-5 m
Qld, NSW, Vic, SA, WA, NT
This wattle is usually bushy to ground level and branches are pendulous. Phyllodes are pale green. Pale yellow, globular flower-heads are produced mainly during June-Oct. Plants can sucker lightly, and it is an ideal species for screens or windbreaks.
H O SS D W L SA CA C2 F2
Charts 4, Chapter 3; 10c, Chapter 14

Acacia saligna, Golden Wreath Wattle
3-10 m x 3-6 m WA
A fast-growing, ornamental species with a profuse display of golden-yellow flower-heads on the ends of the branches in Aug.-Nov. It is hardy to a fairly wide range of conditions.
H O SS D M L SA CA C1 F1
Charts 2c, Chapter 3; 12b, Chapter 16

Acacia sophorae, Coast Wattle
2-8 m x 4-10 m Qld, NSW, Vic, Tas, SA
A bushy plant with narrow phyllodes to 15 cm long. Rod-like yellow flower-heads to 3 cm long are produced during July-Oct. This is a hardy species, used for beach reclamation in some areas. It was previously known as *A. longifolia* var. *sophorae.*
H O SS W L SA G CA C2 F1
Chart 16, Chapter 19

Acacia spectabilis, Glory Wattle; Mudgee Wattle
3-5 m x 2-3 m Qld, NSW
A very showy species with glaucous or silvery bark. Bright golden-yellow, globular flower-heads are produced mainly during July-Oct. This is a popular plant for cultivation. It prefers a sunny position with good drainage.
H O SS D L SA C1 F2
Chart 7c, Chapter 10

Acacia stenophylla, Eumong
5-20 m x 3-8 m
Qld, NSW, Vic, SA, WA, NT
A small to medium tree with pendulous foliage and phyllodes to 50 cm x 0.5 cm. Cream to yellow flower-heads are produced mainly during Dec.-July. Will grow in well-drained and also poorly drained situations.
H O SS M W L SA CA C1 F2
Chart 3, Chapter 3

Acacia suaveolens,Sweet Wattle
1-3 m x 2-5 m Qld, NSW, Vic, Tas, SA
The phyllodes on this species are bluish-green and up to 15 cm long. Fragrant, pale yellow flower-heads are produced in April-Oct. A hardy and adaptable wattle which will grow in most fairly well-drained soils. Responds well to pruning.
H O SS M L SA G CA C1 F1
Chart 1b, Chapter 3

Acacia ulicifolia var. **brownei**, Heath Wattle
0.5-1 m x 1-2 m Qld, NSW, Vic
This shrubby wattle has prickly foliage, with phyllodes to about 1 cm long. Golden-yellow flower-heads are produced mainly during June-Oct. It prefers a well-drained but moist situation with filtered or partial sun. The prickly foliage provides shelter for small birds.
O SS D M L SA C1 F1
Chart 9, Chapter 13

Acacia vestita, Hairy Wattle
3-6 m x 3-5 m NSW
This attractive tree with pendulous branches has soft, hairy, grey-green foliage. Racemes of golden-yellow, globular flower-heads are produced near the ends of the branches in Sept.-Oct. It grows best in moist soils with relatively good drainage.
H O SS D M L SA G C1 F2
Chart 7c, Chapter 10

Acacia victoriae, Bramble Wattle; Gundabluey
3-12 m x 4-6 m
Qld, NSW, Vic, SA, WA, NT
Phyllodes are 2-5 cm long and there can be spines along the branchlets. Globular pale yellow flower-heads are produced in Aug.-Dec. It is an adaptable species, suited to a wide range of fairly well-drained situations.
H O SS D M L SA G CA C1 F1
Chart 10c, Chapter 14

Acmena smithii, Lilly Pilly
10-20 m x 5-15 m Qld, NSW, Vic, NT
This small to medium tree has dark green, shiny leaves. Relatively insignificant cream to greenish flowers are followed by globular, white, pink or purple succulent fruits which are produced during May-Aug. These fruits are edible and can be used for jam making. They are also eaten by birds.
O S SS D M L SA G C1 F1 B
Chart 8c, Chapter 13

61 **Actinotus helianthi**, Flannel Flower
0.3-1.5 m x 0.5-1 m Qld, NSW
A herbaceous plant with soft, grey-green foliage. Has daisy-like flowers to 8 cm diam. The soft, white to cream bracts are tipped with grey-green. They have a texture like that of flannel. The centre of the flower is yellow. Flowering is mainly during Aug.-Feb. Plants can be annual or continue growing for several years. They will frequently self-seed in a garden. Grown as a cut flower.
O S SS D M L SA C1 F1
Chart 18, Chapter 22

Actinotus leucocephalus
0.3-1 m x 0.2-2.5 m WA
The white to cream flower-heads of this species are up to 5 cm diam. Flowering is usually during Sept.-Feb. Seeds germinate readily after bushfires. Plants grow best in semi-shade with a well-drained situation. See also notes for *A. helianthi* (above).
O SS D L SA C1 F1
Chart 18, Chapter 22

Actinotus superbus, Western Flannel Flower
0.3-1 m x 0.2-2.5 m WA
This species is very similar to *A. leucocephalus* (above) but with more hairy bracts. Seed will usually germinate readily. Suitable for cultivation in gardens or containers.
O SS D L SA C1 F1
Chart 18, Chapter 22

Adiantum aethiopicum, Common Maidenhair Fern
0.3 m x 1 m All states
A very well-known fern, with branched fronds and many small, rounded segments. It is a widely cultivated species and is suitable for gardens or containers. Many of the problems experienced by growers result from over-watering.
O SS D M L SA C1 F1
Chart 19, Chapter 23

Agonis flexuosa, Willow Myrtle; Willow Peppermint
8-15 m x 5-15 m WA
A widely cultivated, small to medium tree, with long, narrow leaves. Clusters of small, white flowers are produced along the branches during Sept.-Jan. It is hardy to most conditions with the exception of heavy frosts. Smaller forms are also now obtainable.
H O SS D M L SA CA C2
Chart 16, Chapter 19

Agonis juniperina, Juniper Myrtle
5-10 m x 3-5 m WA
An upright species, with fibrous bark and often pendulous branches. The leaves are small and dense along the branches. Clusters of small, white flowers are produced in Feb.-March and also in Aug.-Nov.
H O SS W L SA G C1 F1
Chart 3, Chapter 3

Albizia lophantha, Cape Wattle
2-8 m x 1-3 m WA
A tall shrub to small tree with ferny leaves. Yellowish-green, soft, bottlebrush flower-heads are produced over a long period mainly during May-Sept. It is a very quick-growing species. It should be grown with other plants if a screen is required as it can suffer damage from borers, which can reduce the life of the plant. Prune after flowering.
H O SS D L SA C1 F1 B
Chart 13, Chapter 17

51 **Allocasuarina littoralis**, Black She-oak
4-8 m x 2-4 m Qld, NSW, Vic, Tas
A slender tree with fine foliage. Rusty-brown, male flower-spikes are produced in March-May. Adaptable to a wide range of well-drained situations. Was known as *Casuarina littoralis.*
H O SS D L SA G C2 F2
Chart 2c, Chapter 3

Allocasuarina luehmannii, Bull-oak
8-25 m x 5-10 m Qld, NSW, Vic, SA
A tree with dark, furrowed bark and long, narrow foliage. Yellowish male flower-spikes are seen mainly in Oct.-Nov. A useful tree for shelter or windbreak purposes, particularly in areas of heavy soils. Is best planted in groups. Was known as *Casuarina luehmannii.*
H O SS M W L CA C1 F1
Chart 3, Chapter 3

Allocasuarina muelleriana, Slaty She-oak
1-4 m x 0.5-1.5 m Vic, SA
A tall, shrubby species, with long, slender, grey-green foliage. Reddish male flowers are produced in Oct.-March. Grows naturally in warm, well-drained areas, and is tolerant of sand or clay soils. Was known as *Casuarina muelleriana.*
H O SS D L SA G CA C1 F2
Chart 10b, Chapter 14

Allocasuarina pusilla, Dwarf She-oak
0.5-3 m x 1-2 m Vic, SA
A bushy, dwarf she-oak, with deep red male flowers, seen during March-Oct. It is an adaptable species, able to grow in clays or sandy soils. Was known as *Casuarina pusilla.*
H O SS M W L SA CA C1 F1
Chart 3, Chapter 3

Allocasuarina torulosa, Forest Oak
8-25 m x 5-10 m Qld, NSW
The variable foliage colour of this species can be reddish or almost black. Trees have a rusty-brown appearance when in flower during March-June. An ornamental and widely cultivated species, adaptable to a range of situations. May reach only 10 m in cultivation. Was known as *Casuarina torulosa.*
H O SS D W L SA G C1 F2
Charts 2c, Chapter 3; 7c, Chapter 10

Allocasuarina verticillata, Drooping She-oak
4-11 m x 3-6 m NSW, Vic, Tas, SA
An attractive tree with an erect trunk and dark, furrowed bark. The long, narrow foliage is pendulous. Yellow-brown male flowers are produced during March-Dec. This species is hardy to a wide range of conditions, including exposed coastal situations. It prefers well-drained situations, but will tolerate wet periods. Was known as *Casuarina stricta.*
H O SS D W L SA G CA C2 F1
Charts 5, Chapter 3; 12b, Chapter 16; 16, Chapter 18

Alyogyne huegelii
1-2.5 m x 1-3 m SA, WA
A large, open shrub with dark green, lobed leaves. Mauve, hibiscus-like flowers of 7-10 cm diam. are produced throughout the year. Prefers a sunny position that is moist with good drainage. Pruning will promote bushy growth.
H O SS D L SA G CA C1 F1 B
Chart 13, Chapter 17

Angianthus tomentosus, Camel-grass; Hairy Angianthus
0.1-0.4 m x 0.2-0.5 m
NSW, Vic, SA, WA, NT
An ornamental, dwarf annual with pale yellow, cylindrical flower-heads to about 1.5 cm long produced mainly during Aug.-Jan. Likes a sunny, well-drained, frost-free situation. Although not widely grown, seed of this species can be obtained through specialist native seed suppliers.
H O SS D SA C1
Chart 18, Chapter 22

Angophora costata, Smooth-barked Apple
10-30 m x 6-15 m Qld, NSW
This species has highly decorative, smooth bark. New bark is bright orange to pink-brown. Profuse white to cream flowers are seen during Nov.-Feb. Hardy to a wide range of soil and climatic conditions. Can suffer frost damage, particularly while young.
H O SS D L SA C1 B
Charts 1c, Chapter 3; 8c, Chapter 13

Angophora floribunda, Rough-barked Apple
10-25 m x 6-15 m Qld, NSW, Vic
A small to medium tree with rough bark. It has a profuse display of white to cream flowers during Sept.-Jan. It will adapt to a wide range of conditions, but can suffer frost damage whilst young.
H O SS D M L SA C1 F1
Chart 12b, Chapter 16

Angophora hispida, Dwarf Apple
3-10 m x 3-6 m NSW
A spreading tree with flaky bark. The branchlets and flower-buds are covered in reddish hairs. Cream flowers of 2 cm diam. are borne in dense clusters during Nov.-Feb. This species grows best in a sunny, well-drained situation.
H O SS D L SA G C1 F1
Chart 12b, Chapter 16

Anigozanthos bicolor, Little Kangaroo Paw
0.3-0.6 m x 0.5-1 m WA
Has strap-like leaves to around 40 cm long. Flower-stems are to 0.6 m tall and the tubular flowers are deep red with green. Suited to a fairly sunny situation. Can be grown in gardens or containers.
H O D L SA G C1 F1 B
Chart 1a, Chapter 3

16 **Anigozanthos flavidus**, Tall Kangaroo Paw
0.5-1 m x 1 m WA
A clump-forming plant with long, strap-like leaves. Flower-stems produced in Oct.-Feb. are up to 3 m tall. The tubular flowers can be green, yellow, orange, pink or red. Likes a sunny situation with moist soil.
H O D M L SA G CA C1 F1 B
Charts 2a, Chapter 3; 8a, Chapter 13

Anigozanthos humilis, Cat's Paw
0.2 m x 0.5-1 m WA
A variable, low growing plant with flower colours of creamy yellow, orange, pink or red. Flowering is mainly during June-Dec. Likes a sunny situation. Excellent for containers, also for gardens provided there is adequate slug and snail control.
H O D M L SA G C1 F1 B
Chart 1a, Chapter 3

Anigozanthos rufus, Red Kangaroo Paw
0.3-0.75 m x 1 m WA
A clump-forming species with leaves to around 60 cm long. Flower-stems are about 1.5 m tall. The tubular flowers are deep red, and are seen mainly during Sept.-Feb. Requires fairly good drainage.
H O D L SA G C1 F1 B
Chart 8a, Chapter 13

Anigozanthos viridis, Green Kangaroo Paw
0.3 m x 0.5 m WA
A clump-forming plant, with yellow-green to emerald green flowers, produced in July-Dec. This Kangaroo Paw will tolerate a moist situation, but flowers best in full or partial sun.
H O D M L SA G C1 F1 B
Chart 1a, Chapter 3

Araucaria bidwillii, Bunya Pine
30-50 m x 10-20 m Qld
A handsome tree with glossy, dark green leaves and woody cones to 30 cm long. Requires adequate space to develop fully. Young plants are often used as indoor container plants.
H O SS D M L SA CA C1 F1
Chart 5, Chapter 3

Asplenium australasicum, Bird's Nest Fern
1-2 m x 1-2 m Qld, NSW
An unusual fern with large, erect, radiating, undivided fronds to 2 m x 0.2 m. It is a nest-shaped plant with a fairly small root system, and often grows in forks of trees. It is suited to cultivation in containers, or in well-drained garden situations with some sunshine.
S SS D M L SA C1 F1
Chart 19, Chapter 23

Asplenium bulbiferum, Mother Spleenwort
1-2 m x 1.5 m Qld, NSW, Vic, Tas, SA
This fern has large, upright or semi-weeping fronds to 1.2 m long. Young plantlets are often produced near the frond tips. Popular for cultivation in gardens or containers. It grows well in hanging baskets.
S SS D M L SA C1 F1
Chart 19, Chapter 23

Asplenium simplicifrons
0.6 m x 0.5-1 m Qld
The fronds on this species are strap-like, to around 60 cm long by 3 cm wide. The species is similar to *A. australasicum* (above), although smaller. It appreciates some humidity.
S SS D M L SA C1 F1
Chart 19, Chapter 23

Astartea fascicularis
1-2.5 m x 2-3 m WA
A decorative shrub, with pink buds which open to white (or sometimes pink), open-petalled flowers. Flowering is over a long period during June-March. It is a hardy plant. It responds well to pruning and is useful as a cut flower.
H O SS W L SA G CA C1 F1
Charts 2b, Chapter 3; 16, Chapter 19

Astroloma ciliatium, Candle Cranberry
0.5-1 m x 1-2 m WA
Small, bright green leaves are tightly packed along the stems of this species. The flowers are cigar-shaped and have a bright red tube tipped with greenish-yellow and black. Main flowering is May-Nov. Light pruning is recommended to promote bushy growth.
O SS D L SA G C1 F1 B
Chart 8a, Chapter 13

Astroloma humifusum, Cranberry Heath
0.1-0.5 m x 0.5-1.5 m
NSW, Vic, Tas, SA, WA
Has narrow, grey-green leaves with pointed tips. Bright red, tubular flowers are produced in March-Oct. A hardy and adaptable low plant suited to a wide range of well-drained situations.
O SS D L SA G C2 F2 B
Chart 1a, Chapter 3

Atriplex cinerea, Coast Saltbush; Grey Saltbush
1-2 m x 2-3 m All states
This species has decorative, silver-grey foliage. The cream to purplish flowers produced in Sept.-March are very small, usually with male and female flowers on separate plants. Prefers full or partial sun with well-drained soils. Excellent for coastal areas and soil erosion control.
H O SS D L SA G CA C2 F2
Chart 4, Chapter 3

Atriplex nummularia, Old Man Saltbush
1-3 m x 2-4 m
Inland areas of Qld, NSW, Vic, SA, WA, NT
A dense shrub with bluish-grey foliage. Small, creamish male and female flowers are borne on separate plants during most of the year. A hardy species, grown mainly for its foliage. Prune for bushy growth. Useful for screens and windbreaks. Is also fire-retardant.
H O SS D L SA G CA C1 F2
Charts 7b, Chapter 10; 12a, Chapter 16; 16, Chapter 19

Atriplex rhagodioides, Silver Saltbush
0.5-2 m x 1-2 m NSW, Vic, SA, WA
The foliage and flowers of this species are similar to *A. cinerea* (above). Flowers are produced for most of the year. A very hardy shrub with decorative silver-grey foliage. Will tolerate hard pruning and foliage can be eaten by stock. Is also fire-retardant.
H O SS D L SA G CA C1 F2
Charts 4, Chapter 3; 10b, Chapter 14

Austromyrtus dulcis, Midgen Berry
0.5-1.5 m x 1-2 m Qld, NSW
A low shrub, with bright pink new growth covered with silky hairs. White flowers of about 1 cm diam. are produced in March-June. These are followed by edible black berries which are enjoyed by birds. Prefers well-drained soils with a sunny position.
H O SS D L SA C2 B
Chart 8a, Chapter 13

Baeckea behrii, Broom Baeckea
0.5-2 m x 0.5-0.8 m NSW, Vic, SA, WA
A slender shrub with small, white or rarely pink, open-petalled flowers, produced mainly during Aug.-Dec. A drought-resistant species native to inland Australia. It prefers a warm situation but will grow in cooler climates.
H O SS D L SA G CA C1 F2
Chart 5, Chapter 3

Baeckea linifolia, Weeping Baeckea
1-3 m x 1-2.5 m Qld, NSW, Vic
An upright or spreading shrub with pendulous branches. The leaves are small and narrow, often with bronze-red tonings. Has a profuse display of small white flowers during Dec.-March. A very attractive species for planting beside ponds.
H O SS M W L SA G C1 F1
Chart 2b, Chapter 3

9 **Baeckea ramosissima**, Rosy Baeckea; Rosy Heath-myrtle
0.3-1 m x 0.3-1.5 m NSW, Vic, Tas, SA
A spreading plant with wiry branches and small leaves. White to deep pink flowers of up to 1.5 cm diam. are produced mainly during June-Feb. It is a variable species with several forms popular in cultivation. Prefers a sunny, well-drained yet moist situation.
O SS D M W L SA G C1 F2
Chart 7a, Chapter 10

Baeckea ramosissima ssp. **prostrata**, Rosy Heath-myrtle
0.1-0.5 m x 1-1.5 m NSW, Vic, Tas, SA
White to deep pink flowers of up to 1.5 cm diam. are produced mainly in July-Nov. Not all forms of *B. ramosissima* will layer, but this prostrate form often puts down roots.
O SS M W L SA G C1 F2
Chart 22, Chapter 28

Baeckea virgata, Tall Baeckea; Twiggy Baeckea
0.2-6 m x 2-3 m Qld, NSW, Vic, NT
Several forms of this species are grown, from groundcovers to tall shrubs. Some have pendulous foliage. There is a showy display of small white flowers produced near the ends of the branchlets in Nov.-March.
H O SS W L SA G C1 F1
Charts 7b, Chapter 10; 11, Chapter 15

Banksia baueri, Koala Banksia; Possum Banksia
2-5 m x 2-4 m WA
A bushy shrub with leaves having toothed margins. Flower-heads of up to 40 cm x 20 cm are produced during June-Nov. They are commonly mauve-grey but can also be orange-brown. Suited to well-drained soils with partial or full sun. The common names refer to the large flower heads.
H O SS D L SA G C1 F2
Charts 1b, Chapter 3; 10b, Chapter 14

17 **Banksia baxteri**, Bird's-nest Banksia
3-4 m x 3-5 m WA
The leaves of this species are up to 15 cm long and have deep triangular lobes. Flower-heads, seen in Nov.-March, are dome-shaped and yellow-green. Grows best in well-drained soils with partial or full sun. Is grown commercially for cut flowers.
H O SS D L SA G C1 F2 B
Chart 1b, Chapter 3

39 **Banksia ericifolia**, Heath-leaved Banksia
3-6 m x 2-5 m Qld, NSW
The leaves of this banksia are small and narrow. Flower-heads of up to 25 cm long are produced in April-Nov. Colours include yellow, orange, deep red and creams. An adaptable species with a preference for well-drained soils. Plants must be propagated from cuttings if flower colour the same as that of the parent plant is desired.
H O SS D L SA G C1 F1 B
Charts 1c, Chapter 3; 8c, Chapter 13

Banksia integrifolia, Coast Banksia
10-20 m x 5-10 m Qld, NSW, Vic, Tas
The leaves of this tree grow to 15 cm long and are dull green above and silvery below. Pale yellow flower-heads to 15 cm long are produced mainly during April-Sept. It prefers a sunny situation and will grow in very exposed coastal areas.
H O SS D L SA CA C2 F1 B
Chart 16, Chapter 19

Banksia marginata, Silver Banksia
1-10 m x 0.5-5 m NSW, Vic, Tas, SA
A variable species with plants often remaining low and bushy under exposed conditions. The leaves have a silvery undersurface. Pale to bright yellow flower-spikes of 4-10 cm long are produced mainly during March-Sept. Responds well to pruning.
H O SS D L SA G CA C2 F2
Chart 17, Chapter 21

Banksia occidentalis, Red Swamp Banksia
3-8 m x 2-5 m WA
Leaves are 5-15 cm long with a white undersurface. Flower-heads, mainly in Dec.-April, are to 15 cm long and are cream to yellow with bright red styles. This species will adapt to moist or well-drained situations. Likes full or partial sun.
H O SS D M L SA C1 F1 B
Chart 1c, Chapter 3

Banksia paludosa, Marsh Banksia
0.5-1.5 m x 0.5-1.5 m NSW
A low, spreading shrub, with yellow to brownish flower-heads to 10 cm long, seen in April-July. This species often grows naturally in moist locations, but it is also suitable for well-drained situations.
H O SS M W L SA C1 F1 B
Chart 11, Chapter 15

Banksia prionotes, Acorn Banksia
4-6 m x 4 m WA
In its natural habitat this species can grow to 12 m x 6 m. It has serrated leaves and highly spectacular whitish-grey buds gradually opening to bright orange flower-heads. Flowering is mainly during Feb.-Aug. The species has a strong preference for deep, sandy soils. It must have a very well-drained situation. An excellent cut flower.
H O D L SA G C1 F2 B
Chart 1c, Chapter 3

Banksia robur, Swamp Banksia
0.5-3 m x 0.5-2 cm Qld, NSW
This species has large, stiff leaves to 30 cm x 10 cm. The flower-buds are a rich bluish-green, with flower-heads being yellow-green at maturity. They can be seen during most of the year. A showy species suited to well-drained or periodically wet situations.
H O SS M W L SA G C2 F1 B
Chart 3, Chapter 3

Banksia serrata, Saw Banksia
10-20 m x 5-12 m Qld, NSW, Vic, Tas
The leaves of this banksia are toothed and to 16 cm long. Greenish-yellow flower-heads to 16 cm x 10 cm are produced in Aug.-April. An adaptable species which occurs naturally in protected or exposed coastal situations.
H O SS D L SA C2 F1 B
Chart 16, Chapter 19

Banksia speciosa, Showy Banksia
3-6 m x 3-8 m WA
This species has serrated leaves to 40 cm long. Flower-heads are up to 15 cm x 12 cm and are greyish, opening to yellow. They are seen from Dec.-Sept. It is a long-flowering banksia, preferring a well-drained situation with full or partial sun. Is grown for cut flowers.
H O SS D L SA G C1 F2 B
Charts 1c, Chapter 3; 16, Chapter 19

50 **Banksia spinulosa**, Hairpin Banksia
3-6 m x 2-4 m Qld, NSW, Vic
This species also has dwarf forms which grow to 1-2 m x 1-3 m. The leaves are serrated and to 8 cm long. Flower-heads, produced during March-Aug, can be yellow or amber with black or red styles. The species is hardy in most well-drained, acid soils.
H O S SS D L SA G C1 F2 B
Charts 2b, Chapter 3; 9, Chapter 13

Bauera rubioides, Wiry Bauera
0.2-3 m x 1-3 m Qld, NSW, Vic, Tas, SA
This species has white to pink, open-petalled flowers of around 2 cm diam. through most of the year. It is a hardy plant, adaptable to a wide range of garden conditions. Responds well to pruning.
H O S SS M W L SA G C1 F2
Charts 7a, Chapter 10; 11, Chapter 15; 21, Chapter 27

Bauera sessiliflora, Grampians Bauera
2-3 m x 2-3 m Vic
This bauera provides a showy display of rosy-purple to magenta flowers of 1-1.5 cm diam. during spring. It is well suited to shaded areas. Responds well to light pruning and should be tip-pruned from an early age to maintain bushy growth.
S SS M W L SA G F2
Chart 21, Chapter 27

Beaufortia orbifolia, Ravensthorpe Bottlebrush
2-3 m x 2-3 m WA
This species is usually of fairly upright habit, but spreading forms are also available. The flower-heads, produced Nov.-July, are lime-green with red tips, maturing to all red. Plants respond well to light pruning.
H O SS W L SA G C1 F2 B
Charts 2b, Chapter 3; 10b, Chapter 14

Beaufortia sparsa, Gravel Bottlebrush; Swamp Bottlebrush
2-4 m x 1-3 m WA
This relatively hardy species has dense green leaves. Bright reddish-orange flower-heads are produced during Dec.-April. Plants are adaptable to a range of garden situations. They respond well to light pruning.
H O SS M W L SA G C1 F1 B
Chart 1b, Chapter 3

Billardiera cymosa, Sweet Apple-berry
Light climber Vic, SA
This species can grow as a small shrub if climbing support is not available. White, cream, green or pink to pale blue, tubular flowers are produced mainly during Aug.-Dec. These are followed by oblong, reddish-green berries. Plants appreciate protection for the root sytem if grown in a hot location.
H O SS D L SA G CA C1 F2
Chart 14, Chapter 17

57 **Billardiera longiflora**, Purple Apple-berry
Light climber NSW, Vic, Tas
This billardiera has dark green, shiny leaves. Greenish-yellow, tubular flowers, seen in Aug.-Dec., are followed by soft, shiny, deep bluish-purple, oblong fruits which are particularly decorative. Plants grow best in relatively shaded situations.
O S SS M L SA C1 F2 B
Chart 14, Chapter 17

Billardiera ringens, Chapman Creeper
Light climber WA
The deep green leaves of this species are to 10 cm long. Flowers are initially orange, then deepen to red. They are seen mainly during Aug.-March. It is a light climber which can also be grown amongst other plants.
H O SS D L SA G C1 F1 B
Chart 14, Chapter 17

42 **Blandfordia grandiflora**, Christmas Bells
0.3-0.8 m x 0.2-0.4 m Qld, NSW
A tufting, grass-like plant with large, very showy, bell-shaped flowers on stems taller than the foliage during Dec.-Jan. The flowers are usually red or orange with yellow. Prefers a moist situation. Suitable for cultivation in gardens or containers.
O SS M L SA G C1 F1 B
Chart 8a, Chapter 13

Blechnum fluviatile, Ray Water-fern
0.5 m x 1 m NSW, Vic, Tas
A prostrate fern with spreading fronds of up to 50 cm long, produced in wheel-like formation. It is quick-growing with a preference for shaded and moist situations.
S SS D M L SA C1 F1
Chart 19, Chapter 23

Blechnum minus, Soft Water-fern
0.5-1 m x 0.5-1 m Qld, NSW, Vic, Tas, SA
This popular species has large, erect or arching fronds with narrow, well-spaced segments. The new growth is often pinkish. Excellent for wet situations.
O S SS D M W L SA C1 F2
Chart 19, Chapter 23

Blechnum nudum, Fishbone Water-fern
1-2 m x 0.5-1 m Qld, NSW, Vic, Tas, SA
This fern can develop a trunk to around 1 m tall after many years. The fishbone-like fronds are around 1 m long. It is a fairly widely grown fern. Has a preference for moist, sheltered situations.
O S SS D M W L SA C1 F2
Chart 19, Chapter 23

Blechnum penna-marina, Alpine Water-fern
0.2 m x 1 m NSW, Vic, Tas
A low, spreading fern, with small, divided fronds to around 20 cm long. The species is ideal for containers or for growing beneath other plants in moist situations.
O S SS M L SA C1 F2
Chart 19, Chapter 23

Blechnum wattsii, Hard Water-fern
0.5-1 m x 0.5-1 m Qld, NSW, Vic, Tas, SA
Has dark green, deeply divided, leathery fronds with broad, serrated segments. The new growth of this species is shiny and can be reddish.
O S SS D M W L SA C1 F2
Chart 19, Chapter 23

Boronia filifolia, Slender Boronia
0.3-0.5 m x 1-2 m Vic, SA
A dwarf shrub with slender leaves which can be purplish. Flowering is mainly during Aug.-Jan. The flowers are pink and around 1 cm diam. Prefers well-drained soils in partial or filtered sun. Responds well to regular light pruning.
O S SS D L SA CA C1 F1
Chart 1a, Chapter 3

31 **Boronia megastigma**, Brown Boronia
1-3 m x 1-2 m WA
A widely grown species with highly fragrant, small, open-bell flowers during July-Nov. They are commonly brown to reddish-brown outside with a yellow or lime-green interior, but other selected forms have burgundy or lime-green flowers. Grows best in moist soil with relatively good drainage. The roots should not be allowed to dry out. It prefers semi-shade or morning sun only, but will grow in full sun.
O SS D M L SA G C1 F2
Chart 7b, Chapter 10

Boronia pinnata, Pinnate Boronia
1-2 m x 1-2 m NSW
A showy plant, popular in cultivation. The leaves are pinnate with a camphor-like fragrance. Bright pink, open-petalled flowers of up to 2 cm diam. are borne in clusters along the branchlets during Sept.-Dec. It is an adaptable species with a preference for semi-shade and relatively well-drained soils.
O S SS D M L SA G C1 F2
Chart 7b, Chapter 10

Brachychiton acerifolius, Flame Tree
10-40 m x 10-15 m Qld, NSW
This rainforest tree is relatively slow-growing and may not reach full height in cultivation. During Oct.-March it sheds nearly all its leaves and becomes covered in bright red, bell-shaped flowers.
H O SS D L SA CA C1 F1
Chart 2c, Chapter 3

46 **Brachychiton discolor**, Lacebark; White Kurrajong
10-30 m x 5-15 m Qld, NSW
This marginal rainforest tree usually grows to a smaller size in cooler areas. It can provide a very profuse display of dull pink to red, bell-shaped flowers during Nov.-March. These are followed by brown, woody fruits of 7-12 cm long.
H O SS D L SA CA C1 F1
Chart 10c, Chapter 14

Brachychiton populneus, Kurrajong
6-20 m x 3-6 m Qld, NSW, Vic, NT
This species has cream or pink, bell-shaped flowers with red markings inside. They are seen mainly during Oct.-Feb. It is an ornamental tree grown widely for shade and shelter or as a street tree. Young plants are grown often indoors.
H O SS D L SA G CA C1 F2
Charts 2c, 5, Chapter 3

Brachychiton rupestre, Bottle Tree
10-20 m x 5-15 m Qld, NSW
This unusual tree has a bottle-shaped trunk and attractive, lobed leaves. It is slow-growing and takes many years to exceed 5-10 m in cultivation. Small, yellowish, bell-shaped flowers are produced in Oct.-Dec. Can be frost-tender.
H O S SS D L SA G CA C1
Chart 10c, Chapter 14

Brachyscome iberidifolia, Swan River Daisy
0.3-0.5 m x 0.3-1 m SA, WA, NT
This brachyscome flowers mainly during Sept.-Feb. with daisy flower-heads to 2 cm diam. They can be white, blue or purple with yellow centres. The species is fairly widely grown both in Australia and Europe. It can be frost-tender and should be cultivated as a summer annual.
O SS D L SA C1
Chart 18, Chapter 22

12 **Brachyscome multifida**, Cut-leaf Daisy
0.5 m x 1-1.5 m Qld, NSW, Vic
A clump-forming plant which can flower throughout the year. The small, daisy flowers are purple, blue-mauve, pink or white. Suited to a wide range of soil and climatic conditions, but flowers best in partial to full sun.
H O SS M L SA G C1 F2
Charts 2a, Chapter 3; 21, Chapter 27

Brachyscome sp. aff. **melanocarpa**
0.05-0.4 x 0.2-1 m NSW
A small, herbaceous suckering perennial with daisy flowers of around 4 cm diam. They are mauve-pink with yellow centres and are seen mainly during Sept.-March. Suited to a wide range of well-drained situations.
O SS D M L SA G C1 F1
Chart 23, Chapter 28

Brachysema lanceolatum, Dark Bush-pea; Swan River Pea
0.5-2 m x 1-3 m WA
The leaves are grey-green to dark green above with a silvery undersurface. Red pea-flowers are produced along the branches mainly during June-Oct. A hardy plant that will grow in a wide range of situations. It flowers best in a sunny position.
H O SS D W L SA G C1 F1 B
Charts 12a, Chapter 16; 17, Chapter 21

Brachysema latifolium see **B.** species

Brachysema praemorsum
Prostrate to 1 m x 1-3 m WA
The leaves of this groundcover are to 3 cm long and appear cut-off at the apex. The pea-shaped flowers, produced mainly during May-Feb., are initially cream then deepen to red. An adaptable plant, suited to most well-drained soils. It prefers filtered or partial sun. Responds well to light pruning.
H O SS W L SA G C1 F1 B
Chart 2a, Chapter 3

Brachysema sericeum
Prostrate to 1 m x 1-4 m WA
A dense groundcover with narrow leaves to 5 cm long. The pea-shaped flowers produced in July-Jan. are usually pale yellow-green, cream or blackish. Has a preference for fairly well-drained soils in filtered or partial sun. Will tolerate full sun.
O SS D M L SA G C1 F1 B
Charts 2a, Chapter 3; 15, Chapter 18

Brachysema sericeum var. **latifolium**, see **B.** species

Brachysema species (currently un-named)
Prostrate x 1-2.5 m WA
This species has dark green leaves which are more-or-less oval. Short red with yellow pea-flowers are produced in Feb.-Oct. A hardy and widely grown plant which does best in well-drained soils with partial sun. There has been confusion regarding the correct name and plants are sometimes sold as *B. latifolium* or *B. sericeum* var. *latifolium*.
O SS D M L SA G C1 F1 B
Charts 8a, Chapter 13; 22, Chapter 28

Callistemon brachyandrus, Prickly Bottlebrush
1-5 m x 1-3 m NSW, Vic, SA
A dense shrub with pointed leaves. Bottlebrush flowers of around 4 cm long are produced mainly during Dec.-April. They are orange-red tipped with gold. This species is frost-tolerant and drought-resistant and grows well in a warm to hot situation.
H O D M L SA G C2 F2 B
Chart 7b, Chapter 10

Callistemon 'Burgundy'
2-4 m x 2-4 m Cultivar
Has deep red to burgundy bottlebrushes of 8-10 cm long. They are produced in Sept.-Dec. and sometimes also in March-April. This cultivar is a selected seedling of *C.* 'Reeves Pink'. It is hardy to a range of situations and responds well to pruning.
H O SS W L SA G C1 F1 B
Chart 2b, Chapter 3

Callistemon citrinus, Crimson Bottlebrush
2-8 m x 2-6 m NSW, Vic
A showy species with several forms. Has bright red bottlebrush flower-heads during Sept.-Dec., and often also in March-April. Plants will flower in autumn, as well as in spring, if they receive some summer moisture. Responds well to pruning.
H O SS W L SA G C1 F1 B
Charts 3, Chapter 3; 11, Chapter 15

Callistemon 'Harkness'
3-6 m x 2-6 m Cultivar
A very showy cultivar. New leaf growth is pink. Bright red flower-spikes to 15 cm long are produced mainly during Sept.-Jan. It is popular in cultivation and adaptable to a wide range of conditions. Responds well to pruning after flowering.
H O SS W L SA G CA C1 F1 B
Charts 5, Chapter 3; 8c, Chapter 13

Callistemon macropunctatus, Scarlet Bottlebrush
2-4 m x 2-4 m NSW, Vic, SA
An open to dense shrub. Flower-spikes are up to 10 cm long and are red tipped with gold. A hardy and adaptable species. Prefers full or partial sun. Responds well to pruning.
H O SS M W L SA C1 F2 B
Chart 1b, Chapter 3

Callistemon 'Mauve Mist'
2-4 m x 2-4 m Cultivar
This cultivar has mauve bottlebrushes of 8-10 cm long. All other comments as for *C.* 'Burgundy' (above).
Chart 2b, Chapter 3

Callistemon pallidus, Lemon Bottlebrush
2-5 m x 2-5 m NSW, Vic, Tas
A dense shrub which has grey-green to dark green leaves with silvery or reddish new growth. Cream to yellow bottlebrush flower-spikes are produced during Sept.-Jan. A hardy species. Withstands winds, frost, periods of waterlogging and moderate coastal exposure.
H O SS W L SA G C1 F2 B
Chart 16, Chapter 19

Callistemon phoeniceus, Lesser Bottlebrush
2-4 m x 3-5 m WA
This species has large flower-spikes to around 12 cm x 5 cm, mainly during Aug.-Jan. They are usually brilliant red, but can be pink. It is a spectacular plant in flower. Responds well to pruning. A prostrate to low spreading form is also cultivated, but not widely available.
H O SS W L SA G C1 F1 B
Charts 2b, Chapter 3; 12a, Chapter 16

Callistemon 'Reeves Pink'
2-4 m x 2-4 m Cultivar
Has bottlebrush flowers of pink tipped with gold. They are 8-10 cm x 6 cm, and are seen during Oct.-Dec. and sometimes also March-April. This cultivar is a selected seedling from *C. citrinus* (above). All *Callistemon* cultivars and forms are commonly propagated from cuttings to retain the characteristics of the parent plants. Variations can ocur in plants grown from seed.
H O SS W L SA G C1 F1 B
Chart 2b, Chapter 3

Callistemon salignus, Pink Tips; Willow Bottlebrush
5-15 m x 3-5 m Qld, NSW, SA
This species commonly grows as a small tree to 8 m high in cultivation. New foliage growth is often bright pink to red. Bottlebrush flower-spikes of white to deep pink are produced in Sept.-Dec. Hardy and suited to a wide range of garden situations.
H O SS W L SA G C1 F1 B
Charts 4, Chapter 3; 12b, Chapter 16

Callistemon sieberi, Alpine Bottlebrush
1-5 m x 1-5 m Qld, NSW, Vic
A variable species with cream to yellow flower-spikes of 2-15 cm long. Main flowering time is Nov.-Feb. It is hardy and adaptable and responds well to pruning. Plants are propagated from cuttings to ensure desired forms.
H O SS M W L SA C1 F2 B
Chart 11, Chapter 15

Callistemon speciosus, Albany Bottlebrush
2-4 m x 1-3 m WA
An erect, stiff shrub with rigid leaves to 15 cm long. The flower-spikes produced in Aug.-March are deep red tipped with gold. Grows best in a sunny position with moist to wet soils. Will also do well in many other situations.
H O SS M W L SA C1 F1 B
Chart 3, Chapter 3

Callistemon subulatus, Tonghi Bottlebrush
2-4 m x 2-4 m NSW, Vic
A branched shrub, with crowded leaves of up to 5 cm long. Deep red flower-spikes of around 6 cm long are produced mainly during Oct.-Dec. Adaptable to a fairly wide range of situations. Pruning after flowering will promote bushy growth.
H O SS W L SA G C1 F1 B
Chart 8b, Chapter 13

Callistemon teretifolius
1-3 m x 2-4 m SA
A fairly open shrub with pointed green leaves and silky new growth. Crimson brushes are produced mainly during Oct.-Feb. This species from the Flinders Ranges, SA, prefers a sunny, well-drained situation.
H O SS D L SA G CA C1 F1 B
Chart 5, Chapter 3

Callistemon viminalis, Weeping Bottlebrush
1-12 m x 1.5-6 m Qld, NSW
Dwarf and tall forms of this species are all popular in cultivation. Red bottlebrush flower-spikes are produced mainly during Nov.-March. A variable species, hardy to a wide range of situations.
H O SS W L SA G C1 B
Charts 8c, Chapter 13; 15, Chapter 18

Callistemon viridiflorus, Green Bottlebrush
1-3 m x 1-2 m Tas
A fairly upright plant with yellow-green brushes produced mainly during Nov.-Jan. Will grow well in moist or even temporarily waterlogged conditions.
H O SS W L SA G C1 F2 B
Chart 2b, Chapter 3

Callitris rhomboidea, Oyster Bay Pine; Port Jackson Pine
3-6 m x 2-3 m Qld, NSW, SA, WA
This conifer-like tree is grown mainly for its neat shape, dense green or glaucous foliage, and drooping branchlets. It is a hardy tree tolerant of poor soils and extended periods of dryness.
H O SS D L SA G C2 F1
Chart 10c, Chapter 14

48 **Calocephalus brownii**, Cushion Bush
0.2-2 m x 0.5-3 m
NSW, Vic, Tas, SA, WA
This species has intertwined, stiff, silvery branches and small, scale-like leaves. Pale yellow and white flower-heads are produced during Sept.-Feb. It is grown primarily for the beauty and unusual colour of the foliage. It is an excellent plant for exposed coastal situations.
H O D L SA G CA C2 F1
Charts 10b, Chapter 14; 16, Chapter 19

Calothamnus gilesii, Giles' Net-bush
2-4 m x 2-4 m WA
An open shrub with finely pointed leaves to 20 cm long. Showy clusters of bright red flowers tipped with gold are produced mainly during July-Feb. This species is hardy and adaptable to a range of conditions, but grows best in full sun. Responds well to pruning.
H O SS D L SA G C1 F2 B
Charts 7b, Chapter 10; 10b, Chapter 14

Calothamnus quadrifidus, Common Net-bush
2-4 m x 2-5 m WA
This variable species has narrow, grey to grey-green leaves. Red flowers are produced in Oct.-March. They are in one-sided spikes or encircle the stems. Will tolerate a range of conditions including both wet and dry soils.
H O SS W L SA G C1 F1 B
Charts 1b, 2b, Chapter 3

Calothamnus rupestris, Cliff Net-bush
1-3 m x 2-3 m WA
A bushy species, with dense, pine-like leaves. Deep pink to red, one-sided flower-spikes are produced on the old wood mainly during Aug.-Nov. It is hardy and best suited to a warm, well-drained situation.
H O SS D L SA G C1 F1 B
Chart 8b, Chapter 13

Calytrix aurea
1-2 m x 1-1.5 m WA
An upright shrub. Has starry, golden-yellow flowers with a spicy fragrance, mainly during Nov.-Jan. Prefers well-drained soils and partial or full sun. Responds well to pruning after flowering.
H O SS D L SA G C1 F1
Chart 1b, Chapter 3

34 **Calytrix tetragona**, Common Fringe-myrtle
1-2 m x 1-2 m
Qld, NSW, Vic, Tas, SA, WA
This species has small narrow leaves. Starry open-petalled flowers in shades of white to pink are produced mainly during Aug.-Nov. It likes a well-drained situation in partial or full sun.
H O SS D L SA G C1 F2
Chart 7b, Chapter 10

Carpobrotus modestus, Inland Pigface
Prostrate x 1-3 m Vic, SA, WA
Has thick, fleshy, juicy, 3-sided leaves to 7 cm long. Daisy-like flowers produced in Aug.-Jan. are light purple shading to white near the centre. *Carpobrotus* plants are well known for their ability to survive in hot, dry situations. Plants are useful as living mulches and for soil erosion control.
H O SS D L SA CA C2 F2
Chart 4, Chapter 3

Cassia artemisioides, Silver Cassia
1-2 m x 1 m NSW, SA, NT
This species has silvery, fern-like foliage. Yellow, bell-like flowers are produced in clusters throughout most of the year. The main flowering is in June-Dec. A hardy and adaptable species. Is frost and drought-tolerant.
H O D L SA G CA C1 F2
Charts 7b, Chapter 10; 10b, Chapter 14

Cassia nemophila, Desert Cassia
1-3 m x 1-2 m NSW, Vic, SA, WA, NT
A bushy shrub with green or silvery leaves. Clusters of yellow flowers are produced mainly during June-Nov. It is a hardy species with many forms and hybrids in cultivation. Will grow in hot, dry conditions and also in cooler climates.
H O D L SA G CA C1 F1
Chart 5, Chapter 3

Castanospermum australe, Black Bean
10-30 m x 5-12 m Qld, NSW
A rainforest tree with attractive foliage, often slow-growing when young. Red with yellow, pea-shaped flowers are produced in Sept.-Nov. Birds are attracted to the flowers which are rich in nectar. Is often used as an indoor foliage plant whilst young.
O S SS D M L SA C1 F1 B
Chart 8c, Chapter 13

Casuarina cristata, Belah
8-25 m x 5-10 m Qld, NSW, Vic, SA, WA
A small to medium tree with fine, green to greyish foliage. Yellowish flower-spikes are produced in Oct.-Jan. Has a preference for heavy soil types and can sucker to form colonies.
H O SS M L SA CA C2 F2
Charts 4, Chapter 3; 10c, Chapter 14

Casuarina cunninghamiana, River Oak
10-30 m x 10-12 m Qld, NSW, NT
A tall tree with fine, pendulous foliage. Light brownish male flower-spikes are produced in Dec.-Jan. A quick-growing tree which occurs naturally beside creeks and rivers. It will also grow in well-drained situations.
H O SS M W L SA G CA C1 F1
Chart 3, Chapter 3

Casuarina equisetifolia, Coastal She-oak; Horsetail She-oak
5-20 m x 5-10 m Qld, NSW, NT
A very graceful tree with drooping branches and fine, she-oak foliage. Flowers are relatively insignificant. It is best suited to tropical or sub-tropical regions. Useful for sand-binding and sand erosion control.
H O SS D SA G CA C2 F1
Charts 1c, Chapter 3; 16, Chapter 19

Casuarina glauca, Swamp She-oak
8-30 m x 4-12 m Qld, NSW
A medium to tall tree. Light brownish male flower-spikes are produced in July-Oct. It is hardy and suited to moist or well-drained situations. Can sucker to form a copse.
H O SS M W L SA CA C2 F2
Charts 3, 4, Chapter 3; 12b, Chapter 16; 23, Chapter 28

Casuarina spp., see also **Allocasuarina** spp.

Cephalipterum drummondii
0.2-0.5 m x 0.2-0.75 m SA, WA
A slender, erect annual with globular flower-heads to about 2.5 cm diam. They are white, yellow, yellow-green or rarely pink, and can be seen through most of the year. Suited to sunny, well-drained situations. Responds well to pruning. Seed germinates readily or plants can be grown from cuttings.
H O SS D L SA G CA C1 F2
Chart 18, Chapter 22

Chamelaucium sp. **'Walpole'**, Walpole Wax
1.5-3 m x 1.5-3 m WA
This decorative species provides a profuse display of open-petalled flowers, of about 1.5 cm diam., during Aug.-Nov. The flowers are initially white then age to pink or purple. It is a relatively hardy species. It responds well to pruning and is grown for cut flowers.
H O SS D M L SA G C1 F1
Chart 1b, Chapter 3

Chamelaucium uncinatum, Geraldton Wax
2-5 m x 2-6 m WA
An open shrub with fine foliage. It has open-petalled waxy flowers, to 1.5 cm diam., mainly during Aug.-Jan. They can be white, pink, mauve or reddish-purple. Grows best in a warm, well-drained position. Responds well to pruning. Grown for cut flower production.
H O SS D L SA G CA C1 F2
Chart 10b, Chapter 14

Cheiranthera alternifolia, Finger Flower
0.5-1 m x 0.5-1 m NSW, Vic, SA
This species has slender branches and narrow leaves. Deep blue flowers with yellow anthers are produced mainly during Oct.-Mar. Plants are relatively insignificant when not in flower, and are best grown amongst other small shrubs. Previously known as *C. cyanea* or *C. linearis*.
H O SS D L SA G C1 F2
Chart 10a, Chapter 14

Chiloglottis trapeziformis, Broad-lip Bird Orchid
0.05-0.12 m x 0.05-0.12 cm Qld, NSW, Vic
A small terrestrial orchid with flower-stems to around 10 cm tall. Each plant has a pair of opposite, basal leaves. The flowers, produced during Sept.-Nov., are purple and green. Container cultivation is recommended.
S SS D M L SA C1 F1
Chart 20, Chapter 24

Chorizema diversifolium
Light twining shrub WA
This species is very showy when in full bloom. Pea-shaped flowers of orange, yellow and pink to purple are produced mainly during Sept.-Oct. It grows well in a shaded situation. Can be frost-tender.
O S SS D M L SA G C1
Chart 14, Chapter 17

Claytonia australasica, White Purslane
Prostrate x 1-2 m NSW, Vic, Tas, SA, WA
A creeping, layering or sometimes suckering, perennial plant, with leaves to 10 cm long. It has fragrant, white, open-petalled flowers of 1-2 cm diam. during Aug.-April. Suitable for gardens or containers.
H O SS M W L SA G C1 F2
Chart 22, Chapter 28

54 **Clematis aristata**, Austral Clematis
Vigorous climber Qld, NSW, Vic, Tas
The leaves of this species are divided into 3 leaflets with toothed margins. It has creamy-white, star-like flowers of about 5 cm diam. during Aug.-March. They are followed by creamy-white, feathery seed-heads. Plants grow best if they have a cool root area.
O S SS D M L SA G C1 F2
Chart 14, Chapter 17

Clematis microphylla, Small-leaved Clematis
A dense climber
Qld, NSW, Vic, Tas, SA, WA
Greenish-cream, star-like flowers are produced during July-Nov. and these are followed by profuse, fluffy seed-heads. This can be a quick-growing plant. Pruning will help to promote bushy growth.
H O SS D L SA G CA C1 F2
Chart 14, Chapter 17

Clianthus formosus, Sturt's Desert Pea
Prostrate x 1-4 m Qld, NSW, SA, WA, NT
A well-known plant of desert areas, with soft, grey-green foliage. Spectacular, large pea-shaped flowers are produced during June-March. They are usually red or red with black. It is the floral emblem of SA. It must have a warm, well-drained situation and should be treated as an annual in cultivation. Grafted plants are also now available.
H O D L SA G CA C1 F2
Charts 10a, Chapter 14; 18, Chapter 22

Commersonia pulchella
0.6-1.5 m x 0.5-1 m WA
A compact shrub, with pink to red flower-buds which are followed by mainly white flowers. Flowering period is during Sept.-March. Likes a warm, well-drained situation. Responds well to regular pruning. Will often sucker lightly.
H O SS D L SA G C1 F1
Chart 23, Chapter 28

3 18 **Conostylis aculeata**
0.2-0.4 m x 0.5 m WA
A clump-forming plant with strap-like leaves that often have spiny margins. Tubular yellow flowers are produced in terminal clusters during Aug.-Feb. It likes a sunny situation with fairly good drainage. Suitable for gardens or containers.
H O SS D L SA G C1 F2 B
Chart 1a, Chapter 3

Conostylis bealiana
0.2 m x 0.3 m WA
A very decorative, small, tufting plant with grass-like leaves. Tubular flowers of 3-4 cm long are produced during May-Sept. They are commonly yellow to orange, but can be greenish. Suited to garden cultivation and also excellent for containers.
O SS D M L SA G C1 F1 B
Charts 1a, Chapter 3; 8a, Chapter 13

71 **Conostylis seorsiflora**
Prostrate x 0.3-0.5 m WA
An attractive matting plant with flat leaves to 15 cm long. Tubular yellow flowers are produced in Sept.-Dec. Adaptable to a range of well-drained but moist soils. Prefers partial sun, but will grow in full sun if soil is moist.
O SS D M L SA G C1 F1 B
Chart 22, Chapter 28

Coprosma quadrifida, Prickly Currant Bush
2-4 m x 1-2 m NSW, Vic, Tas
A small twiggy shrub with prickly foliage. It has very small, greenish flowers during Sept.-Nov. followed by oval, edible, bright red, fleshy fruits of around 0.5-0.8 cm long. Grows well in a cool, moist position. The prickly foliage provides protection for small birds.
O S SS M W L SA C1 F2 B
Chart 9, Chapter 13

Cordyline stricta, Slender Palm Lily
2-5 m tall, erect Qld, NSW
Leaves on the upright stems are to 60 cm long. Sprays of purple-violet flowers are produced in Dec.-Feb., and are followed by purple or blackish berries. Hardy to a range of conditions but can be frost-tender. Useful for narrow, shaded areas. Plants will sucker lightly to form a clump.
O S SS M W L SA G C1 F1
Chart 23, Chapter 28

Correa alba, White Correa
0.5-2 m x 1-2 m NSW, Vic, Tas, SA
A dense shrub with oval, green leaves and sometimes rusty new growth. Starry white, or sometimes pink, flowers are produced mainly during Nov.-May. A hardy species tolerating moist to dry, well-drained soils and also exposed coastal situations. It prefers full or partial sun.
H O SS D M L SA G CA C2 F2
Charts 5, Chapter 3; 12a, Chapter 16; 16, Chapter 19

Correa backhousiana
1-2 m x 2-3 m Vic, Tas
A dense shrub which can grow to 5 m tall in moist situations. It has oval, green, leathery leaves. Cream to pale green, tubular flowers of around 2.5 cm long hang from the branches during May-Nov. Plants respond well to pruning.
O S SS D M L SA G C2 F2 B
Chart 17, Chapter 21

Correa baeuerlenii, Chef's Cap Correa
1-2 m x 2-3 m NSW
A compact, bushy shrub with aromatic, dark green leaves. Flowering is mainly during March-Aug. and each green tubular flower has a flattened calyx, giving it a shape similar to a chef's cap. It is excellent for a shaded situation.
O S SS D L SA G C1 F2 B
Chart 7b, Chapter 10

Correa decumbens
0.2-1 m x 1-3 m SA
A low, spreading shrub with narrow, tubular flowers about 2.5 cm long during Nov.-Feb. The flowers are red with green tips and usually erect. Grows best in moist yet well-drained soils. Responds well to pruning.
O S SS W L SA G CA C1 F2
Chart 7a, Chapter 10

Correa 'Dusky Bells'
0.5 m x 2-3 m Cultivar
A showy plant with bright green leaves and pink, bell-shaped flowers during March-Sept. It is able to grow in a wide range of garden situations.
H O SS D M L SA G CA C1 F2 B
Chart 7a, Chapter 10

Correa glabra, Rock Correa
2-3 m x 1-3 m Qld, NSW, Vic, SA
A variable species with dense foliage. Has tubular flowers of up to 3 cm long. Flowers are usually pale green, but there are also pink to red forms. Main flowering time is May-Aug. Plants respond well to regular light pruning.
H O S SS D L SA G CA C1 F2 B
Chart 8b, Chapter 13

Correa 'Mannii'
1-2.5 m x 1-2 m Cultivar
A widely-grown correa with dark green, oval leaves. Flowering is mainly during March-Sept. with bell-shaped flowers to 4 cm long. They are red with a pale pink interior. Useful for a semi-shade position. Responds well to pruning.
O SS D L SA G CA C1 F2 B
Charts 7b, Chapter 10; 8b, Chapter 13

32 **Correa pulchella**
Prostrate to 1.5 m x 1-3 m SA
This showy species has pendulous, bell-shaped flowers of orange to vermilion, pink or rarely white. Main flowering is in April-Sept. Several different forms of this correa are in cultivation, differing in height and flower colour.
H O SS D L SA G CA C1 F2 B
Chart 7b, Chapter 10

14 **Correa reflexa**, Common Correa
Variable Qld, NSW, Vic, Tas, SA, WA
An extremely variable species, with some forms 0.3-1 m high and others to 3 m. They can be upright or spreading. The colourful, bell-shaped flowers are to 4 cm long and can be in combinations of cream, green, pink and red. Main flowering period is March-Nov. Many different forms of this species are popular in cultivation. They prefer good drainage and will grow in full sun or shade.
H O S SS D L SA G CA C1 F2 B
Charts 2a, Chapter 3; 8a, Chapter 13; 17, Chapter 21

Corybas diemenicus, Slaty Helmet-orchid
A small plant NSW, Vic, Tas, SA
This terrestrial orchid has ground-hugging leaves and helmet-shaped flowers on very short stems. They are purplish with white markings and are seen mainly during June-Oct. Suitable for cultivation in containers, and can also be grown successfully in terrariums.
O S SS M L SA C1 F2
Chart 20, Chapter 24

Corybas dilatatus, Veined Helmet-orchid
A small plant NSW, Vic, Tas, SA, WA
This species is similar to *C. diemenicus* (above) but has veins on the labellum of the flower which end in small points to make a toothed margin. It likes a moist and sheltered situation. Best suited to container cultivation.
S SS M L SA C1 F2
Chart 20, Chapter 24

Crinum flaccidum, Darling Lily; Murray Lily
0.5-1 m Qld, NSW, Vic, SA, NT
This species has long, narrow leaves which die back to the bulb over summer. Large white or yellow, fragrant flowers are produced on stems to around 70 cm tall during Oct.-Jan. It will withstand wet periods but must have relatively good drainage. It is tolerant of drought and frost.
H O SS D W L SA G CA C1 F2
Chart 10a, Chapter 14

Cyathea australis, Rough Tree-fern
To 12 m x 4-6 m Qld, NSW, Vic, Tas
Green fronds to 4.5 m long are produced at the top of a tall but slow-growing trunk. Bases of the fronds are rough to touch. A hardy and easy-to-grow species, but root system must be retained for plants to transplant successfully.
O S SS D M W L SA F1
Chart 19, Chapter 23

64 **Cyathea cooperi**, Scaly Tree-fern
3-12 m x 3-6 m Qld, NSW
This species has a tall, narrow trunk with green fronds to 6 m long. The top of the trunk is covered with long, white, silky scales. An adaptable and popular tree-fern. Quick growing. Fronds can be damaged by heavy frosts.
O S SS D M L SA C1
Chart 19, Chapter 23

Cymbidium madidum
0.3-1 m x 0.2-0.5 m Qld, NSW
This epiphytic orchid has leaves to around 1 m long. Highly fragrant, yellow-green and brown flowers are produced in racemes of up to 70 flowers, mainly during Aug.-Jan. It is an adaptable species which usually grows well in containers. Can be frost-tender.
S SS D M
Chart 20, Chapter 24

Cymbidium suave
Clump-forming epiphyte Qld, NSW
This species has leaves of 0.2-0.45 m long. Racemes of highly fragrant, olive-green flowers are produced during Aug.-Jan. Suitable for container cultivation, but division of established plants is not always successful.
S SS D M
Chart 20, Chapter 24

Dampiera diversifolia
Prostrate x 1-2 m WA
A very showy groundcover with a profuse display of deep blue flowers of around 1 cm diam. between Sept.-Feb. Likes a moist but well-drained situation. Flowers best if in full or partial sun.
O SS D L SA G C1 F1
Charts 21, Chapter 27; 23, Chapter 28

1 5 **Dampiera linearis**, Common Dampiera
9 23 0.3-0.5 m x 1-2 m WA
An extremely variable and complex species. Many different forms are grown. Flowers are usually deep blue, often with a yellow centre. Flowering period is mainly July-Jan. All forms are showy small plants and several spread by suckering lightly.
H O SS D L SA G C1 F1
Charts 15, Chapter 18; 23, Chapter 28

3 70 **Dampiera rosmarinifolia**, Rosemary Dampiera
0.4 m x 1-3 m Vic, SA
A low shrub with leaves like the herb Rosemary. Dense spikes of light blue or mauve-pink flowers are produced in Aug.-Nov. It grows best in a sunny, well-drained situation. Suckers lightly, with new plants sometimes some distance from parent.
H O SS D L SA G CA C1 F2
Charts 2a, Chapter 3; 10a, Chapter 14; 23, Chapter 28

Dampiera teres, Terete-leaved Dampiera
0.3-0.5 m x 0.5-1 m WA
An ornamental dwarf shrub. Flowers are usually blue-mauve, or can be pink. They are produced in spikes mainly during Aug.-Jan. Likes a sunny, well-drained situation. Frost and drought-tolerant. Responds well to hard pruning. Can sucker lightly.
H O SS D L SA G C1 F2
Charts 10a, Chapter 14; 23, Chapter 28

Darwinia citriodora, Lemon-scented Darwinia
1.5 m x 1-2 m WA
The grey-green leaves of this spreading shrub have a spicy fragrance. Flower-heads of yellow-green and red are produced in April-Nov. Plants respond well to pruning. They can be subject to frost damage.
O SS D M L SA G C1 B
Charts 1b, Chapter 3; 8b, Chapter 13

Darwinia glaucophylla
Prostrate x 1-2.5 m NSW
This species can form a dense mat and the leaves can become purplish during winter. Flowers in Nov.-Dec. are insignificant and greenish-cream to pink. Grows best in well-drained soils with partial or full sun. Suitable for gardens or containers.
O SS D L SA G C1 F1
Chart 22, Chapter 28

Darwinia grandiflora
0.1-0.5 m x 1.5-2.5 m NSW
A low, spreading shrub which blooms between May-Dec. The flowers are white then turn dark red as they age. An adaptable plant suited to most well-drained soils. Prefers dappled or partial sun. Can spread by layering. Suitable for gardens or containers.
O SS D L SA G C1 F1 B
Charts 15, Chapter 18; 22, Chapter 28

Darwinia lejostyla
1 m x 1 m WA
This small, bushy shrub has dense, narrow leaves along the branches. Flower-heads are bell-shaped and pinkish-red. They are produced mainly in Aug.-Feb. Prefers a well-drained situation with partial or filtered sun. It is an excellent container plant.
O SS D M L SA G C1 F1 B
Chart 1a, Chapter 3

Darwinia taxifolia ssp. **macrolaena**
0.1-1 m x 1-2 m Qld, NSW
A low, spreading shrub with narrow, grey-green leaves. Clusters of showy, bright pink to red flowers are produced mainly during Sept.-Jan. Grows best in a sunny, well-drained situation. Can be grown in gardens or containers.
H O SS D L SA G C1 F1 B
Chart 8a, Chapter 13

Dendrobium aemulum, Ironbark Orchid; White Feather Orchid
Clump-forming epiphyte Qld, NSW
A variable species with several different forms in cultivation. The leaves are thick, pale to dark green, and 2-5 cm x 1-3 cm. Racemes of fragrant, white, cream or pinkish flowers with slender segments are seen in July-Oct.
O S SS D M
Chart 20, Chapter 24

Dendrobium bigibbum, Cooktown Orchid
Clump-forming epiphyte Qld
This is another variable species which forms slender clumps. The very showy flowers, seen mainly during March-July, can be magenta, mauve, lilac or white. It is the floral emblem of Qld.
H O SS D M
Chart 20, Chapter 24

Dendrobium x **delicatum**
0.3-0.5 m x 0.5-1 m Qld, NSW
A naturally-occurring hybrid between *D. kingianum* and *D. speciosum* (below). It produces arching racemes of white flowers, often tinged with pink or mauve. Main flowering period is Aug.-Oct. Grows well as an epiphyte or in a container.
S SS M C1 F1
Chart 20, Chapter 24

Dendrobium falcorostrum, Beech Orchid
0.2-0.4 m x 0.3-0.5 m Qld, NSW
This species produces racemes of highly fragrant, white to cream flowers during Aug.-Nov. It is a very popular orchid in cultivation and grows well as an epiphyte or in a container.
S SS M C1 F1
Chart 20, Chapter 24

Dendrobium x **gracillimum**
0.3-0.75 m x 0.5-1 m Qld, NSW
A naturally-occurring hybrid between *D. gracilicaule* and *D. speciosum* (below). Small, fragrant, white and yellow flowers are produced in dense, terminal racemes, mainly during Sept.-Oct.
S SS M C1 F1
Chart 20, Chapter 24

Dendrobium kingianum, Pink Rock-orchid
0.2-0.5 m x 0.5-1 m Qld, NSW, Vic
The flowers of this species are usually pink, but can also be white to purple or in various combinations. Flowering is mainly during Aug.-Nov. An adaptable and very commonly cultivated species. It grows well as an epiphyte or in a container.
S SS M C1 F1
Chart 20, Chapter 24

62 **Dendrobium speciosum,** Rock Orchid
0.3-1 m x 0.5-1.5 m Qld, NSW, Vic
This species has large, leathery leaves. Large terminal racemes of white, cream or yellow flowers are produced during July-Nov. It flowers best if in a slightly sunny position. This is one of the hardiest Australian epiphytic orchids. It is suited to cultivation in gardens or containers.
O S SS M C1 F1
Chart 20, Chapter 24

Dendrobium tetragonum, Tree Spider-orchid
0.2-0.3 m x 0.2-0.5 m Qld, NSW
A very fragrant species with racemes of spider-like, green to yellowish flowers with reddish-purple markings. Flowering period is mainly during May-Oct. This epiphytic species is popular in cultivation, but can be slow to establish after division or other disturbance.
O S SS M
Chart 20, Chapter 24

Dianella revoluta, Spreading Flax Lily
0.3-1 m x 0.5-2.5 m
Qld, NSW, Vic, Tas, SA, WA
A clump-forming plant with strap-like leaves to 70 cm long. Flowers in Aug.-Jan. are pale blue, about 1 cm across and in panicles on stems to 1 m tall. This species is hardy and adaptable in cultivation. Several different forms are available.
O S SS M W L SA G CA C1 F2
Charts 17, Chapter 21; 23, Chapter 28

Dianella tasmanica, Tasman Flax Lily
0.6-1.7 m x 0.5-2 m NSW, Vic, Tas
A clumping plant with strap-like leaves to 1 m long. Blue flowers of 1.5 cm diam. are produced in Aug.-Feb., followed by purple-blue berries. Very hardy once established. An ideal plant for full shade or semi-shade. Likes a moist situation.
O S SS M W L SA G C1 F1
Charts 11, Chapter 15; 23, Chapter 28

Dichondra repens, Kidney Weed
Prostrate x 1-2 m All states
A creeping perennial herb with relatively insignificant cream to green flowers during Sept.-Dec. It grows best in well-drained situations and spreads by layering. Useful as a non-mow lawn where there is little or no foot traffic.
H O S SS D L SA G CA C1 F1
Chart 22, Chapter 28

Dicksonia antarctica, Soft Tree-fern
To 15 m x 2-9 m Qld, NSW, Vic, Tas, SA
Fronds to around 4.5 m long are produced at the top of a tall but slow-growing trunk. Bases of the fronds are covered by soft brown hairs. This species, widely grown in cultivation, requires regular watering during hot weather. Can be transplanted by sawing through trunk (see page 134).
S SS D M L SA C1 F2
Chart 19, Chapter 23

Dicksonia youngiae, Bristly Tree-fern
2-5 m x 2-5 m Qld, NSW
This species has a slender trunk with the upper part covered in red, bristly hairs. Fronds are finely divided. It is initially quick-growing. Suited to cultivation in gardens or containers.
O S SS D M L SA C1 F1
Chart 19, Chapter 23

Diplarrena moroea, Butterfly Flag
0.5-1 m x 0.5-1 m NSW, Vic, Tas
A clump-forming plant with long, strap-like leaves. White, 3-petalled flowers are produced on stems of around 1 m tall mainly during Nov.-Jan. A member of the Iris family.
H O SS M W L SA C1 F1
Chart 11, Chapter 15

Diuris longifolia, Donkey Orchid; Wallflower Orchid
To 0.5 m tall NSW, Vic, Tas, SA, WA
A terrestrial orchid with flower-stems to 0.5 m tall. The flowers are yellow or yellow with brown or purple spots. They are seen mainly during July-Nov. A showy species, suited to cultivation in containers.
O S SS M L SA C1 F2
Chart 20, Chapter 24

Diuris maculata, Leopard Orchid
To 0.5 m tall NSW, Vic, Tas, SA
This species is closely related to *D. longifolia* (above) but in this case the flower petals have many dark brown spots. Other comments as for *D. longifolia* (above).
O S SS M L SA C1 F2
Chart 20, Chapter 24

Dodonaea adenophora, see **D. sinuolata** ssp. **acrodentata**

Dodonaea boroniifolia, Fern-leaf Hop-bush
0.5-2 m x 0.7-2 m Qld, NSW, Vic
Flowers are insignificant, but they are followed by a showy display of green, pink or red, 4-winged seed capsules during Sept.-April. This species will grow in most well-drained soils and in partial or full sun. Responds well to pruning.
H O SS D L SA G C1 F1
Chart 7b, Chapter 10

Dodonaea sinuolata ssp. **acrodentata**
2-3 m x 2-3 m Qld, NSW
A shrubby plant, attractive in foliage and fruit. Very small flowers are followed by showy, reddish hops produced mainly during March-Oct. It is a widely grown species. Responds well to pruning. Has been sold as *D. adenophora*, also *D.* sp. aff. *tenuifolia.*
H O SS D L SA G C1 F1
Chart 17, Chapter 21

Dodonaea sp. aff. **tenuifolia**, see **D. sinuolata** ssp. **acrodentata**

63 **Doodia aspera**, Prickly Rasp-fern
0.3-0.6 m x 0.5-1 m Qld, NSW, Vic
This species has erect, often pale green, fish-bone-shaped fronds. New growth is usually bright pink to reddish. A very hardy fern, suited to a wide range of situations.
O S SS D M W L SA C1 F2
Chart 19, Chapter 23

Doodia media, Common Rasp-fern
0.3-0.6 m x 0.5-1 m Qld, NSW, Vic, Tas
This species is similar to *D. aspera* (above).

New growth is purplish-red. A decorative species suitable for gardens or containers.
O S SS D M W L SA C1 F2
Chart 19, Chapter 23

Dryandra formosa, Showy Dryandra
3-8 m x 2-5 m WA
A highly decorative species with attractive, serrated leaves to 10-20 cm long. Orange-yellow flower-heads of 10 cm across are produced mainly in Sept.-Nov. It must have a well-drained situation with full or partial sun. Is grown for cut flower production.
H O SS D L SA G C1 F1 B
Chart 1c, Chapter 3

Dryandra polycephala, Many-headed Dryandra
1-3 m x 1-2 m WA
A small to medium shrub. The stiff leaves are up to 20 cm long and are divided halfway to the midrib with triangular, pointed lobes. Bright yellow flower-heads to 4 cm across are produced during Aug.-Nov. Likes a well-drained position with full or partial sun. The prickly foliage makes this an excellent plant for bird refuge and nesting.
H O D L SA G C1 F1 B
Chart 9, Chapter 13

Dryandra sessilis, Parrot Bush
2-6 m x 1.5-3.5 m WA
Leaves are to 5 cm long with scattered, prickly lobes. Pale yellow flower-heads are produced during July-Nov. This species will adapt to a fairly wide range of well-drained situations. The flowers provide food for native birds and it is also a very popular nesting plant.
H O SS D L SA G C1 F2 B
Chart 9, Chapter 13

Enchylaena tomentosa, Barrier Saltbush; Ruby Saltbush
0.3-1 m x 0.5-1.5 m
Qld, NSW, Vic, SA, WA, NT
A low shrub with succulent, bluish-green foliage. Flowers are fairly insignificant, but colourful small berries are produced almost throughout the year. They are initially yellow then change through various shades to dark red. The species is native to warm, semi-arid to arid regions.
H O D L SA G CA C1 F2
Chart 10a, Chapter 14

Epacris impressa, Common Heath
0.3-2.5 m x 0.2-1 m NSW, Vic, Tas, SA
Usually an upright plant to around 1 m high. Tubular white, pink or red flowers are produced mainly during April-Nov. It is the floral emblem of Vic. Grows best in a well-drained situation with semi-shade or partial sun. Responds well to pruning after flowering.
O S SS D M L SA G C1 F2 B
Chart 7b, Chapter 10

44 **Epacris longiflora**, Fuchsia Heath
0.5-2 m x 0.5-2 m Qld, NSW
A fairly open plant with narrow tubular flowers to 3 cm long, produced through most of the year with main flowering during May-Jan. The flowers are red with white tips and are highly decorative. Plants respond well to light or medium pruning.
O S SS D M L SA G C1 F2 B
Chart 8b, Chapter 13

Epacris microphylla, Coral Heath
0.5-1 m x 0.5-1 m Qld, NSW, Vic, Tas
A dwarf shrub with erect branches. Flower-buds are often pink and then open to mainly white flowers in April-Oct. This species grows naturally in moist, sandy areas. It prefers good drainage if in heavy soils. Responds well to hard pruning.
O SS M W L SA C1 F2 B
Chart 11, Chapter 15

Eremaea beaufortioides, Round-leaved Eremaea
1-2 m x 1-2 m WA
Oval green leaves are crowded along the branches of this species. There is a showy display of orange flower-heads to about 2 cm diam. produced mainly during Sept.-Feb. It likes a warm to hot well-drained situation.
H O SS D L SA G C1 F1
Chart 10b, Chapter 14

Eremophila denticulata, Fitzgerald Eremophila
1-2.5 m x 1-3.5 m WA
This eremophila has tubular flowers to 3 cm long mainly during Sept.-March. They are initially yellow then become red as they age. A hardy and adaptable shrub. Regular pruning is recommended to avoid plants becoming leggy.
H O SS D L SA C1 F1 B
Chart 10b, Chapter 14

19 **Eremophila glabra**, Common Emu-bush; Tar Bush
Prostrate to 1.5 m to 1-3 m
Qld, NSW, Vic, SA, WA, NT
A variable species. Some forms have densely hairy leaves giving a silvery appearance. Yellow to red or green tubular flowers to 5 cm long are produced mainly during June-March. Many forms of this species are widely grown. It will tolerate a range of situations providing there is good drainage. Prefers full or partial sun.
H O D L SA G CA C1 F2 B
Charts 5, Chapter 3; 8a, Chapter 13

Eremophila maculata, Spotted Emu-bush; Native Fuchsia
0.5-3 m x 1-3 m
Qld, NSW, Vic, SA, WA, NT
A variable species. Flowering is mainly during June-Nov. and the flowers can be cream, yellow, orange, pink, red or purplish, with cream or yellow spots inside the tube. A hardy plant with a preference for heavier soil types. Likes a sunny situation with good drainage. Responds well to pruning.
H O SS D L SA G CA C1 F2 B
Charts 5, Chapter 3; 10b, Chapter 14

Eremophila serpens, Creeping Eremophila
Prostrate x 1.5-3 m WA
A vigorous groundcover which flowers for most of the year with purple and lime-green tubular flowers about 2.5 cm long. It is suited to a wide range of conditions. Prefers good drainage and is drought-tolerant but will cope with wet periods. Branches can self-layer.
H O SS D W L SA G CA C1 F2 B
Charts 2a, Chapter 3; 15, Chapter 18

Eriostemon myoporoides, Long-leaved Waxflower
1-2 m x 1.5-3 m Qld, NSW, Vic
The leaves of this species are dark green and aromatic. Flower-buds can be pale to deep pink. White starry flowers are produced during July-Dec. A very widely cultivated species adaptable to a range of situations. Responds well to pruning.
H O S SS D L SA G C1 F2
Chart 17, Chapter 21

Eriostemon spicatus, Pepper and Salt
0.5-1.5 m x 0.5-1.5 m WA
A small, open shrub with small, narrow leaves. Spikes of deep pink to mauve flowers are produced during June-Jan. Plants respond well to pruning. Suited to well-drained garden situations or container cultivation.
O SS D L SA G C1 F2
Chart 1a, Chapter 3

Eucalyptus astringens, Brown Mallet
5-25 m x 4-10 m WA
An upright to spreading tree. Bears a profuse display of cream-yellow flowers mainly during Oct.-Nov. Prefers a well-drained, sunny situation.
H O D L SA G CA C1 F1 B
Chart 2c, Chapter 3

Eucalyptus botryoides, Southern Mahogany
12-40 m x 8-20 m NSW, Vic
This species can grow as an upright forest tree to 30-40 m tall, or in exposed situations it will be a branched tree to around 12 m high. Flowers in summer-autumn are cream. Can be fast-growing. Suitable for coastal situations and able to withstand strong, saline winds. Not recommended for small gardens.
H O SS M W L SA C2 F1 B
Chart 4, Chapter 3

Eucalyptus burdettiana, Burdett Gum
4-10 m x 3-6 m WA
In cultivation this small tree usually has a short trunk and a dense crown. The trunk is smooth with cream, light brown or green-brown bark. Clusters of bright yellow-green flowers are produced during Jan.-March. Will tolerate areas of low rainfall.
H O D L SA G C1 F1 B
Chart 13, Chapter 17

Eucalyptus caesia
5-10 m x 3-5 m WA
A decorative small tree with silvery grey foliage, buds and fruits. Pink flowers tipped with gold are produced in June-Nov. Suitable for a wide range of well-drained situations. A large-flowered form known as 'Silver Princess' is also popular in cultivation. It may need regular pruning and/or staking to avoid damage caused by the weight of flowers, buds or fruits
H O D L SA G CA C1 F2 B
Charts 1c, Chapter 3; 8c, Chapter 13

Eucalyptus camaldulensis, River Red Gum
20-40 m x 10-25 m
Qld, NSW, Vic, SA, WA, NT
A large tree with a thick trunk of 1-2 m diam. The bark can be highly decorative. Flowers are white to cream and produced sporadically. Tolerates wet conditions and is also drought-tolerant. This species is highly regarded for its durable timber, used for posts, stumps and railway sleepers.
H O SS M W L SA C1 F2 B
Charts 3, Chapter 3; 9, Chapter 13

49 **Eucalyptus cladocalyx nana**, Bushy Sugar Gum
6-8 m x 6-8 m SA
This species has a mottled, smooth-barked trunk. Creamy-yellow flowers are seen mainly during Nov.-Mar. Plants can be pruned to encourage bushy growth and the species is widely used for farm and roadside planting.
H O SS D L SA CA C1 F2 B
Chart 12b, Chapter 16

Eucalyptus conferruminata, Bushy Yate
5-10 m x 4-8 m WA
A dense small tree with large clusters of yellow-green flowers mainly during July-Dec. The green buds which precede the flowers are also decorative. The species is useful as a screen or windbreak plant. Previously available as *E. lehmannii*, which is distinguished from this species by its smaller, stalked flower-heads and fruits.
H O SS D M L SA G C2 F1 B
Charts 8c, Chapter 13; 13, Chapter 17; 16, Chapter 19

Eucalyptus cornuta, Yate
6-20 m x 5-10 m WA
Light yellow flowers, in heads of around 8 cm diam., are produced over a long period, with a peak in Sept.-Nov. Will grow in a wide range of soils with good or poor drainage. The root system is better able to resist strong winds in sandy regions.
H O SS D M L SA CA C1 F1 B
Chart 12b, Chapter 16

Eucalyptus crenulata, Silver Gum
6-15 m x 5-10 m Vic
This species has attractive, dense foliage with grey-green, heart-shaped leaves. Clusters of white to cream flowers are produced during Sept.-Dec. Grows well in sun or shade. Withstands pruning.
H O S SS W L SA G C1 F2 B
Charts 3, Chapter 3; 7c, Chapter 10; 13, Chapter 17

Eucalyptus doratoxylon, Spearwood Mallee
3-7 m x 4-7 m WA
A spreading, often densely foliaged species. Bark is smooth and white to cream. Young branchlets are purple-red to red-brown. Profuse cream flowers are seen mainly in Aug.-Oct. This species is hardy to most well-drained situations.
H O SS D L SA G CA C2 F1 B
Chart 12b, Chapter 16

Eucalyptus eremophila, Tall Sand Mallee
3-5 m x 3-6 m WA
This species can be multi-trunked or with one single trunk. Bud-caps are up to 2.5 cm long and are red-brown to red. The flowers, seen mainly during June-Oct., are cream to yellow or can be red. Will grow in a wide range of situations and tolerates both drought and frost.
H O D L SA G CA C1 F2 B
Charts 1c, Chapter 3; 10c, Chapter 14

Eucalyptus erythrocorys, Illyarrie
5-8 m x 3-6 m WA
A very decorative small to medium tree with smooth, white to grey bark. Flowering is mainly during Feb.-May, when bright red bud-caps are shed to reveal yellow flowers. Likes a sunny, well-drained, frost-free situation. Recommended for alkaline soils.
H O D L SA G CA C1 B
Chart 4, Chapter 3

Eucalyptus erythronema, Red-flowered Mallee
4-9 m x 4-7 m WA
An ornamental small tree with a decorative whitish trunk. Has profuse red, or sometimes yellow, flowers during Oct.-Feb. Flowers best in warm climates or situations.
H O D L SA G CA C1 F2 B
Chart 2c, Chapter 3

Eucalyptus ficifolia, Red-flowering Gum
6-10 m x 5-8 m WA
A spectacular flowering gum with colour forms of white to pink, scarlet or deep red. Flowering is usually during Dec.-March. It is a popular tree in cultivation. It must have a well-drained situation and prefers deep, sandy soils.
H O D L SA G C1 F1 B
Chart 1c, Chapter 3

Eucalyptus forrestiana, Fuchsia Gum
4-6 m x 3-5 m WA
A very colourful small tree. The pendulous buds and fruits are bright orange to red and can be seen almost throughout the year. Yellow flowers are produced mainly during Dec.-July. Grows and flowers best in a warm to hot situation. Tolerates moist or well-drained conditions.
H O W L SA G CA C1 F2 B
Chart 5, Chapter 3

Eucalyptus gardneri, low forms, Blue Mallet
2.5-9 m x 3-6 m WA
This is a variable mallee shrub or tree. Leaves can be green or bluish-purple. Clusters of cream to yellow flowers are produced mainly in May-June. Buds and fruits are also decorative.
H O SS D L SA G CA C1 F2 B
Chart 10c, Chapter 14

Eucalyptus globulus, Tasmanian Blue Gum
15-55 m x 10-25 m Vic, Tas
A quick-growing tree with glaucous juvenile foliage. Bears a profuse display of white to cream flowers during Sept.-Dec. It is the floral emblem of Tasmania. Widely planted in various areas of the world for the draining of swamplands.
H O SS M W L SA F1 B
Chart 3, Chapter 3

Eucalyptus kitsoniana, Gippsland Mallee; Bog Gum
3-10 m x 3-8 m Vic
A small mallee species, usually with multiple trunks. Clusters of cream flowers are produced mainly during Aug.-Feb. This species will grow well in moist or fairly well-drained situations. It develops from a large underground lignotuber.
H O SS M W L SA CA C2 F1 B
Charts 7c, Chapter 10; 12b, Chapter 16

Eucalyptus kondininensis, Kondinin Blackbutt
8-15 m x 5-10 m WA
This species has profuse, white to cream flowers mainly during Nov.-Dec. It occurs near salt lakes in WA and is highly tolerant of saline conditions.
H O M L SA G CA C1 F2 B
Chart 4, Chapter 3

Eucalyptus kruseana, Book-leaf Mallee
3-4 m x 3-4 m WA
A much-branched and spreading species. The decorative oval leaves are blue-grey and crowded near the ends of the branchlets. Clusters of yellow flowers are produced mainly during March-Aug. Grows best in a warm, well-drained situation.
H O D L SA G CA C1 F1 B
Charts 5, Chapter 3; 10b, Chapter 14

Eucalyptus lansdowneana, Crimson Mallee; Port Lincoln Mallee
3-6 m x 3-6 m SA
A slender tree or mallee species with smooth, grey-brown bark. The flowers produced in July-Nov., are deep crimson. In the ssp. *albopurpurea* they are whitish-mauve to pink-purple. An ornamental species useful also as a screen or windbreak plant.
H O SS D L SA G CA C1 F1 B
Chart 10c, Chapter 14

Eucalyptus lehmannii, see **E. conferruminata**

10 56 **Eucalyptus leucoxylon**, dwarf forms, Yellow Gum
5-8 m x 5-8 m SA
The dwarf forms of this species have attractive cream trunks and white, cream, or pale to deep pink flowers produced usually during March-Nov. These forms are extremely popular in cultivation. Other forms which can grow to 30 m high occur in NSW, Vic and SA.
H O SS W L SA G CA C1 F2 B
Charts 5, Chapter 3; 8c, Chapter 13

Eucalyptus macrandra, Long-flowered Marlock
5-10 m x 3-6 m WA
This species has a smooth, brown-grey trunk and the leaves are bright green to blue-green. Large clusters of yellow-green flowers are seen mainly during Dec.-March. A very hardy species with flowers rich in nectar.
H O SS W L SA G CA C1 F2 B
Charts 8c, Chapter 13; 10c, Chapter 14

Eucalyptus maculata, Spotted Gum
15-30 m (or taller) x 8-15 m Qld, NSW, Vic
This species is often grown for its spotted, smooth-barked trunk. It has a prolific display of white flowers during May-June. A hardy and adaptable tree, excellent for shade and shelter.
H O SS D M L SA C1 F1 B
Charts 2c, Chapter 3; 8c, Chapter 13

Eucalyptus megacornuta, Warty Yate
6-15 m x 5-10 m WA
Has a smooth, cream to reddish-brown trunk with grey blotches. Large clusters of yellow-green flowers are produced mainly during Oct.-Dec. A decorative small to medium tree.
H O D L SA G CA C1 F2 B
Charts 2c, Chapter 3; 8c, Chapter 13

Eucalyptus nicholii, Narrow-leaved Black Peppermint
8-15 m x 5-10 m NSW
An attractive tree with narrow leaves and often a pendulous habit. New growth can be pink to purplish. Cream flowers are produced mainly during March-May. This species is popular in cultivation within Australia and overseas. It is generally hardy and adaptable to a wide range of situations.
H O SS D M L SA G C1 F2 B
Chart 7c, Chapter 10

Eucalyptus occidentalis, Swamp Yate
12-20 m x 5-10 m WA
This species has a profuse display of pale yellow flowers in March-May. There is also sporadic flowering. It is a hardy tree suited to a wide range of situations, including semi-arid conditions.
H O SS M W L SA CA G C1 F2 B
Charts 3, 4, Chapter 3

Eucalyptus platypus, Round-leaved Moort
4-10 m x 5-10 m WA
Trunk is smooth and grey with pinkish-brown new bark. Profuse yellowish flowers are seen mainly during Oct.-March. This is an excellent low shelter tree. It is drought-resistant, yet tolerant of short periods of waterlogging.
H O SS D L SA G CA C1 F1 B
Chart 12b, Chapter 16

Eucalyptus platypus var. **heterophylla**, Moort
4-10 m x 5-10 m WA
Usually a single-trunked tree in cultivation. It has a profuse display of cream to yellow-green flowers, mainly in Oct.-March. A hardy, drought-tolerant plant. Responds well to pruning. Excellent for screen or windbreak use.
H O D W L SA CA C1 F2 B
Chart 4, Chapter 3

Eucalyptus polybractea, Blue-leaved Mallee
5-10 m x 3-7 m NSW, Vic
This species can be multi-trunked. It has fibrous bark. The leaves are bluish-green and narrow. Many small, white to cream flowers are produced during March-Oct. Plants respond well to pruning. The species is used in the production of eucalyptus oil.
H O SS D M L SA G C1 F2 B
Chart 8c, Chapter 13

4 **Eucalyptus preissiana**, Bell-fruited Mallee
2-5 m x 3-10 m WA
A spreading plant with smooth, grey to cream bark. Spectacular bright yellow flowers are produced mainly during June-Nov. The bell-shaped fruits are also a decorative feature. Plants can be frost-tender whilst young.
H O D L SA G C1 F2 B
Chart 10b, Chapter 14

Eucalyptus pulverulenta, Powdered Gum
6-8 m x 5-8 m NSW
This species is grown primarily for its silvery foliage. The leaves are rounded or heart-shaped. Cream-white flowers are produced mainly during Sept.-Nov or continuing through summer. Grows best in a cool, moist situation. Plants are grown commercially for cut foliage and they respond well to regular pruning.
O SS D M L SA C1 F2 B
Chart 7c, Chapter 10

Eucalyptus robusta, Swamp Mahogany
20-25 m x 10-15 m Qld, NSW
An ornamental, fast-growing tree with a showy display of creamy-yellow (or pink) flowers during July-Nov. An excellent tree for coastal situations, particularly swamplands.
H O SS M W L SA G C2 F1 B
Chart 3, Chapter 3

Eucalyptus sargentii, Salt River Gum
6-12 m x 5-8 m WA
An ornamental tree with a profuse display of cream flowers mainly during Sept-Dec. It is drought-tolerant and also grows in poorly drained areas near salt lakes.
H O M W L SA CA C1 F2 B
Chart 4, Chapter 3

Eucalyptus scoparia, Wallangarra White Gum
9-12 m x 5-8 m Qld, NSW
A slender tree with smooth, pale grey bark. The leaves are long, narrow and pendulous. The small flowers, seen mainly in summer, are cream to white. An attractive and adaptable tree best suited to well-drained situations.
H O SS D L SA C1 F2 B
Chart 7c, Chapter 10

Eucalyptus sepulcralis, Weeping Gum
4-8 m x 3-8 m WA
A graceful tree with a slender, smooth, white trunk. Foliage is pendulous and leaves are up to 9 cm x 1.2 cm. Pale yellow flowers are produced during Nov.-Feb. Suited to a fairly wide range of well-drained situations. It is noted also for its attractive fruits.
H O SS D L SA G C1 F1 B
Chart 1c, Chapter 3

Eucalyptus sideroxylon, Red Ironbark; Mugga
10-20 m x 5-10 m Qld, NSW, Vic
The upright trunk has deeply furrowed, hard, black bark. Leaves are a soft grey-green. The flowers, produced in May-July, are usually light pink. Some forms are cream or deep pink. Adaptable to a fairly wide range of soil and climatic conditions.
H O D L SA G CA C1 F2 B
Charts 8c, Chapter 13; 10c, Chapter 14

8 **Eucalyptus spathulata**, Swamp Mallet
6-12 m x 4-8 m WA
This attractive tree has a smooth trunk with red-brown to grey-brown bark and narrow leaves. Clusters of small cream flowers are produced during June-Nov. It occurs in moist, sandy areas and will also tolerate saline soils.
H O SS M W L SA G CA C1 F2 B
Charts 4, Chapter 3; 11, Chapter 15

Eucalyptus stellulata, Black Sallee
5-15 m x 5-15 m NSW, Vic
Plants can be single-stemmed or multi-trunked. Cream flowers are produced mainly during July-Nov. This species occurs in sub-alpine areas and is excellent for cold districts with frost and snow.
H O SS M S L SA C1 F2 B
Chart 3, Chapter 3

Eucalyptus stricklandii, Strickland Gum
6-12 m x 5-10 m WA
An ornamental tree with smooth, grey to red-brown bark on the upper trunk. Initial growth is upright then branches can spread to form a wide crown. It provides a showy display of bright yellow flowers during Nov.-March. The flower-buds have a powdery, white surface.
H O D L SA G CA C1 F2 B
Charts 3, Chapter 3; 10c, Chapter 14

Eucalyptus stricta, Blue Mountain Mallee Ash
5-12 m x 4-12 m NSW, Vic
This species usually grows as a multi-trunked mallee. Mature bark is shed in long strips to reveal cream or grey new bark. Cream flowers are produced mainly during Jan.-Feb. and often also later in the year. It does best in a well-drained, moist situation.
H O SS D M L SA CA C1 F2 B
Chart 7c, Chapter 10

Eucalyptus tesselaris, Carbeen
10-25 m x 5-12 m Qld, NSW, WA, NT
A graceful tree with smooth, cream bark on upper branches. It has white to cream flowers in summer. Growth habit can vary under different climatic conditions. Grows best in a warm situation.
H O SS D M L SA C1 F1 B
Chart 2c, Chapter 3

Eucalyptus torelliana, Cadaghi
6-15 m x 4-10 m Qld
A medium to large tree with scaly bark on the lower part of the trunk while the upper section is smooth and slaty-green. Large clusters of small, creamy-white flowers are produced during Sept.-Dec. This species, from near coastal areas of tropical Qld, is one of the bloodwood eucalypts.
H O D L SA C1 F1 B
Chart 8c, Chapter 13

Eucalyptus torquata, Coral Gum; Coolgardie Gum
5-9 m x 4-6 m WA
An attractive small tree with decorative, reddish buds and fruits. The flowers, produced in Sept.-Feb., are usually pink but can be cream to red. Best suited to a warm to hot, well-drained position. Is tolerant of slightly saline soils.
H O D L SA G CA C1 F1 B
Chart 1c, Chapter 3

Eucalyptus viridis, Green Mallee
2-10 m x 2-7 m Qld, NSW, Vic, SA
This mallee species has a rough lower trunk with smooth, grey upper branches and ribbony bark. It has narrow, glossy green leaves. Clusters of small white flowers are produced mainly during Nov.-Jan. Grows well in warm to hot regions.
H O SS D SA G CA C1 F2 B
Chart 15, Chapter 18

Eucalyptus websteriana, Webster's Mallee
3-6 m x 3-6 m WA
A spreading shrub with fairly dense foliage. New bark is yellow-green then matures to reddish-brown with curling strips. Has a profuse display of cream to yellow flowers mainly during July-Oct. Likes a warm to hot, well-drained situation. Responds well to pruning.
H O SS D L SA G C1 F1 B
Chart 10c, Chapter 14

Eucalyptus woodwardii, Lemon-flowered Gum
6-15 m x 3-8 m WA
This species has a mainly smooth trunk with grey or pink to white bark. It has showy clusters of bright yellow flowers during July-Nov. Suited to warm to hot, well-drained situations. It is drought-tolerant.
H O D L SA G CA C1 F1 B
Chart 7c, Chapter 10

Eugenia coolminianum, see **Syzygium coolminianum**

Frankenia pauciflora, Common Sea-heath
Prostrate x 1 m All states
A dense mat plant with small, greyish leaves. White to deep pink, open-petalled flowers are produced during Sept.-Dec. Suited to sunny, well-drained situations or to container cultivation. Can spread by layering.
H O SS D L SA G CA C2 F2
Charts 10a, Chapter 14; 22, Chapter 28

Gahnia sieberiana, Red-fruit Saw-sedge
2-3 m x 1-2 m Qld, NSW, Vic, Tas
A large, clump-forming plant. The narrow leaves are 1-2 m long and have sharp margins. Flower-heads are brown and cream and the flowers are followed by small, red, shiny nuts. Plants are hardy and grow particularly well in moist, sunny situations. All members of the *Gahnia* family provide favoured nesting sites for small birds.
H O S SS M W L SA C2 F2 B
Chart 9, Chapter 13

Geijera parviflora, Wilga
4-9 m x 5-9 m Qld, NSW, Vic, SA
A rounded tree, with pendulous foliage often drooping to ground level. Leaves are aromatic when crushed, with a peppermint-like smell. The small white flowers, seen mainly during June-Nov., can have an unpleasant odour. This species is regarded highly as a stock fodder plant during times of drought.
H O D L SA G CA C1 F2
Chart 10c, Chapter 14

Gleichenia dicarpa, Pouched Coral-fern; Tangle Fern
To 2-4 m tall Qld, NSW, Vic, Tas
A wiry fern with forked fronds. This species can be initially slow-growing, but it is hardy once established. Grows best in a fairly sunny and moist position. Plants spread from creeping rhizomes and can form dense, tangled thickets.
O S SS M W L SA C1 F1
Chart 11, Chapter 15

Glishrocaryon behrii, Golden Pennants
0.3-0.5 m x 0.5-1 m NSW, Vic, SA
A clump-forming plant with flower-stems more or less leafless. It provides a showy display of bright yellow flowers usually in Sept.-Feb. Was known as *Loudonia behrii*.
H O SS D L SA G CA C1 F2
Charts 10a, Chapter 14; 23, Chapter 28

Goodenia geniculata, Bent Goodenia
Prostrate x 0.5-1 m NSW, Vic, Tas, SA
A fairly dense mat plant with dark green, oval, toothed leaves. Bright yellow flowers are borne on bent stalks mainly during Oct.-March. A lightly suckering plant, suited to a wide range of garden situations. Prefers a well-drained, sunny position.
H O SS D M L SA G C1 F2
Chart 23, Chapter 28

Goodenia hederacea, Ivy Goodenia
Prostrate x 1-2 m NSW, Vic
This dense mat plant has rounded and toothed leaves. Yellow to orange flowers are seen during Oct.-Feb. It grows best in a well-drained, sunny situation, and can spread by layering or suckering.
H O SS D M L SA G C1 F2
Charts 22, 23, Chapter 28

Goodenia lanata, Trailing Goodenia
Prostrate x 1 m NSW, Vic, Tas
A trailing plant with dark green, toothed leaves and bright yellow flowers produced during Oct.-March. It is a hardy groundcover which spreads readily by rooting at the nodes.
H O S SS M W L SA G C1 F2
Charts 15, Chapter 18; 22, Chapter 28

55 **Goodia lotifolia**, Golden Tip
2-4 m x 2-3 m Qld, NSW, Vic, Tas, SA
A quick-growing shrub with soft, clover-like, greyish-green leaves. Yellow pea-flowers are produced in loose terminal clusters mainly during Sept.-Dec. It is useful for a shaded area.
O S SS D L SA G C1 F2
Chart 13, Chapter 17

Grevillea acanthifolia
0.5-2.5 m x 2-4 m NSW
A variable, spreading shrub with prickly leaves and pink to mauve toothbrush flowers produced during Sept.-March. Some forms of this grevillea are low and spreading while others are more upright. A fairly hardy and adaptable species.
H O SS D M L SA G C1 F2
Chart 1a, Chapter 3

43 **Grevillea alpina**, Grampians low form
0.3-0.5 m x 1-2 m Vic
A species with many different forms. In this form clusters of red and yellow flowers are produced mainly during June-Nov. It prefers a well-drained situation with filtered sun and is ideal as an undershrub beneath taller plants.
O SS D L SA G C1 F2 B
Chart 8a, Chapter 13

Grevillea aquifolium, Variable Prickly Grevillea
0.2-3 m x 1-4 m Vic, SA
Leaves are holly-like. Red and green toothbrush flower-heads are produced mainly during Sept.-Feb. Several different forms of this species are in cultivation. It is suited to warm, well-drained situations and is tolerant of drought and frost.
H O SS D L SA G C1 F2 B
Charts 2b, Chapter 3; 8b, Chapter 13

Grevillea arenaria
1.5-2.5 m x 1.5-2.5 m NSW
This species has oblong, hairy, grey-green leaves. At least two forms are grown, one with reddish and the other with yellow-green flowers. Flowering period is mainly in June-Jan. Although not a spectacular shrub, this species is widely grown for its excellent bird-attracting qualities. Plants respond well to pruning.
H O SS D L SA G C1 F2 B
Charts 8b, Chapter 13; 17, Chapter 21

Grevillea asparagoides
1-2 m x 1-3 m WA
A much-branched shrub with leaves divided into stiff, narrow segments. Bright red flowers are produced mainly during Aug.-Nov. Likes a warm, well-drained situation. Provides protection and nesting sites for small birds and the flowers also supply nectar.
H O D L SA G C1 F1 B
Chart 9, Chapter 13

27 **Grevillea banksii**, Banks' Grevillea
2-5 m x 2-3 m Qld
The leaves of this species are greyish-green and pinnate. Large, usually bright red flower-heads are produced mainly in July-Nov. Likes a sunny, very well-drained and frost-free situation. There are several forms of this species and a number of hybrids with *G. banksii* as one parent.
H O D L SA G C1 B
Chart 1b, Chapter 3

Grevillea barklyana Victorian form
5-8 m x 3-6 m Vic
This species often grows taller in forest situations. It has large, lobed or entire leaves to around 20 cm long. Pale pink toothbrush flower-heads are produced mainly during Aug.-Nov. It is a quick-growing plant which does well in a shaded situation. Another form of this species occurs near Jervis Bay, NSW. Both forms are frost-tolerant.
O S SS M L SA C1 F2 B
Chart 7c, Chapter 10

Grevillea baueri, Bauer's Grevillea
1-2 m x 1.5-2.5 m NSW
Has crowded leaves and bronze to reddish new growth. Terminal clusters of red flowers are produced during March-Nov. This is a relatively hardy shrub, suited to a wide range of conditions.
H O SS D L SA G C1 F2 B
Chart 21, Chapter 27

Grevillea brownii
Usually 0.5 m x 1-3 m WA
A showy, low-growing plant with taller forms also in cultivation. Clusters of very bright red flowers are produced mainly in May-Nov. Ideal for use as a groundcover beneath other shrubs.
O SS D L SA G C1 F1 B
Chart 1a, Chapter 3

Grevillea buxifolia, Grey Spider-flower
2-3 m x 2 m NSW
A fairly upright shrub with oval, hairy leaves and rusty new growth. During July-Dec. flower-heads of an unusual grey and brown combination are borne at the ends of the branchlets. Grows best in a well-drained and semi-shaded situation.
O SS D L SA G C1 F2
Chart 7b, Chapter 10

Grevillea capitellata
Prostrate to 1 m x 0.7-2 m NSW
There are several forms of this ornamental species in cultivation. Has clusters of dark red flowers mainly during July-Nov. Grows best in semi-shaded or sunny, well-drained situations.
O SS D L SA C1 F1
Chart 7a, Chapter 10

Grevillea 'Clearview David'
2-3 m x 2-4 m Cultivar
A bushy shrub with narrow, dark green, prickly leaves. The showy flowers are vivid red with white, and are produced in clusters during July-Nov. Hardy in a range of well-drained situations. Responds well to pruning.
H O SS D L SA G C1 F2 B
Chart 2b, Chapter 3

Grevillea confertifolia, Grampians Grevillea
Prostrate to 0.5 m x 3 m Vic
Taller forms of this species are also in cultivation. The leaves are narrow and slightly prickly. Mauve to pink terminal flower-heads are produced during Aug.-Nov. It is a variable species which has proved adaptable to a range of conditions. Responds well to light pruning which increases the number of flower-heads.
O SS D M L SA G C1 F2
Charts 2a, Chapter 3; 7a, Chapter 10

Grevillea diminuta
0.5-1 m x 1-2 m ACT
An attractive, low, spreading shrub with oval, dark grey to green leaves. Pendant clusters of small red flowers are produced mainly during Jan.-Aug. This species is native to sub-alpine slopes and is highly frost-tolerant.
H O S SS D L SA G C1 F2
Chart 7a, Chapter 10

Grevillea dimorpha, Flame Grevillea
1-2 m x 1-3 m Vic
Several forms of this species are available with broad or narrow leaves. Clusters of brilliant red flowers are produced mainly during April-Nov. A useful undershrub. Responds well to light pruning.
O S SS D L SA G C1 F2 B
Chart 17, Chapter 21

51 **Grevillea** x **gaudichaudii**
0.3 m x 2-5 m NSW
An excellent groundcover with lobed leaves and reddish new growth. Dark red to burgundy toothbrush flower-heads are produced mainly during Sept.-April. This species is very popular in cultivation and certainly deserves to be. It likes a sunny, well-drained but moist position. Responds well to pruning.
H O SS D M L SA G C1 F2 B
Charts 1a, Chapter 3; 8a, Chapter 13

Grevillea glabella, see **G. rosmarinifolia** 'Lara Dwarf'

Grevillea glabrata
2-3 m x 2-4 m WA
Has smooth, grey-green leaves which are lobed and prickly. Loose clusters of small white to cream flowers are produced along the branches during Sept.-Jan. Can be a quick-growing, dense shrub, but responds well to pruning.
H O SS D L SA G C1 F1
Chart 17, Chapter 21

Grevillea hookeriana, Toothbrush Grevillea
2-4 m x 3-4 m WA
This large shrub has green leaves divided into narrow leaflets. Can flower throughout the year with the bright red, toothbrush flower-heads being most prolific in Aug.-Dec. Grows best in a warm, well-drained situation. Responds well to pruning. This form is thought possibly to be a hybrid of unknown origin. Other forms are also in cultivation, although not grown as commonly as the one described here.
H O SS D L SA G C1 F1 B
Chart 8b, Chapter 13

Grevillea ilicifolia, prostrate form, Holly Grevillea
Prostrate to 1 m x 1.5-3 m NSW, Vic, SA
Other forms grow to 2 m tall. Leaves are variable and usually deeply lobed. Cream with red toothbrush flower-heads are produced mainly during March-Nov. Hardy to most well-drained situations. This form grows well as an undershrub beneath taller plants.
H O SS D L SA G C1 F2
Chart 10a, Chapter 14

Grevillea jephcottii, Green Grevillea
2-2.5 m x 1.5-2 m Vic
Leaves are oblong and slightly hairy. Cream to green flowers are produced throughout most of the year. It is a hardy shrub in most well-drained situations. Responds well to pruning. A very popular plant with native honey-eating birds.
H O SS D M L SA G C1 F2 B
Chart 8b, Chapter 13

Grevillea juniperina, Juniper Grevillea
2-4 m x 2-4 m NSW
A bushy shrub with dense, prickly foliage. Orange-red flowers are produced mainly during July-Nov. Responds well to pruning. An excellent species for nectar production and also for bird habitat.
H O SS D L SA G C1 F2 B
Chart 9, Chapter 13

40 **Grevillea juniperina**, prostrate forms, Juniper Grevillea
Prostrate x 1-5 m NSW
A variable species with small, usually prickly leaves. Prostrate forms with buff, yellow or red flowers are available. Flowering is mainly during July-Nov. All forms respond well to pruning and are excellent nectar-producing plants.
H O SS D L SA G C1 F2 B
Charts 8a, Chapter 13; 10a, Chapter 14

Grevillea lanigera 'Mt Tamboritha'
Prostrate x 1-1.5 m Vic
Several forms of *G. lanigera* are widely grown. This is a spreading shrub with greyish-green foliage. Clusters of cream and deep pink flowers are produced over a long period, mainly during May-Oct. Tip pruning while young will encourage dense growth.
H O SS D L SA G C2 F2 B
Chart 8a, Chapter 13

Grevillea laurifolia
Prostrate x 2-4 m NSW
A useful groundcover, with dark red, toothbrush flower-heads produced mainly during Nov.-Jan. Grows best in a well-drained situation with sun or dappled shade.
H O SS D L SA C1 F1 B
Chart 7a, Chapter 10

4 **Grevillea lavandulacea**, Lavender Grevillea
0.5-2.5 m x 0.5-3 m NSW, Vic, SA
A variable species with greyish foliage. Clusters of bright pink to red flowers are produced mainly during June-Nov. It is an adaptable and widely cultivated species. Prefers a warm, well-drained situation. Responds well to pruning.
H O SS D L SA G CA C1 F2 B
Charts 5, Chapter 3; 10b, Chapter 14

Grevillea longifolia, Fern-leaf Grevillea
2-4 m x 3-5 m NSW
A large shrub with horizontal, spreading branches and long, narrow, serrated leaves. Pink-red toothbrush flower-heads are produced mainly in June-Nov. It likes a well-drained situation. Responds well to pruning.
H O SS D L SA G C1 F2
Charts 13, Chapter 17; 15, Chapter 18

Grevillea longistyla
2-5 m x 2-4 m Qld
A bushy shrub with fine, divided, dark green leaves on reddish stems. Clusters of pink to red flowers are produced mainly during June-Nov. Suited to a well-drained situation with full or partial sun. Responds well to pruning.
H O SS D L SA G C1 F1 B
Chart 8b, Chapter 13

Grevillea miqueliana, Oval-leaf Grevillea
2-3 m x 2-4 m NSW, Vic
There are several forms of this species in cultivation. Orange-red to bright red flowers are borne in large, pendulous clusters usually during June-Nov. Will grow in an open situation through to fairly dense shade.
O S SS L SA G C1 F2 B
Chart 8b, Chapter 13

Grevillea mucronulata
1-2 m x 1.5-2.5 m NSW
A dense shrub. New foliage growth is often bronze. Greenish flowers are produced mainly during April-Dec. They are not particularly showy but are highly attractive to honey-eating birds. Very useful as a screen plant. Responds well to pruning.
O SS D L SA G C1 F2 B
Chart 8b, Chapter 13

Grevillea pilulifera
1 m x 1 m WA
A small, fairly compact plant with narrow, hairy leaves. The flowers are mainly cream with yellow, orange or red styles. The stigmas deepen in colour as they mature. Flowering is during July-Nov. Plants respond well to pruning.
O SS D L SA G C1 F1
Chart 17, Chapter 21

Grevillea pinaster
1.5-2.5 m x 2-4 m WA
A bushy shrub with soft, narrow, green leaves. Pendant clusters of bright red flowers are produced mainly during June-Dec. Hardy to most well-drained situations. Flowers best in full or partial sun.
H O SS D L SA G CA C1 F1 B
Chart 10b, Chapter 14

41 **Grevillea 'Pink Pearl'**
2-4 m x 2-4 m Cultivar
A vigorous shrub with short, narrow, pointed leaves. Clusters of bright pink flowers are produced throughout most of the year, with a peak during July-Oct. Responds well to pruning. Provides protection and nesting sites for small birds.
H O SS D L SA G C1 F2 B
Chart 9, Chapter 13

Grevillea 'Poorinda Constance'
1.5-3 m x 1.5-3 m Cultivar
A large shrub with clusters of bright red flowers produced almost throughout the year. Peak flowering is in July-Oct. Plants can be pruned successfully to a smaller size if desired. An excellent bird-attracting grevillea.
H O SS D L SA G C1 F2 B
Charts 2b, Chapter 3; 8b, Chapter 13

Grevillea 'Poorinda Firebird'
1.5-3 m x 1.5-3 m Cultivar
A showy plant with clusters of bright red flowers produced mainly in June-Dec. This hardy hybrid grevillea is suited to most well-drained situations. It responds well to pruning.
H O SS D L SA G C1 F2 B
Chart 2b, Chapter 3

Grevillea 'Poorinda Queen'
2-4 m x 2-4 m Cultivar
Pale orange to apricot flowers are produced in clusters along the branches almost throughout the year. Peak flowering time is July-Nov. Hardy to most well-drained situations. Responds well to pruning. An excellent bird-attracting plant.
H O SS D L SA G C1 F2 B
Chart 8b, Chapter 13

Grevillea repens, Creeping Grevillea
Prostrate x 2-4 m Vic
This dense, groundcovering plant has holly-like leaves and often reddish new growth. Deep red to burgundy toothbrush flower-heads are produced mainly during Oct.-Feb. Suited to a situation with semi-shade or even full shade. There are at least two forms of this species in cultivation.
O S SS D L SA G C1 F2 B
Chart 10a, Chapter 14

Grevillea robusta, Silky Oak
10-25 m x 6-15 m Qld
Can grow to a large tree of around 40 m in its natural habitat. It has attractive, deeply divided leaves and provides a showy display of bright orange flowers usually during Nov.-Jan. Plants can take some years to flower initially.
H O SS D W L SA G C1 F2 B
Chart 10c, Chapter 14

1 **Grevillea 'Robyn Gordon'**
1-2 m x 2-3 m Cultivar
A showy hybrid with deeply lobed leaves and terminal clusters of bright red flower-heads for most of the year. Adapts to a range of situations. Prefers a sunny position with good drainage, but tolerates high moisture levels.
H O SS D W L SA G C1 F1 B
Chart 1b, Chapter 3

Grevillea rosmarinifolia, Rosemary Grevillea
2-3 m x 2-4 m NSW, Vic
A large shrub, with narrow, prickly, green leaves. Bears clusters of pink to red with cream flowers during June-Dec. Adaptable to a wide range of situations and useful as a screen plant. An excellent bird-attracting species.
H O SS D L SA G C1 F2 B
Charts 8b, Chapter 13; 12a, Chapter 16; 21, Chapter 27

Grevillea rosmarinifolia 'Lara Dwarf'
0.5-1 m x 1-2 m Vic
A small shrub with narrow, slightly prickly leaves. Pink to red with cream flowers are produced mainly during June-Oct. Likes a sunny, well-drained situation. An excellent container plant. This plant was for some time botanically included under *G. glabella*.
H O SS D L SA G C1 F2 B
Chart 8a, Chapter 13

Grevillea sericea, Pink Spider-flower
2.5 m x 2.5 m NSW
This species has narrow leaves and a slightly open growth habit. Plants are hardly ever without some flowers. Colour forms of pink to mauve or white are available. Likes a well-drained position with partial or full sun.
H O SS D L SA G C1 F2
Chart 1b, Chapter 3

Grevillea shiressii, Blue Grevillea
3-8 m x 2-5 m NSW
A quick-growing, bushy plant. The flowers, seen mainly in July-Dec., are a bluish-green. The flowers are often hidden within the foliage but honey-eaters have no trouble at all in locating them. An excellent bird-attracting species.
H O S SS W L SA G C1 F2 B
Charts 8c, Chapter 13; 13, Chapter 17; 17, Chapter 21

Grevillea speciosa, Red Spider-flower
1.5-3 m x 1.5-3 m NSW
A large shrub of slightly open habit, with oblong leaves which can be hairy. Bright red flowers are produced in attractive wheel-like heads mainly during June-Dec. Plants respond well to pruning.
H O SS D L SA G C1 F1 B
Chart 1b, Chapter 3

70 **Grevillea thelemanniana**, Spider-net Grevillea
Prostrate or 1-2 m x 2-3 m WA
A variable species with green or greyish foliage. The flowers are usually bright red and are produced during May-Dec. The prostrate forms of this grevillea are very popular garden plants. They grow best in sunny, well-drained situations.
H O SS D L SA G CA C1 F1 B
Charts 1a, Chapter 3; 8a, Chapter 13

Grevillea tridentifera, prostrate form
0.5 m x 2-4 m WA
A dense groundcover with finely divided, light green leaves. Scented cream flowers are produced in dense clusters, on often upright branches, during Aug.-Nov. These upright branches should be removed after flowering to retain prostrate growth habit.
H O SS D L SA G C1 F2
Chart 2a, Chapter 3

45 **Grevillea tripartita**
2-3 m x 2-3 m WA
A large, open shrub with very prickly leaves on the long, stiff stems. Clusters of red and cream flowers are produced mainly during July-Nov. Grows best in a sunny situation with good drainage. Needs a large area to develop well. Responds well to pruning. An excellent shelter plant for birds.
H O SS D L SA G C1 F1 B
Charts 9, Chapter 13; 12a, Chapter 16

Grevillea vestita
2-3 m x 2-3.5 m WA
A large shrub with pointed, lobed, greyish-green leaves. Clusters of small, white flowers are produced mainly during Aug.-Nov. This species is hardy to a wide range of positions, with a preference for good drainage. It responds well to pruning. An excellent shelter plant for birds.
H O SS D M L SA C1 F1
Chart 9, Chapter 13

Hakea cinerea, Grey Hakea
1-2 m x 1-2 m WA
A decorative shrub with blue-green foliage and clusters of yellowish-green flowers produced mainly during Aug.-Oct. It is an adaptable species which prefers good drainage but will tolerate moist conditions.
H O SS D L SA C1 F2 B
Chart 10b, Chapter 14

Hakea laurina, Pincushion Hakea
3-6 m x 3-5 m WA
A large, bushy shrub to small tree. Cream and red flower-heads in March-July are pin-cushion-shaped. Grows best in a well-drained situation. Frost can damage flower-buds. Young plants are strengthened by light pruning.
H O SS D L SA G C1 F1 B
Chart 1c, Chapter 3

Hakea multilineata, Grass-leaf Hakea
3-5 m x 1.5-3 m WA
A bushy plant with long, narrow leaves. Flowering is mainly during June-Nov. when very showy, pale to deep pink spikes of about 4 cm long are produced along the branches Likes a well-drained situation with partial or full sun.
H O SS D L SA G C1 F1 B
Chart 1c, Chapter 3

Hakea nitida, Shining Hakea
1-2.5 m x 2-2.5 m WA
This species has prickly green leaves. Profuse cream flower-spikes are seen mainly during Sept.-Nov. It is usually a somewhat open shrub but becomes more dense in exposed positions. Requires good drainage.
H O SS D L SA G CA C1 F1 B
Chart 12a, Chapter 16

Hakea nodosa, Yellow Hakea
2-3 m x 2-3 m Vic, Tas, SA
Often an upright shrub but can be spreading. Has narrow, pine-like leaves. Fragrant yellow flowers are produced mainly during Feb.-May. Will tolerate moist to wet conditions.
H O SS W L SA G CA C1 F2
Chart 2b, Chapter 3

Hakea purpurea
1-2 m x 1-1.5 m Qld
The leaves are divided into narrow, needle-like segments. Clusters of bright red flowers are produced usually during June-Nov. This species flowers best in a sunny situation. The flowers provide nectar and small birds often choose this plant for nesting.
H O D L SA G C1 F1 B
Chart 9, Chapter 13

Hakea salicifolia, Willow Hakea
3-7 m x 2-5 m Qld, NSW
A bushy, quick-growing shrub to small tree. Has long smooth leaves, often with reddish new growth. Clusters of small, white to cream flowers are produced mainly during July-Nov. Plants can become open as they mature, but pruning will promote dense growth. Previously known as *H. saligna.*
H O SS W L SA G C1 F2
Chart 13, Chapter 17

Hakea saligna, see **H. salicifolia**

Hakea sericea, Silky Hakea
2-4 m x 1-3 m NSW, Vic, Tas
An open to bushy shrub with short, needle-like leaves. White to pink flowers are produced mainly during April-Sept. It is drought-tolerant but will also grow in moist situations. An excellent nesting and refuge plant for birds.
H O SS D M L SA G CA C1 F2
Chart 9, Chapter 13

Hakea suaveolens, Sweet-scented Hakea
3-6 m x 3-5 m WA
The leaves of this species are smooth with narrow, prickly segments. White to cream flower-heads are produced mainly during April-June. Will grow in a wide range of well-drained situations. Useful as a screen or windbreak plant and a good nesting shrub for birds.
H O SS D L SA G CA C2 F1
Charts 5, Chapter 3; 9, Chapter 13; 12b, Chapter 16

73 **Halgania cyanea**, Rough Halgania
0.5 m x 0.5-1 m NSW, Vic, SA, WA, NT
A low shrub which will often spread by suckering. Leaves are small, toothed and slightly rough. Flowers, in Sept.-Feb. are open-petalled, deep blue and produced in clusters. Responds well to light or hard pruning which should be done annually.
H O SS D L SA G CA C1 F2
Chart 23, Chapter 28

Hardenbergia comptoniana, Native Lilac
Dense climber WA
Profuse racemes of bluish-purple to mauve pea-flowers are produced usually during Aug.-Nov. There is also a white-flowered form. It is a quick-growing species, best suited to a warm, well-drained situation. Can be frost-tender.
O SS D M L SA C1
Chart 14, Chapter 17

Hardenbergia violacea, False Sarsaparilla; Purple Coral-pea
Climber or trailer Qld, NSW, Vic, Tas, SA
Has dark green leaves. Racemes of usually mauve-purple pea-flowers are produced during July-Oct. White and pink forms are available and there are also shrubby forms in cultivation. Best suited to a well-drained situation.
H O SS D L SA G CA C1 F2
Charts 14, Chapter 17; 15, Chapter 18

56 **Hardenbergia violacea 'Happy Wanderer'**
Vigorous climber Cultivar
Purple pea-flowers are produced in long racemes during July-Oct. This is a selected form of *H. violacea* (above). It is a vigorous and floriferous climber or groundcover. Plants should be pruned after flowering and possibly again in summer.
H O SS D L SA G C1 F2
Chart 14, Chapter 17

13 **Helichrysum apiculatum**, Common Everlasting
0.3-0.6 m x 1-2 m All states
The stems and leaves of this species have a silvery appearance. Clusters of bright yellow flower-heads are produced mainly during Sept.-Feb. A species with many forms. Prefers a sunny, well-drained situation. Valuable for foliage colour contrast.
H O SS D L SA G CA C1 F2
Chart 2a, Chapter 3

2 6 **Helichrysum baxteri**, Fringed Everlasting
0.5 m x 1 m Vic, SA
A showy, clump-forming plant with daisy-like everlasting flowers during spring and summer. They are white with yellow centres. Best suited to sunny, relatively well-drained situations.
H O SS D M L SA G C1 F2
Charts 1a, Chapter 3; 21, Chapter 27

Helichrysum bracteatum, Straw Flower
0.5-1.5 m x 0.3-1 m All states
There are annual and also perennial forms of this species. Plants can flower over a long period, mainly during Sept.-May. The papery flower-heads are to 6 cm diam. and can be white, yellow, deep gold or pink. Flowers best in a sunny situation. Plants are widely grown and are excellent cut flowers.
H O SS D L SA G C1 F2
Chart 18, Chapter 22

6 **Helichrysum bracteatum 'Dargan Hill Monarch'**
0.5-1 m x 1 m Cultivar
Has large, soft, greyish leaves and large golden-yellow everlasting daisies for most of the year. Likes a sunny, moist but well-drained position. Responds well to regular light fertilising and regular pruning.
H O SS D M L SA G C1 F2
Chart 21, Chapter 27

Helichrysum cassinianum, Pink Cluster Everlasting
0.3-0.5 m x 0.1-0.3 m SA, WA, NT
A showy small annual, producing many stems from a leafy base. Clusters of small, pink, everlasting flowers are seen mainly during Aug.-Dec. Suitable for massed garden planting or for cultivation in containers.
H O D L SA G C1 F2
Chart 18, Chapter 22

Helichrysum semipapposum, Clustered Everlasting
0.2-1 m x 0.5-1.5 m All states
A variable species with green to greyish stems and leaves. Dense terminal clusters of golden-yellow flower-heads are produced mainly during Oct.-Feb. Responds well to pruning.
H O SS D M L SA G C1 F2
Chart 7a, Chapter 10

Helipterum albicans
0.2-0.3 m x 0.2-0.3 m
Qld, NSW, Vic, Tas, SA
An annual or perennial plant with yellow or white papery flower-heads to around 3 cm diam. Flowering is mainly during Nov.-Feb. This species has a wide distribution throughout eastern Australia. It likes a sunny situation and is frost-hardy. Can be grown from seed or cuttings.
H O SS D L SA C1 F2
Chart 18, Chapter 22

Helipterum floribundum
0.2-0.4 m x 0.1-0.3 m NSW, SA, WA, NT
A stiff, annual species. Many white, papery flower-heads of up to 2 cm diam. are produced mainly during Sept.-Dec. Best suited to a sunny situation.
H O SS D L SA C1 F1
Chart 18, Chapter 22

Helipterum humboldtianum
0.3-0.6 m x 0.2-0.3 m WA
The leaves of this species have wavy edges. Clusters of yellow, everlasting flowers are produced mainly during Sept.-Jan. This annual is grown to a limited extent in Australia and also overseas.
H O SS D L SA C1 F1
Chart 18, Chapter 22

59 **Helipterum manglesii**, Pink Everlasting
0.3-0.5 m x 0.3 m WA
Has stem-clasping leaves. Pink, papery flower-heads of about 2.5 cm diam. are produced mainly during Oct.-Jan. A widely grown everlasting daisy which prefers a sunny situation. It is an annual species which will self-seed under favourable conditions. An excellent dried flower.
H O SS D M L SA G C1 F1
Chart 18, Chapter 22

Helipterum roseum, Everlasting
0.5-1 m x 0.5 m WA
The pink or white flowers of this showy annual species are up to 4 cm diam. They are seen mainly during Aug.-Jan., and are excellent for cutting and drying. It is a very popular species and will commonly self-seed in a garden.
H O SS D M L SA G C1 F1
Chart 18, Chapter 22

Hemiandra pungens, Snake Bush
Prostrate x 1-2 m WA
Has narrow, prickly leaves and a profuse display of usually mauve-pink flowers in Oct.-April. Several forms of this species are grown with some more bushy than others. There are also white-flowered forms. Likes a sunny, well-drained situation.
H O D L SA G C1 F1
Chart 1a, Chapter 3

9 70 **Hibbertia pedunculata**, Guinea-flower
Prostrate x 0.5-1 m NSW, Vic
Has profuse bright yellow flowers of around 2 cm diam. mainly in Oct.-April. It is a relatively hardy mat plant suited to a wide range of well-drained situations, or to cultivation in containers. Can spread by layering.
H O SS D L SA G C1 F2
Chart 22, Chapter 28

Hibbertia scandens, Climbing Guinea-flower
Vigorous climber Qld, NSW
Has long, trailing stems and shiny green leaves. Bright yellow, open-petalled flowers of about 7 cm diam. are produced almost throughout the year with a peak in Nov.-Jan. Can be initially slow-growing but then usually a vigorous plant. Can suffer frost damage.
H O SS D M L SA CA C2
Charts 14, Chapter 17; 16, Chapter 19

Homoranthus darwinioides
0.5-1 m x 0.5-1 m NSW
A compact shrub with small, bluish-green, aromatic leaves. Small pink, yellow and green tubular pendant flowers are produced in pairs, mainly during Jan.-July. Responds well to light pruning. Previously known as *Rylstonea cernua*.
H O SS D L SA G C1 F1 B
Chart 8a, Chapter 13

Homoranthus papillatus
0.5-1 m x 1-2 m Qld
An ornamental, low, spreading plant with horizontal branches. Has small, smooth greyish-green leaves. Clusters of small, yellow flowers are produced mainly during Oct.-Feb. This species has been sold as *H. flavescens* which differs in having slightly rough leaves.
H O SS D M L SA G C1 F1
Chart 2a, Chapter 3

Hovea lanceolata, Lance-leaf Hovea
1-2 m x 1 m Qld, NSW
An open shrub with leaves to 6 cm long. Blue to purple pea-flowers are produced mainly during July-Nov. This species grows best in a semi-shaded and well-drained garden situation.
O SS D M L SA C1 F2
Chart 7b, Chapter 3

11 26 **Hymenosporum flavum**, Native Frangipani
5-10 m x 1.5-5 m Qld, NSW
An upright tree with shiny, dark green leaves. Has a profuse display of fragrant, yellow and cream flowers during Oct.-Dec. Hardy to a fairly wide range of conditions.
H O SS D M L SA G CA C1 F1 B
Chart 2c, Chapter 3

60 **Isopogon anethifolius**, Conebush
1.5-3 m x 1-2 m NSW
Has upright branches and finely divided leaves. Yellow flower-heads of around 4 cm diam. are produced mainly during Aug.-Nov. Prefers a well-drained situation. Although often of upright habit, dense bushy growth can be encouraged by pruning from an early age.
H O SS D L SA G C1 F2
Chart 17, Chapter 21

72 **Isotoma fluviatilis**
Spreading, prostrate plant Qld, NSW, Vic
This mat plant has small green leaves and small, blue, star-like flowers in spring and summer. Plants spread by layering. Grows best in moist situations and will flower well if in partial or full sun.
H O SS M W L SA C1 F1
Chart 22, Chapter 28

Jacksonia scoparia
3-5 m x 1.5-3 m Qld, NSW
An upright shrub with narrow, greyish foliage. Profuse orange to yellow, fragrant pea-flowers are produced during Sept.-Nov. An eye-catching plant when in flower. Prefers a warm, well-drained situation.
H O SS D L SA G CA C1 F2
Chart 2c, Chapter 3

Jasminum suavissimum, Sweet Jasmine
Slender climber Qld, NSW
A comparatively light climber which can also act as a groundcover. It has slender green leaves. Highly fragrant, white flowers are produced in clusters mainly during Oct.-Feb. Will grow in a wide range of well-drained situations. Responds well to pruning.
H O S SS D L SA C1 F2
Chart 14, Chapter 17

Kennedia beckxiana
Climber WA
A fairly strong twiner, climber or groundcover with green to blue-green leaves divided into 3 leaflets. Bright red with green pea-flowers of up to 5 cm long are produced mainly during Aug.-Dec. Likes a well-drained situation and is a good bird-attracting plant.
H O SS D L SA G C1 F1 B
Charts 14, Chapter 17; 15, Chapter 18

5 **Kennedia glabrata**
Prostrate x 1-2 m WA
Leaves are shiny and dark green. Fragrant, brick-red pea-flowers are produced on stems above the foliage around Nov.-Dec. A very quick-growing plant although often short-lived. Useful for initial quick cover in new garden areas. Plants flower and seed profusely.
O SS D L SA G C1 B
Chart 8a, Chapter 13

Kennedia macrophylla
Climber WA
A strong climber, twiner or groundcover. Has large, bright red with yellow pea-flowers which are produced in racemes of up to 15 cm long mainly during Nov.-Dec. It is an adaptable species suited to well-drained situations. Tolerates drought and also coastal exposure.
H O SS D L SA CA C2 F1 B
Charts 14, Chapter 17; 15, Chapter 18

Kennedia nigricans, Black Coral-pea
Vigorous climber WA
The pea-flowers of this species are deep purple-black with greenish-yellow. They are seen mainly during Sept.-Nov. A vigorous plant excellent for large areas but able to strangle smaller plants if given the opportunity. Can suffer frost damage.
H O SS D L SA CA C1 B
Chart 14, Chapter 17

Kennedia retrorsa
Vigorous climber NSW
Racemes of purple pea-flowers provide a showy display mainly during Sept.-Oct. This is a vigorous species. It grows well in semi-shade. As with *K. nigricans* (above) it can strangle smaller plants.
O SS D L SA C1 F1
Chart 14, Chapter 17

Kennedia rubicunda, Dusky Coral-pea
Vigorous climber or groundcover
Qld, NSW, Vic
The pea-flowers of this species are a dusky-pink to dark red. They are seen mainly during Oct.-Jan. Excellent for coastal situations but can be frost-tender. This is another vigorous kennedia which can strangle smaller plants if given the opportunity.
O SS D M L SA G CA C2 B
Charts 14, Chapter 17; 15, Chapter 18

Kunzea ambigua, White Kunzea
1-3 m x 1-2 m NSW, Vic, Tas
A bushy, tea-tree-like shrub with small, often crowded leaves. Profuse, small, white, honey-scented flowers are produced mainly during Oct.-Jan. Suited to a range of situations including exposed coastal conditions.
H O SS D M L SA C2 F1
Charts 12a, Chapter 16; 16, Chapter 19

Kunzea baxteri
2-4 m x 2-4 m WA
A bushy shrub with very showy, red, bottlebrush flower-spikes tipped with gold. They are seen mainly during May-Oct. Grows and flowers best in well-drained to dry situations. Pruning will encourage dense growth.
H O SS D L SA G C2 F1 B
Chart 16, Chapter 19

4 **Kunzea pomifera**, Muntries
0.5 m x 1-3 m Vic, SA
A dense, spreading plant with crowded leaves and clusters of white to cream flowers in spring. These are followed by bluish berries. It is hardy, although sometimes initially slow-growing. Prefers a well-drained situation.
H O SS D L SA G CA C2 F2 B
Charts 10a, Chapter 14; 17, Chapter 21; 21, Chapter 27

Lagunaria patersonii, Norfolk Island Hibiscus
8-13 m x 3-6 m Qld
An attractive, single-trunked tree. Flowering is during Dec.-April when pink, open-petalled flowers to 6 cm diam. are produced. Ideally suited to coastal situations. Usually grows as a small to medium tree in cultivation.
H O SS D L SA G CA C2 F1 B
Charts 1c, Chapter 3; 16, Chapter 19

15 **Lambertia formosa**, Mountain Devil
2-3 m x 2-3 m NSW
This species has dark green, pointed leaves and orange-red to bright red tubular flowers. Plants can flower throughout the year, with a peak in Feb.-April, and contain a good supply of nectar for honey-eating birds. The rigid foliage also provides excellent nesting sites.
H O SS D L SA G C1 F2 B
Charts 1b, Chapter 3; 9, Chapter 13

Lambertia inermis, Chittick
2-4 m x 1.5-2.5 m WA
A large shrub producing clusters of yellow to red flowers over a long period during July-Dec. Likes a well-drained and sunny situation. This species is usually of open habit but plants respond well to pruning.
H O D L SA G C1 F2 B
Chart 1b, Chapter 3

6 **Lechenaultia biloba**, Blue Lechenaultia
0.5-1 m x 0.5-1 m WA
A small shrub with small, narrow leaves. Spectacular blue flowers are produced during July-Dec. Very deep blue, pale blue and white forms are also in cultivation. Likes a sunny, well-drained position. Plants can be short-lived but some forms sucker naturally, and all strike readily from cuttings. Suitable for gardens or containers.
O SS D M L SA G C1 F1
Charts 1a, Chapter 3; 21, Chapter 27; 23, Chapter 28

1 21 **Lechenaultia formosa**, Red Lechenaultia
22 68 0.1-0.6 m x 0.5-1 m WA
A variable plant in growth habit and also flower colour. Flowering period is March-Nov. and flowers can be in combinations of yellow, orange, pinks and reds. Responds well to pruning. Flowers best in a sunny situation. Some forms sucker lightly. Suitable for gardens or containers.
H O SS D M L SA G C1 F1
Charts 1a, Chapter 3; 21, Chapter 27; 23, Chapter 28

Leptospermum flavescens, Tantoon
3-4 m x 3-4 m Qld, NSW
A large shrub with branchlets often pendulous. Profuse white to cream tea-tree flowers can almost cover the foliage during Sept.-Dec. Responds well to pruning.
H O SS M W L SA G C1 F1
Chart 12a, Chapter 16

Leptospermum 'Horizontalis'
0.5-1 m x 2-4 m Cultivar
A dense, spreading shrub with prickly pointed leaves. Has profuse, white, tea-tree flowers during Oct.-Dec. A hardy and reliable low shrub which will tolerate a fairly wide range of conditions.
H O SS W L SA G CA C2 F1
Charts 12a, Chapter 16; 15, Chapter 18; 21, Chapter 27

Leptospermum humifusum
0.2-1 m x 1-2 m Tas
A variable, spreading, dwarf shrub. Leaves are small and dark green. Has small, white, tea-tree flowers mainly during Sept.-Nov. Likes a well-drained situation in full or partial sun.
H O SS W L SA G CA C1 F2
Chart 2a, Chapter 3

Leptospermum laevigatum, Coastal Tea-tree
3-6 m x 3-6 m Qld, NSW, Vic, Tas, SA
A bushy shrub or small tree, often with a twisted and gnarled trunk. White flowers are produced mainly during Sept.-Dec. Excellent for exposed coastal situations. Many birds nest in the branches of this species. The bark is papery and provides good nesting material.
H O S SS D M L SA CA C2 F1
Charts 9, Chapter 13; 16, Chapter 19

Leptospermum nitidum 'Copper Sheen'
2.5 m x 2-3 m Cultivar
Has reddish foliage with bright deep red new growth. Lime-yellow flowers of around 2.5 cm diam. are produced during Sept.-Nov. This plant is worthy of cultivation for its foliage alone. Flowers are also attractive. Pruning will promote the new growth.
H O SS M W L SA G C1 F1
Chart 2b, Chapter 3

Leptospermum phylicoides, Burgan
3-6 m x 2-4 m Qld, NSW, Vic
This species has crowded, narrow, green leaves. Clusters of white (or sometimes palest pink) tea-tree flowers are produced near the ends of the branchlets in a showy display during Nov.-Feb. A very useful plant for moist to wet situations.
H O SS M W L SA G C1 F2
Chart 7c, Chapter 10

Leptospermum scoparium, Manuka
1.5-2.5 m x 2-3 m NSW, Vic, Tas
Has white to pale pinkish or purplish flowers of 2-3 cm diam. mainly during Oct.-Dec. A variable species with many different forms and botanical varieties. All are hardy to a wide range of situations.
H O SS M W L SA G C1 F2
Chart 12a, Chapter 16

Leptospermum scoparium var. **rotundifolium**, Round-leaf Tea-tree
1.5-2.5 m x 2-3 m NSW
Flowers can be white or various shades of pink, even merging into purple. Flowering is during Oct.-Dec. One form from Jervis Bay, NSW, has bluish-mauve flowers of 2-3 cm diam. A hardy and attractive shrub suited to a wide range of conditions and uses in cultivation.
H O SS M W L SA G C1 F2
Chart 21, Chapter 27

Leptospermum squarrosum, Peach Tea-tree
1-3 m x 1-3 m NSW
A bushy shrub with narrow, prickly, dark green leaves. Profuse white to deep pink flowers are produced along the older branches mainly during Feb.-April. This is a hardy and adaptable species.
H O SS M W L SA G C1 F2
Chart 11, Chapter 15

Lipparis reflexa, Yellow Rock-orchid
0.2-0.5 m x 0.2-0.5 m Qld, NSW
This lithophytic orchid has broad leaves to 30 cm long. It produces racemes of small, pale greenish-white to yellow-green flowers mainly during March-May. It is an adaptable species and grows well in containers.
O S SS M C1 F1
Chart 20, Chapter 24

Lippia nodiflora, see **Phyla nodiflora**

Lophostemon confertus, Brush Box
10-35 m x 6-12 m Qld, NSW
A small to medium tree with shiny, dark green leaves to 15 cm long. Feathery white flowers are produced mainly during Dec.-Feb. It is a hardy species which rarely reaches its full size in cultivation. It is widely used as a street tree. Was known as *Tristania conferta.*
H O SS D M L SA C1 F1
Charts 2c, Chapter 3; 12b, Chapter 16

Mazus pumilio, Swamp Mazus
Prostrate x 1-2 m Qld, NSW, Vic, Tas, SA
A colourful mat plant with shiny, oblong, green leaves. Tubular mauve or white flowers are produced mainly during Nov.-April. Likes a moist, sunny situation and spreads by suckering.
H O SS M W L SA CA C1 F1
Chart 23, Chapter 28

50 **Melaleuca armillaris**, Bracelet Honey-myrtle
4-8 m x 3-6 m Qld, NSW, Vic
A bushy large shrub to small tree with dark green, narrow leaves to 2.5 cm long. Flower-buds can have prominent reddish bracts. Cream flower-spikes are produced mainly during Aug.-Jan. A hardy and quick-growing species suitable for use as a screen or wind-break plant.
H O SS M W L SA G C2 F2 B
Charts 7c, Chapter 10; 12b, Chapter 16; 13, Chapter 17

Melaleuca decussata, Totem Poles
2-4 m x 2-4 m Vic, SA
A dense shrub. Has small, grey-green leaves and some forms have pendulous foliage. Pale to deep mauve brushes are produced during Sept.-Jan. Will grow in moist or well-drained situations.
H O SS M W L SA G CA C1 F2
Charts 3, Chapter 3; 11, Chapter 15

Melaleuca diosmifolia
2-4 m x 2-4 m WA
A dense, bushy shrub with crowded green leaves. Lime-green bottlebrush flower-heads are produced during Oct.-Dec. It is an adaptable species which flowers best in well-drained situations. Plants can be frost-tender.
H O SS M W L SA G C1 B
Chart 12a, Chapter 16

Melaleuca elliptica, Granite Honey-myrtle
3-5 m x 2-5 m NSW
A dense shrub with pendulous branches. The oval, grey-green leaves can become reddish during cold weather. Orange-red to deep red flower-spikes of up to 8 cm long are produced on the older wood mainly in Sept.-Feb. This species will grow in a wide range of situations.
H O SS W L SA G C1 F1 B
Charts 5, Chapter 3; 12a, Chapter 16

Melaleuca ericifolia, Swamp Paperbark
4-8 m x 2-4 m NSW, Vic, Tas
An upright shrub to small tree with papery bark. The leaves are small and crowded on the branchlets. Cream flower-brushes about 4 cm long are produced around Oct.-Nov. Grows best in a moist situation with full or partial sun.
H O SS W L SA G CA C1 F2
Chart 3, Chapter 3

Melaleuca fulgens, Scarlet Honey-myrtle
1.5-3 m x 1.5-3 m WA
A slightly open shrub with narrow, greyish-green leaves. The open bottlebrush-type flower-heads, seen in Sept.-Dec., can be scarlet, deep pink, or salmon-pink tipped with gold. Adaptable to a fairly wide range of garden situations.
H O SS D W L SA G C1 F1 B
Chart 1b, Chapter 3

Melaleuca halmaturorum
4-6 m x 2-4 m Vic, SA
A large shrub to small tree with attractive papery bark. White flower-spikes are produced mainly during Sept.-Dec. This hardy species will tolerate a range of conditions including salt spray. Prefers a sunny situation.
H O SS M W L SA CA C2 F1
Chart 4, Chapter 3

Melaleuca hypericifolia, Hillock Bush
3-6 m x 2-5 m NSW
A dense shrub with pendulous branchlets. The leaves can become reddish during cold weather. Orange-red flower-spikes of up to 8 cm long are produced on the older wood mainly in Sept.-Feb. Will grow in a wide range of situations.
H O SS W L SA G C1 F1 B
Charts 8c, Chapter 13; 17, Chapter 21

Melaleuca incana, Grey Honey-myrtle
2-3 m x 2-3 m WA
An attractive plant with grey-green, pendulous foliage. Pale yellow brushes of up to 5 cm long are produced during Sept.-Dec. Suited to moist or well-drained situations.
H O SS M W L SA G CA C1 F1
Chart 2b, Chapter 3

Melaleuca lanceolata, Moonah
3-8 m x 2-6 m Qld, NSW, Vic, SA, WA
This species has a dark, hard-barked trunk. It has white to cream brushes in Oct.-Feb. and flowering can be profuse. It is a relatively slow-growing small tree. Prefers a sunny, well-drained situation and will tolerate exposed coastal conditions and alkaline soils.
H O SS L SA G CA C2 F1
Chart 4, Chapter 3

Melaleuca lateritia, Red Robin Bush
2-4 m x 1.5-3 m WA
Has narrow leaves to 1-2 cm long. Bright orange-red flower-spikes of up to 10 cm long are produced on the older wood mainly in Nov.-April. Plants are adaptable to sun or semi-shade in moist or well-drained situations.
H O SS M W L SA G C1 F2 B
Charts 8b, Chapter 13; 12a, Chapter 16

Melaleuca leucadendron
15-25 m x 8-15 m Qld, WA, NT
A medium to large tree with papery bark and broad leaves. Cream flower-spikes to 15 cm long are produced mainly during June-Feb. with sporadic flowering at other times. Will tolerate moist or even waterlogged situations.
H O SS M W L SA G CA C2 F1 B
Charts 2c, 3, Chapter 3; 9, Chapter 13

Melaleuca linariifolia, Snow in Summer
5-10 m x 3-6 m Qld, NSW
This attractive tree has papery bark and white, feathery flowers produced in clusters during Nov.-Feb. It is a hardy species which will grow in moist or well-drained positions. It is often grown as a street tree. The papery bark provides excellent nesting material for birds.
H O SS W L SA G C1 F2
Charts 9, Chapter 13; 13, Chapter 17

Melaleuca nesophila, Showy Honey-myrtle
3-6 m x 2-5 m WA
A dense shrub with globular flower-heads of about 2.5 cm diam. They are mauve-pink tipped with gold, and can be seen mainly during Dec.-March. Hardy to a wide range of conditions including moderate coastal exposure. Responds well to pruning.
H O SS W L SA G CA C1 F1
Chart 16, Chapter 19

Melaleuca quinquenervia
15-25 m x 3-10 m Qld, NSW
An upright tree with papery bark and broad leaves. Cream bottlebrush flower-spikes are produced mainly during June-Dec. with sporadic flowering at other times. Plants are hardy to a wide range of situations but can be damaged by frosts.
H O SS M W L SA C2 B
Chart 3, Chapter 3

Melaleuca squamea, Swamp Honey-myrtle
1-3 m x 1-1.5 m NSW, Vic, Tas, SA
A fairly upright shrub with terminal heads of colourful, mauve flowers produced mainly during Sept.-Dec. Hardy to a wide range of soil types and able to tolerate poor drainage.
H O SS D M W L SA C1 F2
Chart 7b, Chapter 10

Melaleuca styphelioides, Prickly-leaved Paperbark
4-15 m x 3-8 m NSW
A large shrub or small tree with papery bark. Has creamy white flower-spikes, mainly during Dec.-Jan. An adaptable species suited to situations with good or poor drainage.
H O SS D M W L SA CA C1 F1
Charts 2c, 4, Chapter 3; 13, Chapter 17

Melaleuca thymifolia, Thyme Honey-myrtle
0.5-1.5 m x 1-1.5 m Qld, NSW
A compact shrub with mauve to purple flowers during Oct.-April. Excellent for a sunny, moist situation. Will withstand periods of waterlogging.
H O SS M W L SA CA C1 F1
Charts 2a, Chapter 3; 11, Chapter 15

Melaleuca violacea
1-2 m x 1-2 m WA
Leaves are greyish-green and heart-shaped. Purple to violet flowers are produced mainly during Sept.-Oct. A variable species, with a prostrate form also available. Grows well in moist situations.
H O SS W L SA G C1 F1
Charts 2b, Chapter 3; 12a, Chapter 16

Melaleuca viridiflora
8-18 m x 4-10 m Qld, WA, NT
A large shrub to medium tree with leaves to 15 cm long. Pale green or red flower-spikes are produced throughout most of the year. A variable species both in habit and flower colour. Best suited to tropical or sub-tropical areas.
H O SS D M W L SA G C1 B
Chart 2c, Chapter 3

47 **Melaleuca wilsonii**, Violet Honey-myrtle
1-2.5 m x 1-3 m Vic, SA
An open to fairly dense shrub with short, narrow leaves. Lilac to reddish-pink flowers are produced in clusters of up to 10 cm long along the older branches mainly during Sept.-Oct. Hardy to a wide range of well-drained or moist situations.
H O SS W L SA G CA C1 F2 B
Charts 10b, Chapter 14; 12a, Chapter 16; 15, Chapter 18

Melia azedarach var. **australasica**, White Cedar
6-8 m x 4-6 m Qld, NSW
This is one of the few Australian deciduous trees. It has small, fragrant, purple and white flowers during Nov.-Dec. They are followed by yellow-orange berries which are retained on the tree for many months. Parrots enjoy these fruits. This species can grow much taller in its natural habitat.
H O SS D M L SA CA C1 F1 B
Chart 10c, Chapter 14

Mentha diemenica, Slender Mint
0.2 m x 0.5-1 m NSW, Vic, Tas, SA
Has highly aromatic leaves of 2-3 cm long. Spikes of small, mauve flowers are produced during Sept.-Feb. This native mint spreads by layering. It grows well in a wide range of situations and can cover a large area if conditions are favourable.
H O SS W L SA G CA C2 F2
Chart 22, Chapter 28

20 **Micromyrtus ciliata**, Fringed Heath-myrtle
0.1-1 m x 1-2 m Vic, SA
A variable species with prostrate and low, shrubby forms. Leaves are very small and crowded. Buds are white to pink, then white flowers deepen with age to red. Flowering period is May-Nov. Likes a moist yet fairly well-drained situation. An excellent cut flower.
O SS M W L SA G C1 F2
Charts 1a, Chapter 3; 7a, Chapter 10

Montia australasica, see **Claytonia australasica**

Myoporum floribundum, Slender Myoporum
2.5-4 m x 2-3 m NSW, Vic
A graceful shrub with horizontal branches and drooping leaves to 10 cm long. Clusters of small, white flowers are produced on the upper side of the branches mainly during Nov.-Jan.
O SS D L SA G CA C1 F2
Chart 5, Chapter 3

Myoporum insulare, Boobialla
3-5 m x 4-8 m NSW, Vic, Tas, SA, WA
A bushy shrub with foliage to ground level. White starry flowers are produced mainly during Sept.-Dec. An excellent screen or windbreak plant for exposed situations.
H O SS M W L SA G CA C2 F2
Charts 4, Chapter 3; 16, Chapter 19

Myoporum parvifolium, Creeping Myoporum
0.2-0.4 m x 1-3 m Vic, Tas, SA, WA
A hardy groundcover with bright green or purplish leaves. Many small, white or pale pink flowers are produced during Nov.-March. Grows best in partial to full sun. Plants can spread by layering. Dwarf, shrubby forms are also available.
H O SS W L SA G CA C2 F2
Charts 10a, Chapter 14; 15, Chapter 18; 21, Chapter 27; 22, Chapter 28

Myoporum viscosum, Sticky Boobialla
1-2 m x 1-2 m NSW, Vic, SA
The leaves of this species are shiny dark green and new growth is often sticky. Flowers are to 1.5 cm diam. and are white with small purple spots. Flowering is mainly during Sept.-Dec. A hardy shrub suited to coastal or inland areas.
H O SS D L SA C2 F1
Chart 15, Chapter 18

Myriocephalus stuartii, Poached Egg Daisy
0.5 m x 0.1-0.2 m Qld, NSW, Vic, SA, NT
An erect plant with flower-heads to 5 cm diam. The large centre is yellow, surrounded by white, papery bracts. Flowering is mainly during Sept.-Dec. This is an annual species with a wide natural distribution in low rainfall regions. It must have a sunny situation. The flowers are showy and dry well.
H O D L SA G C1 F1
Chart 18, Chapter 22

Nephrolepis cordifolia, Fish-bone Fern
0.5-1 m x 0.5-2 m Qld, NSW, WA, NT
A commonly cultivated fern with fronds to 1 m long. It spreads by creeping rhizomes to create a dense clump. It is a hardy species adaptable to a wide range of conditions. It can tolerate full sun provided the root system is moist.
O S SS D M L SA C1 F1
Charts 15, Chapter 18; 19, Chapter 23

Nothofagus cunninghamii, Myrtle Beech
5-15 m x 3-6 m Vic, Tas
This relatively slow-growing tree is cultivated mainly for its attractive foliage. It has shiny, oval, toothed leaves and bronze to reddish new growth. Small brownish flowers are produced in Nov.-Jan. Best suited to a shaded location. Can be used as an indoor container plant whilst young.
O S SS M W L SA C1 F2
Charts 1c, Chapter 3; 7c, Chapter 10

Olearia floribunda, Heath Daisy-bush
1-1.5 m x 0.5-1 m NSW, Vic, Tas, SA
A bushy shrub which produces a showy display of small white to bluish daisy flowers usually during Sept.-Dec. This species is adaptable to a fairly wide range of garden situations. Pruning after flowering is recommended.
H O SS D L SA C1 F2
Chart 7b, Chapter 10

30 **Olearia phlogopappa**, Dusty Daisy-bush
1.5-2.5 m x 1-2 m NSW, Vic, Tas
Has greyish-green and hairy leaves which are oblong with wavy edges. White, pink, blue or purple daisy flowers are profuse mainly during July-Nov. A widely grown species with many different forms. All are showy. Plants are fairly quick-growing and regular light pruning is recommended.
O SS D M L SA G C1 F2
Chart 7b, Chapter 10

Pandorea jasminoides, Bower Climber
Strong climber Qld, NSW
Has shiny, dark green, divided leaves. The trumpet-flowers are white to pink with deep red throats or all white. They are produced mainly during Dec.-March. It is an attractive species with selected forms (such as 'Bower of Beauty') also now available. Responds well to pruning.
O SS D M L SA C1 F1
Chart 14, Chapter 17

Pandorea pandorana, Wonga Vine
Strong climber Qld, NSW, Vic, Tas
The tubular flowers are usually cream to brown with cream to reddish throats. Flowering is mainly during July-Nov. Selected forms of this species are available including forms with white or yellow flowers. A useful plant for semi-shaded situations where it can be quite vigorous.
O SS D M L SA C1 F1
Charts 14, Chapter 17; 17, Chapter 21

Passiflora cinnabarina, Red Passion-flower
Usually vigorous climber NSW, Vic
Bright coppery-red flowers of up to 5 cm diam. are produced mainly during Sept.-Dec. followed by oval green fruits. The fruits are edible but without a pleasant taste. An adaptable species suited to a wide range of situations.
O S SS D M W L SA G C1 F1
Chart 14, Chapter 17

2 **Patersonia occidentalis**, Purple Flags
0.5-0.8 m x 0.5 m Vic, Tas, SA, WA
A clump-forming plant with narrow, rush-like leaves. Purple, 3-petalled flowers are produced during Oct.-Feb. There is also a white-flowered form. This hardy species grows best in a moist, sunny position.
H O SS M W L SA G CA C1 F2
Charts 2a, Chapter 3; 11, Chapter 15

Pellaea falcata, Sickle Fern
0.3-0.6 m x 0.5-1 m Qld, NSW, Vic, Tas
This fern has fishbone-shaped fronds with narrow segments and undulating margins. It is a hardy species which spreads by creeping rhizomes.
O S SS D M L SA C1 F2
Chart 19, Chapter 23

51 **Persoonia pinifolia**, Pine-leaved Geebung
3-5 m x 2-4 m Qld, NSW
A very attractive large shrub with fine green foliage and often reddish new growth. Long spikes of small yellow flowers are produced during Dec.-May. These are followed by clusters of green to purplish, fleshy fruits called geebungs. Likes a well-drained, warm situation. Responds well to light pruning. Fruits were eaten by Aborigines.
O SS D L SA G C1 F2
Chart 1b, Chapter 3

Petrophile serruriae
2-3 m x 2-3 m WA
A bushy shrub with finely divided, prickly leaves. Has clusters of pink to yellow flowers produced in the upper leaf axils mainly during Oct.-Dec. Seed can germinate readily in a garden if conditions are suitable.
H O SS D L SA G C1 F2
Chart 10b, Chapter 14

Phyla nodiflora
Prostrate, spreading plant Qld, SA, NT
This mat plant spreads by rooting at the nodes. Heads of pink flowers are produced throughout most of the year. Prefers a sunny position with well-drained soils. Can be used as a lawn if there is little or no foot traffic.
H O SS D L SA G CA C2 F2
Charts 10a, Chapter 14; 22, Chapter 28

1 **Pimelea ferruginea**
0.5-1.5 m x 0.5-1.5 m WA
An attractive small shrub with shiny, oblong leaves crowded along the branches. During

July-Oct. there is a spectacular display of terminal, pink flower-heads. Plants respond well to light pruning after flowering.
O SS D M L SA CA C2 F1
Chart 1b, Chapter 3

Pimelea humilis, Common Rice-flower
0.1-0.3 m x 0.3-1 m NSW, Vic, Tas, SA
A clump-forming plant with crowded, grey-green leaves. Heads of white to cream flowers are produced during Sept.-Nov. It is a lightly suckering species recommended for semi-shaded situations. It grows well at the base of tree trunks.
O SS D M L SA C1 F2
Chart 23, Chapter 28

Pittosporum phylliraeoides, Butterbush
3-6 m x 1.5-3 m
Qld, NSW, Vic, SA, WA, NT
An upright small tree with pendulous branches. Yellow, open-petalled, fragrant flowers are produced in Sept.-Nov. These are followed by decorative yellow fruits. This species is often found in extremely arid situations. Former spelling *P. phillyraeoides.*
H O SS D L SA G CA C1 F2
Chart 10c, Chapter 14

Pittosporum undulatum, Sweet Pittosporum
4-14 m x 2-6 m Qld, NSW, Vic, Tas, SA
A bushy tree with shiny, dark green leaves. The fragrant, cream-white flowers in Sept.-Nov. are followed by globular orange fruits with sticky seeds. Will grow in open or shaded situations. It adapts to a wide range of conditions and in some areas will form dense thickets through self-seeding.
H O S SS D M L SA C1 F1
Chart 12b, Chapter 16

Platycerium bifurcatum, Elkhorn
Clump-forming epiphyte Qld, NSW
This fern has large, irregular fronds. It is usually cultivated as an epiphyte and attached to slabs, trees or tree-fern trunks. It is the most common elkhorn fern in Australia. It is hardy and is widely cultivated.
S SS D C1 F1
Chart 19, Chapter 23

Polyscias sambucifolius, Elderberry Panax
4-6 m x 1-3 m Qld, NSW, Vic
A fairly upright small tree with olive-green, pinnate leaves to 30 cm long. Small greenish flowers are produced in Sept.-Dec., followed by translucent bluish berries. Suitable for use in a shaded location. Was known as *Tieghemopanax sambucifolius.*
O S SS D M W L SA C1 F2
Chart 1c, Chapter 3

Polystichum proliferum, Mother Shield-fern
0.5-1.5 m x 1-2 m NSW, Vic, Tas
This hardy and adaptable fern has arching, dark, dull green fronds. New plants are often produced at the frond tips. Grows best in cool, moist situations.
O S SS D M L SA C1 F2
Chart 19, Chapter 23

Pratia pedunculata, Pratia
Prostrate x 0.5-2 m NSW, Vic, Tas
A dense carpeting plant with small, oval leaves. It has profuse blue or white starry flowers during Oct.-April. Likes a moist position in sun or semi-shade and spreads by layering. It is an attractive plant and is suitable for gardens or containers.
H O SS M W L SA C1 F2
Charts 2a, Chapter 3; 22, Chapter 28

33 **Prostanthera aspalathoides**, Scarlet Mint-bush
0.5 m x 0.3-1 m NSW, Vic, SA
Has fine, strongly aromatic foliage. Tubular flowers of red, orange or yellow are produced over a long period, mainly during Sept.-Feb. Grows best in a warm, well-drained situation (unlike many other *Prostanthera* species which prefer shade and moisture). Responds well to tip pruning.
O SS D L SA G C1 F2 B
Chart 7a, Chapter 10

Prostanthera cuneata, Alpine Mint-bush
0.3-1.5 m x 0.5-1.5 m NSW, Vic, Tas
A shrubby *Prostanthera* with aromatic foliage. Has a showy display of white (or pale pink) flowers with purple or yellow markings during Oct.-March. This variable shrub, from sub-alpine areas, is well suited to semi-shaded situations.
O S SS D M L SA C1 F2
Chart 21, Chapter 27

Prostanthera lasianthos, Vic. Christmas Bush
2-6 m x 2-3 m Qld, NSW, Vic, Tas
This upright shrub has aromatic, dark green leaves to about 10 cm long with toothed margins. It provides a good display of tubular flowers in Nov.-Jan. Flowers are commonly white with purple markings in the throat. Pale mauve and pink forms are also available. Ideal for shaded situations. It is quick-growing and pruning will encourage bushy growth.
O S SS D M W L SA C1 F2
Charts 7c, Chapter 10; 13, Chapter 17

Prostanthera melissifolia, Balm Mint-bush
1.5-3 m x 1-2 m Vic
A bushy shrub with highly aromatic, dark green leaves. Violet to deep lilac (or sometimes pink) flowers provide a showy display during Oct.-Jan. A useful plant for a shaded situation. It is fairly quick-growing and responds well to pruning.
O S SS D M W L SA C1 F2
Chart 7b, Chapter 10

Prostanthera microphylla, see **P. serpyllifolia** ssp. **microphylla**

Prostanthera monticola, Monkey Mint-bush
1 m x 2 m NSW, Vic
This species usually grows as a dense, bushy plant with dark green leaves. Tubular flowers to 2-3 cm long are produced mainly during Nov.-Feb. They are an unusual shade of green streaked with purple. Responds well to pruning. Previously sold as *P. walteri* which has hairier stems and leaves.
O S SS D L SA G C1 F2 B
Charts 8a, Chapter 13; 17, Chapter 21

67 **Prostanthera rotundifolia**, Round-leaf Mint-bush
1.5-2.5 m x 1-3 m NSW, Vic, Tas, SA
This species has round to oval, aromatic leaves. Bears a profuse display of mauve-purple flowers during Aug.-Nov. Pink forms are also available. Excellent for shaded situations. Growth is usually compact and plants respond well to light pruning.
O S SS D M L SA C1 F2
Chart 21, Chapter 27

Prostanthera serpyllifolia ssp. **microphylla**, Small-leaf Mint-bush
0.3-0.5 m x 1 m NSW, Vic, SA, WA
A dwarf shrub of fairly open habit with small, hairy, aromatic leaves. Has pink to red or bluish-green tubular flowers scattered over the plant mainly during Sept.-Feb. Likes a well-drained situation. Previously known as *P. microphylla.*
H O SS D L SA G CA C1 F2 B
Chart 8a, Chapter 13

Pterostylis concinna, Trim Greenhood
To 0.3 m high Qld, NSW, Vic, Tas
This small terrestrial orchid has a basal rosette of leaves and a flower-stem to 0.3 m high. The flowers are green with white and brown markings and are seen mainly during May-Oct. Protection from slugs and snails is essential. Is cultivated with best success in containers.
O S SS L SA C1 F2
Chart 20, Chapter 24

Pterostylis curta, Blunt Greenhood
To 0.3 m high Qld, NSW, Vic, Tas
A small terrestrial orchid with a basal rosette of wavy leaves. The flowers, produced during July-Oct., are green with red and brown markings. Cultivation as for *P. concinna* (above).
O S SS L SA C1 F2
Chart 20, Chapter 24

Pterostylis nutans, Nodding Greenhood
To 0.3 m high Qld, NSW, Vic, Tas, SA
This small terrestrial orchid has about 5, wavy-edged leaves in a basal rosette. Nodding, translucent, green flowers are produced on stems to 0.3 m tall, mainly during July-Nov. This colony-forming species is one of the most adaptable of the Australian terrestrial orchids. Cultivation as for *P. concinna* (above).
O S SS L SA C1 F2
Chart 20, Chapter 24

Pterostylis pedunculata, Maroonhood
To 0.3 m high Qld, NSW, Vic, Tas, SA
The basal rosette has 3 to 6 leaves which are heavily veined. The flowers of this small terrestrial orchid usually have green and white stripes with the hood tip mainly maroon or reddish-brown. They are produced on stems to 0.3 m high during July-Nov. See *P. concinna* (above) for cultivation comments.
O S SS L SA C1 F2
Chart 20, Chapter 24

Pultenaea gunnii, Golden Bush-pea
1-1.5 m x 1-1.5 m Vic, Tas
A quick-growing small shrub with small green leaves. Has a showy display of orange-yellow pea-flowers produced in clusters during Aug.-Nov. Plants benefit from light pruning from an early stage. The seeds, produced in pods following flowering, provide food for parrots and pigeons.
H O SS D M L SA C1 F2 B
Chart 8b, Chapter 13

Pultenaea humilis, Dwarf Bush-pea
0.2-0.4 m x 0.5-1 m NSW, Vic, Tas
A small shrub with dense, hairy leaves. Heads of orange and yellow, or orange and brown, pea-flowers are produced mainly during Aug.-Nov. Although often a fairly insignificant plant when not in bloom the flowers can provide a very showy display of colour. Plants respond well to light pruning after flowering.
O SS D L SA G C1 F2
Chart 7a, Chapter 10

Pultenaea pedunculata, Matted Bush-pea
0.5 m x 1-2 m NSW, Vic, Tas, SA
A quick-growing groundcover with crowded, small green leaves giving a dense foliage cover. Has a profuse display of usually orange or yellow with red pea-flowers during Sept.-Dec. Will tolerate shade but flowers best in sun or partial sun. Plants can spread by layering.
H O SS D M L SA G C1 F2
Charts 1a, 2a, Chapter 3; 7a, Chapter 10; 22, Chapter 28

Pultenaea pedunculata 'Pyalong Gold'
0.5 m x 1-2 m Cultivar (Vic)
This selected form of *P. pedunculata* (above) has profuse, golden pea flowers.
H O SS D M L SA G C1 F2
Chart 22, Chapter 28

Pultenaea pedunculata 'Pyalong Pink'
0.5 m x 1-2 m Cultivar (Vic)
This selected form of *P. pedunculata* (above) has attractive, pink pea-flowers.
H O SS D M L SA G C1 F2
Chart 22, Chapter 28

Regelia ciliata
1.5-2.5 m x 2-3 m WA
A hardy shrub with small, stem-hugging leaves. Mauve to purple, globular flower-heads are produced during Nov.-March. Adaptable to a wide range of conditions. Responds well to pruning.
H O SS M W L SA G C1 F1
Charts 12a, Chapter 16; 17, Chapter 21

Regelia velutina, Barrens Regelia
2.5-4 m x 1-2 m WA
A highly decorative species with greyish foliage and bright red flower-spikes tipped with gold. Flowering is mainly during Aug.-Jan. Prefers a warm to hot, well-drained situation. Plants can be slow to flower initially.
H O SS D L SA G C2 F1 B
Chart 10b, Chapter 14

Restio tetraphyllus, Tassel-cord Rush
1.5-2 m x 1-2 m Qld, NSW, Vic, Tas, SA
A decorative rush with upright stems bearing soft foliage at the tips. Tassels of brown or reddish flowers are produced mainly during Sept.-Dec. A very attractive plant for use beside a pond.
H O SS M W L SA C1 F2
Chart 11, Chapter 15

Rhagodia spinescens
Prostrate to 1 m x 1.5-3 m
Qld, NSW, Vic, SA, WA, NT
A dense groundcover with greyish, hairy, triangular leaves. Flowers are insignificant. It occurs in inland regions of Australia and is tolerant of very hot, dry conditions. Plants withstand clipping. Foliage is fire-retardant.
H O SS L SA G CA C2 F2
Charts 10a, Chapter 14; 12a, Chapter 16

Rylstonea cernua, see **Homoranthus darwinioides**

Scaevola 'Mauve Clusters'
Prostrate x 1-2 m Cultivar
A dense groundcover with bright green leaves. Has profuse clusters of small, fan-shaped, mauve flowers during Sept.-March. It is quick-growing and suitable for gardens or containers. Plants can sucker lightly.
O SS D M L SA C1 F1
Charts 2a, Chapter 3; 21, Chapter 27

58 **Scaevola striata**, Royal Robe
0.2-0.5 m x 1-2 m WA
The leaves of this species have toothed margins and foliage is usually quite dense. Showy mauve to bluish-purple flowers to around 2.5 cm diam. are produced mainly during Oct.-Feb. A useful groundcover which can spread by lightly suckering.
O SS D M L SA C1 F1
Chart 15, Chapter 18

Scleranthus biflorus, Knawel
0.1-0.3 m x 0.5-1 m Qld, NSW, Vic, Tas
A dense, moss-like plant with bright, light green foliage. Flowers insignificant. A somewhat unusual plant, ideal for use in rockeries. The foliage colour contrasts well with other shades of green in the garden. Suitable also for cultivation in a container.
H O SS D M L SA C1 F2
Chart 7a, Chapter 10

Sollya heterophylla, Bluebell Creeper
Hardy climber WA
A relatively dense, bushy climber. Clusters of blue, pink or white bell-shaped flowers hang from the branchlet tips, mainly during Sept.-Feb. These are followed by elongated green to bluish fruits. It is a hardy species, adaptable to a wide range of situations. Responds well to pruning.
H O SS M W L SA C1 F1
Charts 14, Chapter 17; 17, Chapter 21

Sowerbaea juncea, Vanilla Lily; Rush Lily
0.3-0.5 m x 0.3-0.5 m Qld, NSW, Vic
A small, clump-forming plant with grass-like leaves. During Oct.-Dec. globular clusters of mauve flowers are borne on stems taller than the foliage. The flowers have a fragrance similar to chocolate or caramel. Suitable for cultivation in gardens or containers.
H O SS M W L SA C1 F1
Chart 11, Chapter 15

Sprengelia incarnata, Pink Swamp-heath
1-2 m x 0.5-0.7 m NSW, Vic, Tas, SA
An erect plant with small, pointed leaves. Dense terminal clusters of small, star-like, pale pink flowers are produced mainly during Sept.-Dec. Pruning will encourage bushy growth.
H O SS M W L SA C1 F1 B
Chart 11, Chapter 15

Spyridium parvifolium 'Austraflora Nimbus'
Prostrate x 0.5-1 m Cultivar
The small, white to cream flowers, produced mainly during Sept.-Feb. are surrounded by grey floral leaves. This decorative groundcover is a selected form of *S. parvifolium* which usually grows to 3 m tall.
O SS D L SA G C1 F2
Charts 2a, Chapter 3; 10a, Chapter 14

Stenocarpus sinuatus, Firewheel Tree
6-15 m x 3-5 m Qld, NSW
This species can grow much larger in its natural habitat. It has large, shiny, dark green leaves. Spectacular, red, wheel-like flower-heads are produced during Jan.-May. Likes a warm situation. Can be frost-tender, particularly when young.
H O SS D M W L SA G C1 B
Chart 1c, Chapter 3

35 **Stylidium graminifolium**, Grass Trigger-plant
0.1-0.2 m x 0.2-0.3 m Qld, NSW, Vic, Tas
A tufting plant with grass-like leaves. Numerous pale to dark pink flowers are produced on stems to 1 m tall during Nov.-Jan. The flowers have an unusual trigger-like pollinating mechanism. It is a widespread species including some forms from sub-alpine regions.
O SS D M L SA G C1 F1
Chart 7a, Chapter 10

Stypandra caespitosa, Tufted Lily
0.3-0.5 m x 0.5 m Qld, NSW, Vic, Tas
This tuft-forming plant has grey-green, grass-like leaves. Blue or sometimes cream flowers are borne on branched stems above the foliage in Oct.-Feb. This species is suitable for a wide range of moist or well-drained situations.
O SS D M L SA G C1 F2
Charts 2a, Chapter 3; 11, Chapter 15

Swainsonia maccullochiana, Ashburton Pea
1.5-2 m x 1-2 m WA
This annual species has ferny, pinnate leaves and heads of rose-pink pea-flowers produced mainly during Nov.-Feb. It is an attractive plant and likes a sunny, well-drained situation. Has only been cultivated to a limited extent to date.
H O SS D L SA C1 F1
Chart 18, Chapter 22

Syzygium coolminianum, Lilly Pilly
5-10 m x 3-5 m NSW
An attractive small to medium tree with shiny, dark green leaves. White flowers are produced in Sept.-Dec., followed by globular, succulent pink to blue-purple fruits. Responds well to pruning. It is often grown as a street tree and the fruits can be used for jams. Is sometimes sold as *Eugenia coolminianum.*
H O S SS D M L SA C1 F1 B
Charts 1c, Chapter 3; 8c, Chapter 13

Telopea oreades, Gippsland Waratah
3-5 m x 2-4 m NSW, Vic
A large, open shrub to small tree with tough, green leaves. It has terminal, red flower-heads mainly during Sept.-Dec. The flower-heads are more open than those of the NSW Waratah, *Telopea speciosissima.* Prefers fairly good drainage and is best suited to a position with partial sun.
O S SS D M L SA C1 F2 B
Chart 7c Chapter 10

Telopea speciosissima, NSW Waratah
3-5 m x 2-3 m NSW
This species has spectacular, red flower-heads produced usually during Sept.-Nov. It is the floral emblem of NSW. Prefers a cool root area with some sun on the foliage area of the plant to encourage good flowering. Responds well to pruning after flowering.
O SS D M L SA C1 F2 B
Chart 8b, Chapter 13

Templetonia retusa, Cockies Tongues
1.5-2.5 m x 1-2 m SA, WA
This is usually an upright shrub. It has grey-green, wedge-shaped leaves. Showy, large, bright pink or red (rarely white) pea-flowers are produced during May-Oct. Plants prefer a relatively open situation.
H O SS D W L SA G CA C2 F1 B
Chart 5, Chapter 3

Tetratheca ciliata, Pink Bells
0.2-0.5 m x 0.5-1 m Vic, Tas, SA
A small, clump-forming plant with pendant, mauve-pink (or white) flowers, produced near the branchlet ends in July-Dec. It is ideally suited as an undershrub, growing beneath taller plants. Responds well to pruning.
O SS D M L SA G C1 F2
Chart 7a, Chapter 10

Tetratheca thymifolia
0.5-1 m x 0.5-1 m Qld, NSW, Vic
This species is similar in form, flower and cultivation requirements to *T. ciliata* (above). It is slightly hardier and is also more vigorous.
O SS D M L SA G C1 F2
Chart 7a, Chapter 10

66 **Thryptomene saxicola**, Rock Thryptomene
0.5-1.5 m x 1-2 m WA
A bushy, arching plant with profuse clusters of small, pale to deep pink flowers. Flowering period is mainly during April-Oct. Hardy to a range of garden situations. It responds well to regular light pruning and is excellent for cut flowers.
H O SS D L SA G C1 F1
Chart 21, Chapter 27

Tieghemopanax sambucifolius, see **Polyscias sambucifolius**

Todea barbara, King Fern
2-3 m x 2-4 m Qld, NSW, Vic, Tas, SA
This large fern has a short, broad trunk from which multiple heads of fronds to 2 m long can develop. The fronds are leathery, divided, and bright shiny green. Plants are slow to reach full size.
O S SS D M W L SA C1 F2
Charts 11, Chapter 15; 19, Chapter 23

Trachymene caerulea, Rottnest Daisy; Blue Lace Flower
0.5-1 m x 0.3-0.5 m WA
A fairly widely grown annual. Delicate blue flowers are produced in soft heads of up to 6 cm diam. on the tips of branching stems. Main flowering time is Sept.-Jan. Requires frost protection when plants are young. Early pruning will encourage bushy growth and more flower-heads.
H O SS D M L SA C1
Chart 18, Chapter 22

Tristania conferta, see **Lophostemon confertus**

Tristania laurina, see **Tristaniopsis laurina**

Tristaniopsis laurina, Kanooka; Water Gum
Usually 3-15 m x 2-15 m Qld, NSW, Vic
Has attractive, smooth, grey-barked trunk or trunks and glossy green leaves. Yellow flowers are produced mainly during Aug.-Feb. Adaptable to a range of different situations. Very old plants can grow larger than dimensions above. Was known as *Tristania laurina*.
H O S SS D M W L SA C1 F1
Charts 2c, Chapter 3; 12b, Chapter 16

Verticordia plumosa
1 m x 1 m WA
A small, bushy shrub with grey-green aromatic leaves. Dense globular heads of mauve-pink flowers are produced in Sept.-Dec. Suited to a sunny, well-drained situation. Responds well to pruning after flowering.
H O SS D L SA G C1 F1
Chart 1a, Chapter 3

Viminaria juncea, Native Broom
4-6 m x 2-4 m Qld, NSW, Vic, Tas, SA, WA
Upright plant with fine, pendulous branchlets. Sprays of light yellow pea-flowers create a showy display in Sept.-Nov. It is a quick-growing plant ideal for garden planting in moist situations.
H O SS M W L SA CA C1 F2
Chart 3, Chapter 3

6 **Viola hederacea**, Ivy-leaved Violet; Native Violet
0.1 m x 1-2 m Qld, NSW, Vic, Tas, SA
A spreading herb with green, kidney-shaped leaves. The small, violet flowers are purple-blue and white. They can be seen for most of the year. Ideal for a moist, shaded or semi-shaded location. Suitable for gardens or containers.
O S SS M W L SA C1 F2
Charts 11, Chapter 15; 22, Chapter 28

Wahlenbergia gloriosa, Royal Bluebell
Prostrate x 0.5-1 m NSW, Vic, Tas
This alpine species has leaves of 2-3 cm long with wavy margins. Showy, deep blue-purple flowers are produced on slender stems mainly in Nov.-March. It is the floral emblem of the ACT. Likes a sunny yet moist position. Spreads by suckering.
H O SS D M L SA C1 F2
Charts 7a, Chapter 10; 23, Chapter 28

Waitzia acuminata, Everlastings
0.3-0.6 m x 0.3-0.6 m
NSW, Vic, SA, WA, NT
An annual with toothed lower leaves to 8 cm long. Papery flower-heads are produced on branched stems, mainly during Sept.-Dec. They are usually golden-yellow but can be white or pink. This species has a wide natural distribution and has potential for greater use as a garden flower. Seed is available commercially.
H O D L SA G C1 F1
Chart 18, Chapter 22

Waitzia aurea, Golden Waitzia
0.4 m x 0.1-0.3 m WA
This annual species is of erect habit. It has golden everlasting flower-heads produced mainly during Sept.-Dec. It is not widely grown at present but seed is obtainable.
H O D L SA G C1 F1
Chart 18, Chapter 22

Waitzia suaveolens, Fragrant Waitzia
0.3-0.6 m x 0.1-0.3 m WA
The flower-heads of this annual species are commonly white but may have pink tonings. They are seen mainly in Sept.-Dec. As with other waitzias this species has garden potential and is well worth trying.
H O D L SA G C1 F1
Chart 18, Chapter 22

Westringia fruticosa, Coast Rosemary
2-3 m x 2-3 m Qld, NSW
A dense shrub with dark green leaves to 3 cm long. White flowers with purple marks are produced throughout the year, but mainly during Sept.-Nov. A very hardy species with many landscape uses. There is also a variegated form, *W. fruticosa* 'Morning Light' which is less vigorous than forms with green foliage.
H O SS W L SA G CA C2 F2
Charts 12a, Chapter 16; 21, Chapter 27

Westringia glabra, Violet Westringia
1-2 m x 1-2 m Qld, NSW, Vic
A bushy shrub with mauve-purple flowers produced over a long period mainly during Aug.-Dec. This is a hardy species suited to a range of garden situations. Plants respond well to light or medium pruning.
O SS D M L SA G C1 F1
Charts 13, Chapter 17; 21, Chapter 27

Glossary

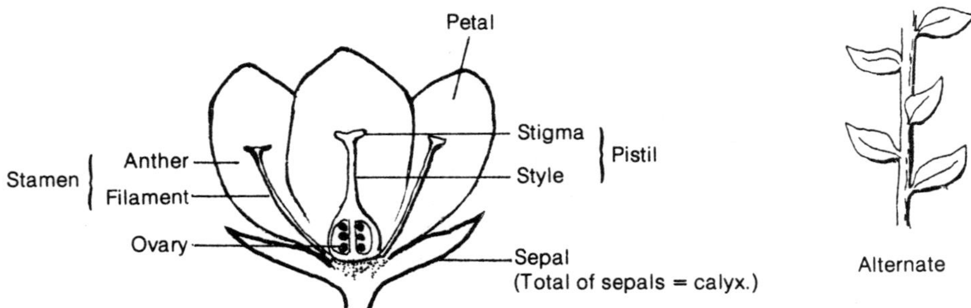

Parts of a flower.

acute Bearing a short, sharp point.

alternate Of leaves, occurring first on one side of a branch and then on the other.

annual A plant that completes its life cycle within one year.

anther The pollen-bearing part of a stamen.

axil The angle formed by a leaf and the stem which bears it.

axillary Produced within the angle of a leaf and a stem.

basal At the base.

Nerve or midrib
Apex
Axillary bud
Margin
Blade
Vein

Parts of a leaf.

Basal leaves

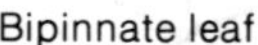
Bipinnate leaf

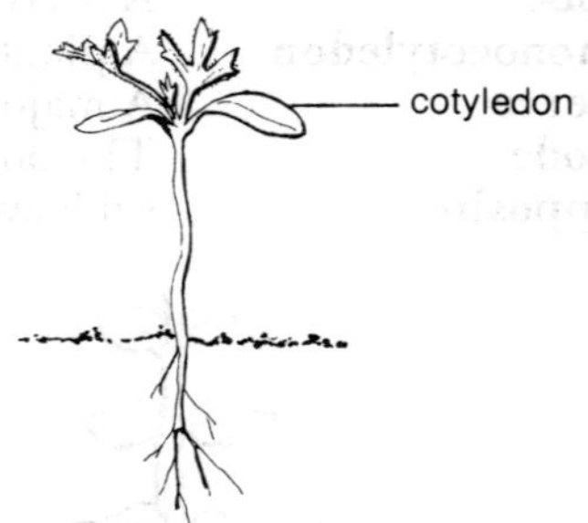

A dicotyledon seedling.

bipinnate Of leaves or fronds; twice divided.

bracts Modified leaves at the base of a flower-stalk, or surrounding clusters of small individual flowers.

calcareous With a high lime content.

calyces Plural of calyx.

calyx Outer covering of flower-base; protector of buds.

compound leaf A leaf divided into separate leaflets.

cotyledon The primary leaf or seed-leaf of a plant.

cultivar Horticultural variety of a plant.

decussate Leaves in opposite pairs, alternately at right angles along the stem.

dicotyledon A plant with two cotyledons, or seed-leaves.

epiphyte A plant which grows on another plant but is not parasitic.

friable Easily crumbled.

frond The leaf of a fern.

genus A classification of plants below the level of a family, and above the level of a species, e.g. *Acacia*, *Grevillea.*

glabrous Smooth, without hairs.

gland A fluid-secreting organ, usually on leaves.

glaucous Covered with a bloom, giving a white, pale blue or greyish lustre.

labellum Modified front petal of an orchid; appears as a'lip' or 'tongue'.

lignotuber A woody swelling bearing dormant buds, at the base of a trunk at or below ground level.

linear Long, narrow, with parallel edges.

lithophyte A plant which grows on rock or stone in its natural habitat.

Decussate leaves

A lobed leaf

lobe A division of a leaf, petal or sepal.
monocotyledon A plant with a single cotyledon or seed-leaf.
nerve A major vein or midrib of a leaf.
node The point on a stem where leaves or bracts arise.
opposite Of leaves; arranged opposite each other on a stem.

Opposite leaves

An ovate leaf

ovate Somewhat egg shaped, widest below the middle with the tip tapering to a point.
panicle A branched formation of flowers.
pendant Hanging down.
phyllode Modified leaf stalk acting as a leaf, as in most *Acacia* species.
pinna First division of a compound leaf.
pinnae Plural of pinna.
pinnate Of compound leaves or fronds; divided once.

A panicle

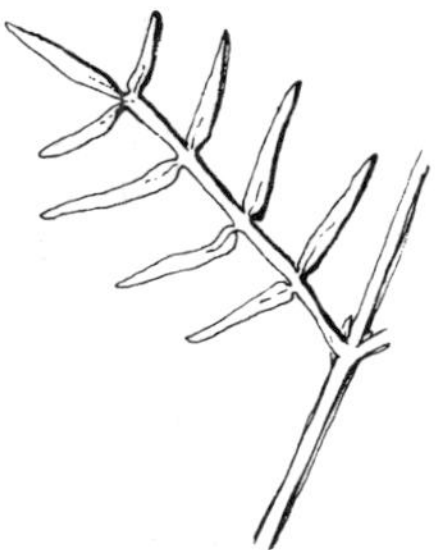
A pinnate leaf

pinnules The smallest divisions of a compound leaf.
pod A dry, non-fleshy fruit that splits when ripe to release its seed.
prostrate Lying flat on the ground.
prothalli Plural of prothallus.
prothallus A growth resulting from the germination of spore, as in ferns.
pungent Sharply pointed.
raceme Equally-stalked flowers along a single stem.

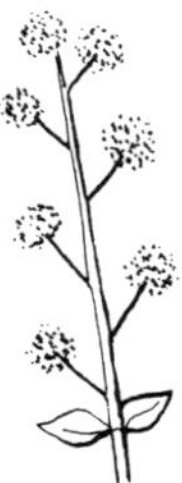
A raceme

rhizome An underground stem on which new rhizomes grow as extensions in subsequent seasons.

ringbarking The removal of a ring of bark and cambium tissue from a stem or trunk, thus restricting sap flow to the limb.

segment A subdivision or part of an organ.

sepal A lobe that is a portion of the calyx.

serrated With sharp teeth along the margins.

simple Of leaves, undivided.

sp. Species: classification of closely related plants within a genus. **spp.** Species, plural.

spike Of flowers; stalkless flowers arranged along a single stem.

ssp. Subspecies: a sub-group within a species.

stamen A floral segment, made up of a pollen-bearing anther and a supporting filament.

stigma A floral segment. The tip of a style, carrying pollen-receptive tissue.

style A floral segment. Usually a filament connecting the stigma with the ovary.

taproot A perpendicular main root of a plant.

terminal At the apex or end.

trifoliolate A compound leaf with three leaflets.

tuber The swollen end of an underground stem, independent of tubers formed in previous seasons.

var. A subdivision of a species.

vein A strand of liquid-conducting tissue within a leaf.

whorl A ring of flowers or leaves around a stem.

x Used in the naming of plants to indicate a hybrid that has occurred in the natural habitat of the parent plants.

A simple leaf

Leaves in whorl formation

Bibliography

This selected bibliography is by no means a complete listing of all the books currently obtainable on Australian native plants. There are many others including books on particular Australian plant genera, such as *Acacia, Banksia* and *Eucalyptus*, as well as very detailed technical publications on plant identification, cultivation, and related subjects such as pests and diseases. A more detailed listing of these publications will be found in each volume of *The Encyclopaedia of Australian Plants Suitable for Cultivation* by Elliot and Jones (Lothian, Melbourne).

GENERAL PUBLICATIONS

Blombery, A.M. (1980) *A Guide to Native Australian Plants*, Angus & Robertson, Sydney.

Elliot, W.R. & Jones, D.L. (1980-1984) *Encyclopaedia of Australian Plants Suitable for Cultivation*, Volumes 1-3, Lothian, Melbourne.

Society for Growing Australian Plants, *Australian Plants*, Quarterly journal, S.G.A.P., Sydney.

Wrigley, J.W. & Fagg, M. (1983) *Australian Native Plants*, Collins, Sydney.

LANDSCAPING AND THE SELECTION OF PLANTS

Adams, G.M. (1980) *Birdscaping Your Garden*, Rigby, Adelaide.

Australian Plant Study Group (1980) *Grow What Where*, Nelson, Melbourne.

Australian Plant Study Group (1982) *Grow What Wet*, Nelson, Melbourne.

Australian Plant Study Group (1983) *Grow What Basic*, Nelson, Melbourne.

Blombery, A.M. (1972) *What Wildflower Is That?* Hamlyn, Sydney.

Brown, A. & Hall, N. (1968) *Growing Trees on Australian Farms*, Forestry & Timber Bureau, Canberra.

Canberra Botanic Gardens (1971-) *Growing Native Plants* (Series), Australian Government Publishing Service, Canberra.

Elliot, G.M. (1982) *Australian Plants For Small Gardens and Containers*, Hyland House, Melbourne.

Elliot, G.M. (1984) *Colour Your Garden With Australian Plants*, Hyland House, Melbourne.

Elliot, W.R. and Jones, D.L. (1980-84) *Encyclopaedia of Australian Plants Suitable for Cultivation*, Volumes 1-3, Lothian, Melbourne.

Hall, N. (1972) *The Use of Trees & Shrubs in the Dry Country of Australia*, Forestry & Timber Bureau, Canberra.

Harris, T.Y. (1977) *Gardening With Australian Plants — Shrubs*, Nelson, Melbourne.

Harris, T.Y. (1979) *Gardening With Australian Plants — Small Plants and Climbers*, Nelson, Melbourne.

Harris, T.Y. (1980) *Gardening With Australian Plants — Trees*, Nelson, Melbourne.

Jones, D.L. (1984) *Palms In Australia*, Reed, Sydney.

Jones, D.L. & Gray, B. (1977) *Australian Climbing Plants*, Reed, Sydney.

Lord, E.E. & Willis, J.H. (1982) *Shrubs and Trees for Australian Gardens*, 5th Edition, Lothian, Melbourne.
Molyneux, B. (1980) *Grow Native*, Anne O'Donovan, Melbourne.
Molyneux, B. & Macdonald, R. (1983) *Native Gardens — How to Create an Australian Landscape*, Nelson, Melbourne.
Wilson, G. (1975) *Landscaping With Australian Plants*, Nelson, Melbourne.
Wilson, G. (1980) *Amenity Planting in Arid Zones*, School of Environmental Design, College of Advanced Education, Canberra.

GARDEN MAINTENANCE

Bradley, J. (1971) *Bush Regeneration*, Mosman Parklands & Ashton Park Association, Sydney.
Breckwoldt, R. (1983) *Wildlife in the Home Paddock*, Angus & Robertson, Sydney.
Elliot, W.R. (1984) *Pruning, A Practical Guide*, Lothian, Melbourne.
Elliot, W.R. & Jones, D.L. (1983) *Encyclopaedia of Australian Plants Suitable for Cultivation*, Volume 1, Lothian, Melbourne.
Hadlington, P.W. & Johnston, J.A. (1977) *A Guide to the Care and Cure of Australian Trees*, NSW University Press, Kensington, NSW.
Handreck, K.A. (1979) *When Should I Water?* Discovering Soils Series No. 8, CSIRO, Melbourne.
Hockings, F.D. (1980) *Friends and Foes of Australian Gardens*, Reed, Sydney.
Inall, N. & Drynan, R. (Ed.) (1983) *Caring For Young Trees*, Australian Broadcasting Commission, Sydney.
McCubbin, C. (1981) *Australian Butterflies*, Nelson, Melbourne.

WEEDS

Bradley, J. (1971) *Bush Regeneration*, Mosman Parklands & Ashton Park Association, Sydney.
Buchanan, R.A. (1981) *Common Weeds of Sydney Bushland*, Inkata Press, Melbourne.
Burbidge, N.T. (1984) *Australian Grasses*, Angus & Robertson, London.
Kleinschmidt, H.E. (1983) *Suburban Weeds*, Qld. Department of Primary Industries, Brisbane.
Kleinschmidt, H.E. & Johnson, R.W. (1977) *Weeds of Queensland*, Qld. Department of Primary Industries, Brisbane.
Lamp, C. & Collet, F. (1976) *Weeds in Australia*, Inkata Press, Melbourne.
Parsons, W.T. (1973) *Noxious Weeds of Victoria*, Inkata Press, Melbourne.
Whibley, D.J.E. & Christensen, T.J. *Garden Weeds, Identification and Control*, Botanic Gardens of Adelaide, Adelaide.

FERNS AND ORCHIDS

Jones, D.L. & Clemesha, S.C. (1981) *Australian Ferns and Fern Allies*, Reed, Sydney.
Jones, D.L. & Goudey, C.J. (1981) *Ferns in Australia, Common, Rare & Exotic*, Reed, Sydney.
Rentoul, J. (1980) *Growing Cymbidiums & Slippers*, Lothian, Melbourne.
Rentoul, J. (1982) *Growing Vandas, Dendrobiums & Others*, Lothian, Melbourne.
Richards, H., Wootton, R. & Datodi, R. (1984) *Cultivation of Australian Native Orchids*, Australasian Native Orchid Soc. (Vic. Group), Melbourne.

PROPAGATION AND POTTING MIXES

Elliot, G.M. (1981) *Fun With Australian Plants*, Hyland House, Melbourne.
Elliot, W.R. & Jones, D.L. (1983) *Encyclopaedia of Australian Plants Suitable for Cultivation*, Volume 1, Lothian, Melbourne.
de Fossard, R.A. (1979) *Tissue Culture for Plant Propagators*, University of New England, Armidale, NSW.
Handreck, K. & Black, N. (1984) *Growing Media for Ornamental Plants & Turf*, NSW University Press, Kensington, NSW.
Plumridge, J. (1977) *How To Propagate Plants*, Lothian, Melbourne.

FLORA OF PARTICULAR AREAS

Australian Systematic Botany Society (Jessop, J. Ed.) (1981) *Flora of Central Australia*, Reed, Sydney.
Beadle, N.C.W., Evans, O.D. & Carolin, R.C. (1982) *Flora of the Sydney Region*, Reed, Sydney.
Burbidge, N.T. & Gray, M. (1970) *Flora of the A.C.T.*, Australian National University Press, Canberra.
Cochrane, G.R., Fuhrer, B.A., Rotherham, E.R., Simmons, J. & M. & Willis, J.H. (1980) *Flowers & Plants of Victoria & Tasmania*, Reed, Sydney.
Costermans, L. (1981) *Native Trees and Shrubs of South-Eastern Australia*, Rigby, Adelaide.
Costin, A.B., Gray, M., Totterdell, C.J. & Wimbush, D.J. (1979) *Kosciusko Alpine Flora*, CSIRO, Melbourne.
Cunningham, G.M., Mulham, W.E., Milthorpe, P.L. & Leigh, J.H. (1981) *Plants of Western New South Wales*, Soil Conservation Service, NSW.
Erickson, R., George, A.S., Marchant, N.G. & Morcombe, M.K. (1973) *Flowers and Plants of Western Australia*, Reed, Sydney.
Rotherham, E.R., Briggs, B.G., Blaxell, D.F. & Carolin, R.C. (1975) *Flowers & Plants of New South Wales & Southern Queensland*, Reed, Sydney.
Williams, K.A.W. (1979) *Native Plants — Queensland*, Volume 1, K.A.W. Williams, North Ipswich, Qld.
Williams, K.A.W. (1984) *Native Plants — Queensland*, Volume 2, K.A.W. Williams, North Ipswich, Qld.

Index to Plant Common Names

For index to Botanical Plant Names, see alphabetical listing of plant descriptions in Section 2.

Index

See also Index to Plant Common Names.
For index to Botanical Plant Names see alphabetical listing of plant descriptions in Section 2.